CARAVANSERAI

Journey Among Australian Muslims

A completely revised and updated edition, including compelling discussion of September 11, the Bali bombing and the Australian Government's stance on asylum seekers.

An outstanding contribution to Australian literature.

Caravanserai, winner
NSW Premier's Literary Award 1996
Judges' comments

Deen shines a light into rarely explored corners of the Muslim culture and lifestyle.

Elle

Caravanserai *challenged my view of Islam; it is an interesting, beautifully written and emotional account of one person's journey.*

Australian Book Review

In memory of my parents,
who taught their children that those who
deny their identity, have no identity.

CARAVANSERAI

Journey Among Australian Muslims

HANIFA DEEN

Fremantle Arts Centre Press

Australia's finest small publisher

Published 2003 by
FREMANTLE ARTS CENTRE PRESS
25 Quarry Street, Fremantle
(PO Box 158, North Fremantle 6159)
Western Australia.
www.facp.iinet.net.au

First edition published in 1995 by Allen & Unwin Australia Pty Ltd.

Consultant Editor Janet Blagg.
Production Coordinator Cate Sutherland.
Cover Designer Marion Duke.
Printed by Griffin Press.

National Library of Australia
Cataloguing-in-publication data

Deen, Hanifa.
Caravanserai: journey among Australian Muslims.

New ed.
Includes index.
ISBN 1 86368 388 7.

1. Muslims — Australia. 2. Islam — Australia. I Title.

305.697094

The State of Western Australia has made an investment in this project through ArtsWA in association with the Lotteries Commission.

Contents

Author's Note

Along the way this book has changed directions more than once, although the intention has always remained the same. I wanted to give Muslims a human face, to show them as ordinary people at a time in history when their identity as Australian Muslims was evolving. Writing in the shadow of the Gulf War of 1991, I wanted to engage the interest of an untouched, unmoved audience whose images of Muslims were really reflections from a 'distorted mirror'. Ten years on and today everyone has an opinion about Muslims. The audience is no longer untouched or unmoved, but the distortions and one-dimensional images still persist.

Since the World Trade Centre tragedy on 11 September 2001, language has changed, definitions have been reshaped and mindsets have hardened. At the time of my original journey however, we in Australia seemed to live in a world untouched by outside world events and most people were indifferent towards Muslims: voices of prejudice spoke mainly in whispers; they were hidden out of sight; for the most part they were not respectable.

I recall that as I travelled around Australia, many Muslims asked me what should have been an easy question to answer: what kind of book was I writing? Answering this was harder than I expected. I found it much easier to talk about the kind of book I wasn't writing! I wasn't writing a religious book; neither was I writing an academic book or a Who's Who of the Muslim world in Australia. I wanted to move away from the usual emphasis on religious identity and theological explanations — and anyway I am not the person to write such books. Coverage of Muslims in Australia, whether in the electronic media, the press, academic dissertations or community newsletters, concentrated mainly on a 'followers of Islam' approach — a ritualistic rendering in many ways as concentrated and unswerving as Muslims at prayer.

Recent world events have shifted this portrayal and today in the eyes of the West, the words Muslim and Arab have become synonymous with 'terrorist', 'fanatic' and 'extremist'. While ten years ago Muslims were a 'problem', seen to have little in common with other Australians, today they have graduated into becoming a problem with potential enemy status. Seldom are they thought of as people who mow their lawns, are preoccupied with losing weight, worry about their jobs and mortgages, play sport, swap jokes or tell their children bedtime tales.

This book is based on two separate journeys: the first began in 1993 two years after the first Gulf War; the second, incorporated into the revised edition of the book, took place in the shadow of September 11 and the Bali bombings of 2002. Both my journeys were odysseys of the mind and the heart. And there were times when I wasn't sure what I was looking for until I actually found it; until I met a particular person or shared an old dream or felt a certain tug, a certain resonance.

Often I stumbled, but gradually the narrative took shape. I have met and talked with about three hundred people. The book is based on the stories and experiences they shared with me, together with my own personal reflections and sometimes my own imagination. As time passed I came to feel less and less an interviewer and more a collector and interpreter of stories. A style seemed to be emerging: a combination of commentary and storytelling

— more like the style of traditional storytellers of long ago, whose repertoires were as deep as their memories. This led me to the idea of the caravanserai, with its many levels of meaning, relating to people, journeys and interaction. Caravanserais were not the place for maintaining a social distance; travellers from different lands did not keep one another at arm's length.

Last year I picked up the threads of my original journey once more and revisited old friends and familiar places where I found my Muslim and Arab comrades acknowledging 2001 as a defining moment in their existence in Australia. I discovered them reeling from events near and far which had impacted on all our lives. They were stunned that, almost overnight, people were repulsed by them and doubted their commitment and loyalty to Australia.

I myself was not untouched; my emotions fluctuated: I was full of anger and yet terribly saddened by what I was witnessing and for many months I simply could not find the words to express myself. Finally I came to my senses at the time of the Tampa incident and the deliberate attempts to demonise asylum seekers. I now have new friends who do not live in Perth, Adelaide, Melbourne or Sydney. Some of them are trapped behind the wires in our shameful detention gulags in remote areas, out of sight. This is not the welcoming caravanserai that I envisaged for them. Their experiences are yet another reason for me to break my silence.

This book is written from the point of view of a Muslim who has grown up in Australia and, rightly or wrongly, has the confidence to state what she sees and hears. Years ago I wrote, in the original preface, that *Caravanserai* was written out of pride; that in a strange way I had been waiting all my life to write that narrative — a story without an ending I called it. This still holds true for me. I continue to hope it will strike a chord with some of the approximately three hundred thousand Muslims living in Australia, and that other Australians will find something of value.

Many people have helped me. They contributed in diverse ways and without them there would have been no journey and consequently no book. I thank them all for their patience, their support and their strong belief that what I was doing mattered, though I understand that not everyone will agree with everything I have written. There are so many people to thank that I cannot mention them all. Not everyone appears under their own name — the reasons are obvious.

I wish to thank: Iman Partoredjo, Wafa Chafic and family, Ali Roude, Leila Allush, Farida Hasim, Nada Nasser, the Reverend John Baldock, Eric Lloga, Steve Mark, Ahmad Hammoud, Farida Karolla, Hisam Sidaoni, Sawsan Madina, Majida Aboud, Hurriyiat Babacan, Dr Aziz Kazi, Shaykh Rashid Raashed, Charlie Coorie, Irene Donohoue-Clyne, Dorothy Hoddinot, Mary Jones, Fariha Gurakan, Madenia Abdurahim and family, and all my friends in Campbelltown. I am indebted to Dr Franz Oswald, Elizabeth Weiss and Brian Johns.

The following publications were particularly useful: Fatima Mernissi, *Beyond the Veil* (Al Saqi Books, 1985) and *Women and Islam* (Oxford University Press, 1985); James Jupp (ed.), *The Australian Encyclopedia of Australian People* (Angus & Robertson, 1988); and *Studies in Hadith Methodology and Literature* by M M Azami (American Trust, 1977). I have made extensive use of the *Australasian Muslim Times* 1992–94 and wish to thank Dr Ashfaq Ahmad and Najia Khalil. My revised edition has been informed by access to the writings of Dr Greg Fealy, Research Fellow in Indonesian Politics, Australian National University.

I would also like to acknowledge the support of the Arts Council of Australia.

Every attempt has been made to obtain copyright permissions for the quotations used.

I am also grateful to publisher Ray Coffey from Fremantle Arts Centre Press who believed in 'the new *Caravanserai*' right from the start, and let me also thank Janet Blagg for her editorial assistance. I also acknowledge the Australian Arabic Council, Amnesty International in Sydney and the Refugee Council of Australia for their help — they are all busy organisations and I thank them for their generosity in making time for me.

HANIFA DEEN
December 2002

The Caravanserai

Once Khidr went to the king's palace and made his way right up to the throne.

Such was the strangeness of his appearance that none dared to stop him.

The king, who was Ibrahim ben Adam, asked him what he was looking for.

The visitor said: 'I am looking for a sleeping-place in this caravanserai.'

Ibrahim answered: 'This is no caravanserai, this is my palace.'

The stranger said: 'Whose was it before you?'

'My father's,' said Ibrahim.

'And before that?'

'My grandfather's.'

'And this place, where people come and go, staying and moving on, you call other than a caravanserai?'

— *Idries Shah,* The Way of the Sufi

The storyteller

In days gone by, caravans of merchants, pilgrims and other wanderers would travel together as one band for mutual protection. There was safety in numbers, so it was believed, and brigands, robbers and wild animals often preferred to lie in wait for easier prey, unless desperation, greed or hunger overcame good sense. Such caravans were common sights in desert and mountain areas of south Asia, northern Africa and the Levant, moving slowly against the dunes and rocky mountains, with beasts of burden — camels, donkeys and horses — plodding along, loaded with valuable cargo.

The sands of time moved slowly as the caravans wended their way along the rough trails. From a distance they seemed to be crawling; barely moving against the dunes and the friendly rays of the early desert sun, or silhouetted against windswept, rugged hills. Draw nearer and the purposeful but restrained movement, the energy lying beneath the surface, held in check and rationed out as assiduously as water from a canteen, became clearer. Experienced men knew better than to squander their energy in hurried, wasteful movements. Man and beast were welded together as one, for the fate of the master often lay in the strength and loyalty of his animals, while they in turn depended upon their master's courage and knowledge of the terrain ahead.

If good fortune smiled down at them and evil *djinns* (genies) with fiery bodies or illusory shapes were kept at bay by talismans, prayers or a Beneficent Allah, they might well reach the protective walls of a caravanserai by nightfall. These enormous, walled medieval caravan inns were scattered along the trade routes, in less remote areas at intervals of one day's journey on the roads, providing a welcome haven and accommodation for weary travellers at night. It was a thrilling sight when the huge, dark shape of the caravanserai wall and its solitary gate loomed out of the dusk. There was an unwritten law that whoever entered for the night would enjoy sanctuary and protection. Even blood enemies who found themselves locked inside the enormous gate were safe from each other.

Many caravanserais were gargantuan structures, large enough to enclose a spacious courtyard the size of a football field, where camels could be unloaded and fed, and herds of animals sheltered. Smaller, two-storeyed inns with open-arcaded galleries could be found in cities near the bazaars and served as a kind of stock exchange for different goods. But in architectural splendour and atmosphere, they were dwarfed by the monumental, sandstone caravanserais found in the remote parts of Turkey, or the mud-walled, fortress-style structures of Afghanistan.

In inclement weather, men and their animals might even sleep together in one enormous common sleeping hall, with doorways built high enough for animals to enter, and all would emerge better tempered when the sun rose the next morning. After breakfasting on steaming cups of green Chinese tea or sweetened black Indian tea that washed down rough wheat cakes, they parted with a handful of coins to the smiling innkeeper before moving on. The more profitable and usually better kept caravanserais lay at major trading crossroads, where trade caravans from many lands and provinces converged for a night's sanctuary before continuing on their different ways.

But in the evening, the special magic of the caravanserai drifted through the ranks, beguiling young and old alike. Travellers from a dozen far-off lands lounged around on their *charpoys* noisily slurping tea, drawing cool, scented smoke into their lungs from the communal *nargeelahs,* or water pipes, placed on the ground before them by lowly serving boys. Eager to exploit these occasions, men exchanged news of the trails ahead, of bazaars and local wrestling contests and horse competitions, while often a master storyteller would emerge with tales of wise men, despotic caliphs, great warriors and horsemen or malicious *djinns* — all of which made men more mindful of their prayers and almsgiving. Omens, curses and other dread portents were part of the wayfarers' realm, for they faced not only physical dangers but also an unpredictable, often malevolent spirit world. Listening to the amazing tales of the professional storyteller was a favourite form of entertainment wherever one went in the Muslim world. Masters of the art possessed extraordinary powers to excite the imagination of their audience. Their repertoire was as vast as their memories and at their disposal lay a treasure chest filled with marvels. Some of these they made up as they went along, but more often the fabric of their stories came from tales of *The Thousand and One Nights* and other old coffee-house favourites, which they embellished in countless ways, transporting enthralled listeners to distant lands and ancient kingdoms.

Muslims were great travellers in the past. Motivated by trade, conquest, adventure and a strong feeling of mission, journeying was a way of life — for men. Women found themselves confined to houses, villages and towns and familiar paths, where their lives unfolded predictably, with only the pain and the mystery of childbirth their property alone. This was the lot of most women in the Middle Ages, irrespective of their religion or ancestry. Now and then the monotony of their lives was broken by a religious festival, or a visit to a local holy shrine or a famous mystic to ask for the granting of a secret wish or the cure of a terrible disease.

Caravanserais were unsuitable places for women, unless you happened to be a serving girl, or the landlord's wife, or a gypsy woman wandering across borders with her clan and its ostracised caravans.

Many years ago, in a book whose title I can no longer recall, I stumbled across a description of a caravanserai. I have remained fascinated by the imagery it evoked and the secrets I imagine these archaic structures still house, even though they have been replaced by modern lorries and roads and now stand as ghostly reminders of a way of life since past. The more I read, the more I wanted to know about these vast lonely structures and the travellers they sheltered.

Somewhere along the way, the enchantment of the caravanserai and an engrossment in global movements and cultural diversity have converged, in a curious way, with my desire to record modern stories about Australian Muslims. Consequently, the caravanserai has acquired for me a different shape and meaning, part of the continuing drama of human movement and social change.

Muslims, great travellers in the past, today continue to make their way through borders and across continents and oceans, bringing their caravans to rest in a new desert country far to the south — a vast desert land fringed by green coastal oases. Muslim men, women and children have journeyed together and made Australia a caravanserai with a difference — a sanctuary of more permanent abode.

In the eighteenth century and perhaps even earlier, Muslim fishermen came to our shores. Fishermen from the eastern islands of modern Indonesia sailed along northern and north-western Australia, fishing for trepang and trading with the Aborigines. This interaction continued for almost three centuries, but the Indonesians and Malays came and went like the winds which assisted their canoes and trawlers. Muslims did not settle in Australia until the nineteenth century when a new breed was drawn to these shores, as determined in their way — and as stubborn — as the camels they came to tend.

Caravans fired by imagination headed towards a caravanserai of dreams ... a long, lonely chain of travellers.

It is written that to understand ourselves today, we must visualise ourselves in the past — investigate the 'once upon a time' of our lives. Through listening to people I have learnt that they alone determine for themselves when their pasts end and when their presents commence. I found that this decision has little to do with geographical or political boundaries or dates on a calendar. It is made of more delicate, whimsical stuff — the stuff of dreams and memories and the painful, often heart-breaking, ritual of rending ties forever.

I

Southern caravans

'By Allah,' the king thought to himself, 'I won't slay her until I hear some of her wondrous tales.'

Richard F Burton (adapted by Jack Zipes),
Arabian Nights: The Marvels and Wonders of The Thousand and One Nights

1

The road from Jallander

Muhammad Hanif was his name. He offered his story to me with all the charm of a born storyteller, shaking off the dust and burnishing it brightly like a shiny brass *hookah* or *nargeelah* ready for its audience to inhale its heady tobacco. He was secretive about his age, and my transparent attempts to pry this secret from him were futile. I was being too greedy; everything else he shared generously with me. It was enough that our names were the same and that we shared similar backgrounds — Pakistani ancestry with hawker 'pedigrees' — and, as I soon learnt, a weakness for a good story and an ear for the theatrical twist.

In the past the true teller of tales used a gift for embellishment and editing in ways that amazed the listener — two warriors became 'ten thousand warriors', a pretty woman 'an exquisite beauty, as lovely as the moon'. A poignant pause, a gesture or a rolling of the eyes, important details dear to the heart of any storyteller, were all treated with more respect then.

He must have been in his early seventies, but he looked at least fifteen years younger. His memory was sharp and he demonstrated a phenomenal ability to recollect small details, giving rich colour to the times he had lived in and the grand sweep of his personal history.

Lively and good-humoured eyes revealed a man who enjoyed a laugh and a good cup of strong country tea. His skin was smooth and almost unlined, a brown contrast to snowy white hair, but it was his speech which fascinated me. There was a lazy, drawling quality to his diction, and his pronunciation and accent signalled that he might well have grown up in the Australian countryside.

But Muhammad Hanif's past began in the small village of Kotlee in the district of Jallander, which once lay in an undivided Punjab before Partition in 1947 split British India into two nations, India and Pakistan. His father and hundreds of other eager young men travelled in ones and twos along dusty roads on foot or by bullock cart, to sail across oceans for the adventure of a lifetime. The enticing descriptions of older men just returned from a strange but wonderful land to the south drew these shy, uneducated young men away from their villages towards the excitement of the unknown.

Haji Sher Muhammad was one of those older men who had recently returned from Australia. Like others who had accompanied the early camel teams in the mid-nineteenth century, he came home after a few years when his contract ended. Let the others remain, he had lived his adventure and new lands beckoned. With the money he had saved, he made the pilgrimage, or *haj*, to the holy city of Mecca before returning to his village with the honourable title of *haji* and the status due to one who has performed this special pillar of Islam and can face his Maker with a clear conscience.

Haji Sher Muhammad found himself invited as an honoured guest and teller of tales to one village after another. Only twenty or so years had passed since the so-called 'Indian mutiny', and British rule was well entrenched. Young men came from far and wide to squat or sit cross-legged in front of him and listen to the celebrated *haji* tell of his journey, his pilgrimage to Mecca and best of all, his exploits in the exotic south land.

'The people are white with yellow hair and they have

strange pale eyes,' he told his captivated listeners. 'It is a wonderful new country, a huge land, full of adventure and sights to behold like you have never imagined. Fortunes can be made; money earned to send home to your families. You can eat meat every day and wear fine clothes. You must see this place!'

Young men in particular listened to his urging. People were poor in Jallander. The district was full of small farming villages and, while everybody knew that Punjabis were good farmers — growing wheat, cotton and corn — there was just not enough land; holdings were small and extended families large. By now it had become customary for the eldest son to leave home and travel over the ocean, working hard to send money home to support other family members.

Muhammad Hanif's father was one of many who set out for Australia, their imaginations captured, their eyes shining and eager, while the eyes of mothers, sisters and perhaps here and there a young bride, were red from weeping. At this time, ships were boarded at Bombay or Calcutta, but adventure came at a price: men who sailed to Perth, Sydney or Melbourne often disembarked at Singapore or Hong Kong and took whatever labouring jobs they could find to earn money for the rest of their passage to Australia. Young, strong and robust, their hopes soared as high as the serpent-eagle in the sky. Some worked their way to Australia as ship's stokers (like my mother's father), dreaming as they toiled and sweated in the engine room. These were the years before Federation and the subsequent Immigration Restriction Act, better known as the White Australia policy. In a scene repeated year after year, the young men from Jallander were met at the Sydney docks by older men from their home district who had already settled there. Two of these elders had opened a small warehouse-cum-boarding house in the inner-city area of Redfern. Imam Deen and Abdullah Muhammad supplied haberdashery goods to a small but growing number of Indian hawkers, mainly Muslims. Hawking or peddling in those days was also done by Christian Syrians and Lebanese, a few Turks, some Chinese and some Australian-born men.

Why did the young Punjabis — including his father — take to hawking so enthusiastically, I asked Muhammad Hanif. Piecing together the information we had unearthed, we concluded that the trade had several advantages: you could start with very little, there were others to stake you and advise you, and it was a way of seeing this exotic country, with its strange plants, birds, animals and people.

Hawking in rural India was a common occupation. Shops and bazaars belonged to cities and large towns, not to small villages, where every penny was guarded scrupulously and only after harvest, or the feast of Eid which marked the end of the fasting month of Ramazan, or for a wedding, might there be cash money. Australia had a widely dispersed population and settlements were often isolated, so hawking readily found a place.

Perhaps the peculiar chain of mutual dependency, illustrated in a line of credit arrangements, also appealed to young Indian hawkers. Large Australian warehouses sold goods on credit to Imam and Abdullah and other small-scale Indian wholesalers. They in turn supplied their countrymen with goods to hawk around the country, again on credit. The hawkers sold work shirts and trousers, boots, fabric, dishcloths, safety pins, sewing needles, sweets and a hundred other lines to their customers in isolated country districts — all on credit. In those days it might take as long as six months, or even a year, for a farmer or his farmhands to pay off a bill of six shillings and six pence.

Long ago I found an old notebook among my father's

papers. In it he had recorded his sales in his beautiful handwriting when, as a young man, he travelled with his horse and cart through the Latrobe Valley in Victoria during the Depression. Each page held its own little story:

Kilmany 4 November 1931
Second house from the School.
Bought 1 tin of curry powder, paid 1-6. Bal. 6

Sold Mrs Jones 23 September 1931
2 Pr. Sheetings 0-17-0
2 Pr Pillow slips 4-6
2 Boys ties 2-0
1-3-6
1-0-0 Paid by cheque 14/11/31
Balance 3-6 paid 5/2/32

The pioneers of the nineteenth century, who came out forty years or so before my father, were mainly peasants with little or no education. Most were illiterate in their own language, Punjabi, possessed few skills other than those of a peasant farmer, and came with empty pockets. Men like Imam Deen and Abdullah would help these newcomers settle in: smooth the way for them in this strange new environment; read and write letters for them; help them with their paperwork and frustrating contacts with the bureaucracy; and give them credit for the supplies they needed to begin — often in a very small way on foot. Without the hawkers, the wholesalers had no outlet; without the wholesalers, the hawkers had no goods or guides. Each depended on the other.

Muhammad Hanif, who came to Australia as a young child in the early 1930s to help his father, told me that the hawkers' aim was financial independence. They made their money, sent some home and saved up to buy property.

'How did they manage the bookkeeping if they were illiterate?' I asked. I wanted to know the small details, find answers to the questions I'd forgotten to ask my father when I still had the chance years before.

'They would give a book and pencil to the farmer and ask him to write down his order and how much he still owed.'

Although I'm prepared to believe in the honesty of farmers and everyone else in those days, it must have been tempting to some to cheat the illiterate, itinerant hawkers. Later I asked my mother, now in her eighties, whose Kashmiri father had also hawked in Victoria in the 1890s. She recalled, as a very young girl, helping some of her father's friends read their accounts. One poor man had been hoodwinked by a barmaid at a country pub. Instead of recording her debts for goods received, she had written down the words to a popular song!

If these were the days of White Australia, were there signs of racial discrimination?

'Yes, there were hidden signs, but there were good people too,' Hanif said. 'The types who didn't like you never invited you inside or made you camp well away from the homestead.'

Some of the types who didn't like you might also sit in parliament, I learnt. According to researcher Dr Trevor Batrouney, parliamentary debates in 1901 and 1903 refer disparagingly both to the practice of hawking — 'for being neither honest nor productive labour'— and to Syrian hawkers themselves, for assuming threatening and menacing attitudes and 'forcing poor women to buy their goods.' ('Syrians' may have been a term for hawkers generally in some areas, just as 'Afghans' stood for camel men.) So 'sinister' hawkers forced poor country women to take credit, I thought; compelled them to take up to a year to pay a bill of one shilling for a pair of baby's booties and a yard of elastic!

Not everyone liked hawking. Muhammad Hanif's father

belonged to a group of men who went to northern New South Wales in about 1910 and worked on farms. Punjabis who were not happy hawking were advised by elders like Imam Deen and Abdullah to go to Lismore or Casino: 'The Australians are opening up the land; there's a lot of cedar to be cleared and jobs for the taking.'

The days were long and hard. They cleared the land, chopping down trees and cutting prickly lantana to build fences for their bosses, the cattle farmers, who needed paddocks for grazing. Fencing the paddocks was exhausting. There was no machinery then, only axes, hard labour, dreams and sweat. But the jobs were there, and more and more went north to work and to settle. At one time, Hanif estimates, there were close to two hundred Muslims working in the area and 'maybe one hundred Sikhs.'

Eventually they were able to buy land on leasehold from big graziers. One day in 1927, Hanif's father bought forty acres from the Armstrong family to set up his own banana plantation and market garden at Caniaba, near Lismore. Did he know anything about bananas?

'He learnt as he went along,' came the answer. I am left to imagine that slowly he prospered.

Around 1920 immigration authorities started to allow the entry of families of Indians who were resident in Australia, and men were able to sponsor sons and 'real brothers', Hanif said. Fear of Japan and a need for Indian support at Imperial conferences forced concessions, but this made no real dent in White Australia, for in those days there were only around two thousand Indians in the whole country.

'Sons could stay as long as they liked and could become citizens. Life was tougher for "real brothers", who could only remain for three years.' Hanif remembered all of the restrictions.

He joined his father in about 1936 as a boy of ten — his mother had died at his birth. He attended primary school and Lismore High for a while, but his schooling was interrupted and he finally gave it away when his father became ill and he had to tend the bananas.

Banana growers like Hanif and his father would take their produce to Lismore or Casino; any not sold there would go to Sydney and Melbourne. Before 1948 all the east coast's bananas, peas and beans came from these places. Railway tracks snaked through the hills and horse trolleys were used to transport produce.

'Beautiful to see those places then,' Hanif said wistfully.

After the Second World War, the Australian government brought in thousands of Italian workers, many of whom eventually came to the north coast and bought land, often living cheek by jowl with both Indian leaseholders and big pastoralists. The Italians settled down with either Italian brides they brought out or local wives. And the Muslims?

'It was too hard to bring our women out.'

I wondered if it also had something to do with the dream of striking it rich and returning home a local hero of largesse and wealth, just like Haji Sher Muhammad all those years ago.

Many Indians, especially the older ones, went back home after the war, but some of the younger people drifted to the cities of Brisbane or Sydney.

'We never sold our farm. We always intended to come back,' Hanif insisted. But for reasons left unsaid, Hanif and his father departed for India in 1946 and Hanif found himself unable to return for forty years.

What was it like for Indians in 1946 in Australia, knowing that they had to make a choice — India or Pakistan? Independence and Partition were nearing.

'One Australian friend, Perce Frederick, pleaded with me, "Don't go back. There will be trouble in your country. You people are going to fight like cats and dogs. Now is the worst possible time to return."'

'"Come on, Perce," I said. "We have to go back — my sisters are all there. Don't worry, nothing is going to happen; there'll be no trouble in the Punjab." After I went back, I wrote him a letter, saying, "You were right."'

Chaos was everywhere on the eve of Partition: Muslims trying desperately to reach Pakistan; Hindus and Sikhs moving in the opposite direction towards the redefined India — and everyone racing against the clock. It took Hanif and his family three months to travel the hundred and fifty kilometres from their village of Kotlee, now within the new India, to the Punjabi capital, Lahore, which was now in Pakistan. Refugees could not travel without military convoys to protect them. They would stay in a camp for a week, move along a few kilometres, and find themselves forced to stop and anxiously wait another month for yet another military convoy.

Arriving in Lahore, Hanif found himself with thirty-five rupees in his pocket and the shirt and trousers he was wearing. On his feet, he still wore a pair of Dunlop sandshoes from 'home'. An Australian friend came to his aid. Gordon Murphy, his old schoolmate in Caniaba, answered his desperate telegram and sent enough money for Hanif and his family to survive on for the next year.

'We made little huts, small houses out of mud bricks to live in — we had to make the bricks by hand, too. How I regretted leaving Australia! I couldn't even speak Punjabi properly. Thirteen years of living in a hovel and working for other people,' he says bitterly. For the first time the smile fades and the genial Australian countryman disappears. 'We were landless until 1960, when we got some land in compensation for what we'd lost. My poor father died in 1952, when we were still struggling along from day to day.'

Land compensation in 1960 was limited and an administrative nightmare for the new Pakistani government, and a nightmare of waiting and hoping for the landless dispossessed like Hanif. Some farmers would receive land left behind by Sikh and Hindu farmers who had fled to India and who themselves might spend the rest of their days farming land that once belonged to a Muslim farmer — a farmer who tended the same crops and spoke the same language but practised another religion.

'We had one stroke of good luck. Land records for the Punjab had always remained in the capital, Lahore, so at least we could prove we were landowners.' But it was not until 1975 that Hanif was declared the legal owner and finally felt safe.

Just after the land business was settled, a fresh quarrel broke out — this time with the Australian government over his status. Hanif had always believed that he was an Australian citizen. To his terrible distress, he was now told that he wasn't — despite his Australian passport and the farm he still owned in New South Wales. The wrangle was only resolved in 1993, by which time Hanif was living back in Sydney, and waiting for his family to join him.

For more than thirty years he'd believed he was an Australian citizen and then, through some administrative error, he discovered that he wasn't.

'You've bloody ruined my life!' he told them at immigration.

And they said he wasn't Australian?

Latifa Ali is Hanif's niece. Whereas his father 'went a-farming', Latifa's father, Rahmatullah, was a true hawker; a man who turned his back on the farming tradition for the freedom and uncertainty of life on the open road.

Latifa adored him, in particular his great sense of humour and love of a good time. A 'good time' meant circuses, for he never missed a circus or a carnival that came to town. He liked 'the Charlie Chaplin silent movies, zoos and listening to the speakers at the Domain.'

From photographs he looks a dapper figure, with a homburg hat pulled over his eyes. Latifa, with her dark hair, no-nonsense air and quick, economical movements, resembles him, I think.

Eighteen was the typical age for young men to leave their village. With his youthful ways and happy personality, Rahmatullah got on well with the young Australian men he met in the country, and often went on hunting parties with them. Starting out with money lent by a friend, he hawked with a case in his hand as he tramped the roads on foot. It must have been in the early 1900s, although Latifa believes that he came out in 1898.

Contracting for fencing work from local farmers and sleeping rough at night was a favourite way of earning extra money, but if a man was serious about hawking, sooner or later he needed a horse and cart. Within a year or so, with the extra money, Rahmatullah bought a horse and built himself a cart with special drawers of different sizes for the assortment of items he sold.

All the men in those days knew each other's routes and each had his special round. A full circuit took about three months and sometimes their paths would cross, which brought a welcome respite from the roads and the dust and the sound of your own voice. Life was better with a horse and cart. For one thing you could make longer trips, with your wagon piled high with goods. It was also easier to ride along the dirt tracks than to tramp them on foot. Bourke, Dubbo and Broken Hill were Rahmatullah's territory for many years — vast tracts of hard, dry land for a man to traverse on horse and cart. A horse was a good mate for a lonely man.

'They were more religious than the next generation,' Latifa said. 'During Ramazan, the month of fasting, they never worked; they would come in from the country and congregate together for the festival of Eid ul-Fitr; they gave their *qurbani*, the annual sacrifice of meat or money, as donations to poor Australians. For the whole month they fasted and rested.' In Ramazan, or Ramadan, as Arabic speakers pronounce it, you are not supposed to travel and fast at the same time. So this enforced holiday for thirty days of the year became a time of prayer and friendly gathering for men who spent most of their days alone.

They would pray by themselves with their prayer mats out on the country roads, or when they came to Sydney, they would pray together with others in a room or a house, for there were no mosques then.

Times were hard and people were careful with their money, but the hawkers provided an essential service. Rahmatullah encountered no trouble because of his skin colour, though Latifa remembers him telling her that Aborigines were badly treated by white men.

'Some of his customers were Aborigines. They would call out to him, "Here comes our countryman!" when he appeared, because they were the same colour.'

Business prospered. Rahmatullah bought a second horse and built a special canvas-covered wagon for living and sleeping in. By then he had made up his mind to return to India, marry and return with his bride. It was 1934 and he was in his fifties. Like many others, he had delayed marrying until his fortunes took a turn for the better.

'He's come back with a wife!'

Word got around the properties that their old friend 'Jack' had been as good as his word and gone and got married. When the bridal couple first turned up at the stations, everyone rushed to see Jack and his new bride. There stood the bride in strange, uncomfortable western clothes, because her husband had insisted that she dress like the locals. She stood shyly to one side, surrounded by people she could not understand, strange men grinning at her, children squealing and dogs barking … warm, friendly people, but oh, so strange! Of course Latifa's mother found life on the road hard, but who would protect her when her husband was out working the roads if she stayed behind in the city?

As a young child, Latifa travelled with her parents in the two wagons — one serving as a haberdashery shop and the other as a sleeping caravan. The wagons trundled along, the pots and pans, kettles and crockery, lamps and tins clanging away. Rahmatullah would slaughter their meat out on the stations the *halal* way, according to proper religious ritual. The farmers never minded — they ate it anyway and never charged him for his portions.

'My mother would cook chapattis and curry over an open fire while my father brushed and fed the horses. They all had special names — I have no idea where he got the names from! By then he had four horses,' Latifa said counting them on her fingers. 'There was Smiler, Bonny, Kate — and Dhal. Yes, dhal, the favourite curried lentil dish he loved so much. And then we had a foal called Betty. They probably sounded exotic names to him …

'All the Indian men treated their horses like children and talked to them in Punjabi. The horses definitely understood my father. When he returned from the city he would go to their paddock and they would come cantering across, jealously vying to get his attention first.

'Horses were always bought from the property owners and he broke them in himself — I remember the scars on his legs. He would also give a hand helping to muster the brumbies for the owners.

'It was a good life,' Latifa sighed. 'Hard, but good. I still remember my father singing as we rode along. "If you sing," he always said, "you never get sick." He had some favourite songs: "Ramona", and a whole lot of country and western tunes.'

By 1948 another daughter had been born and the children needed schooling, so Rahmatullah said goodbye to his old life and the family settled back in Sydney, living comfortably in the Gladesville house he had bought with his accumulated savings long before but in which they had hardly ever lived.

They had to leave the horses behind, but managed to bring Wally, Rahmatullah's pomeranian, with them to Gladesville. But the days of Latifa's father making her kites out of newspaper and twigs were long gone, and there was no need to make her little hats with bobbing corks to keep the flies away. Latifa's country childhood was over.

Even after coming back to Sydney, Rahmatullah made the local rounds with his suitcase just as he had done at the start as a young man, all those years ago.

'He had itchy feet and after hawking for nearly fifty years, it was in his blood,' Latifa said. 'He couldn't stop, although by then the days of the hawkers were really over. Small shops were opening up and taking the business. Grace Brothers had their mail-order catalogues, people used cars and the roads were better ... But still he went on as long as he could.'

Muslims were great travellers in the past and there were some wayfarers who wanted the caravan to go on for ever ... A special breed, the Muslim hawkers; fired by imagination and true to their religion, against the odds; their journey but a prelude to others who would follow after a long interlude.

2

Rose carpets of Isparta

Turkish–Cypriot Muslims first settled in Australia in the late 1940s, their entry eased because, as residents of a British territory, they held British passports. This magical document allowed them to circumvent the White Australia policy, which held other Turks to be Asian. Immigration from the Turkish mainland did not begin until 1968, after the signing of an agreement between Australia and Turkey.

Ibrahim Dellal, an exceedingly polite Turkish–Cypriot community leader, eloquent and well versed in English, told me about those early years. At his suggestion we met at a Turkish pizza parlour in Sydney Road, Brunswick, an inner-city, working-class suburb of Melbourne, crowded with Turkish clubs, restaurants, coffee houses, bakeries — everything *halal*, of course.

'It's a miracle that you're here!' he said to me. By now I was growing used to Ibrahim's colourful language, although people do not usually associate me with miracles. Pleasantly but firmly, he insisted I use the Turkish word *Turkei* when talking about his ancestral land, and coached me in my pronunciation until my tongue became obedient.

Ibrahim, a man of firm convictions and a full head of snowy white curls, talked with great gusto of his experiences in the 1950s 'When Australia was more disciplined, there was full employment and I was eighteen years old and full of fire!'

One day in November 1968, a group of 168 immigrants from mainland Turkey landed in Sydney. Ibrahim flew from Melbourne to Sydney on this great occasion to greet them.

'I was with Shaykh [Sheikh] Fahmi and one of the old camel men, a Turk called Mustapha Anjahn who was blind and very old. As they came off the plane Mustapha tugged at my sleeve.

'"Tell me, they are tall, aren't they?" he said.

'They weren't particularly tall, but I didn't want to disappoint him, so I said, "Yes, they're tall."

'"Are their costumes beautiful, my son?"

'"Yes," I answered, wanting him to remember them as they were in his youth. There were two or three other such questions and I kept answering "yes" all the time.

'"It's great," he said. "They haven't changed a bit!"'

Those first mainland Turks, and many who followed them, soon disappeared into automobile assembly plants and clothing and textile factories.

That day in 1968 marked the most significant contact between Australians and Turks since the battle of Gallipoli in the First World War, commemorated each year in Australia on Anzac Day, 25 April. 'Johnny Turk' had finally arrived in Australia. Because of the respect between Turkish and Australian and New Zealand soldiers that grew out of their wartime encounters, Turkish immigrants in Australia were not generally regarded as 'typical Muslims'. 'Johnny Turk' was seen as a friendly figure, quite unlike the terrifying 'Turkish conqueror' image that had been used to frighten little children as the 'Muslim hordes' advanced on Europe.

At its zenith the Ottoman Empire ruled south-eastern Europe, North Africa, most of the lands around the Mediterranean Sea and Arabia. The five hundred years from the fall of Constantinople in 1453 to the collapse of the Turkish Empire in 1918 are not part of Australia's historical memory. Our own threatening stereotypes stem from the English crusade romances or television fairytales of Arabs in Bedouin dress at prayer, or Iranian clerics complete with black robes, turbans, flowing beards and piercing eyes.

Ten years old and, like many of her generation, quick-witted and dependable, Sema became an 'interpreter' right from the beginning. In the late 1960s there was no government telephone interpreter service, in fact there weren't many migrant services at all. So the new Turkish arrivals were forced to improvise. Young Sema often interpreted for others, with her parents' encouragement. Everyone knew how hard it could be trying to make sense of an alien world as you stumbled along, your tongue thick and useless, trying to form new sounds in situations which confounded and threatened you.

'Why didn't they learn English?' the uninformed and unfair have cried for decades. Perhaps those critics have never tried learning Arabic, or Turkish, or Italian, or Greek at the end of a long day on the assembly line, or after a night shift, when you want nothing more than to cry and you wonder if the desperate dream driving you along has turned into a nightmare.

Word quickly made the rounds that with young Sema by your side, your problems were solved. Soon everyone seemed to be knocking on Sema's door, especially as her services were free. Other 'voluntary' interpreters charged around $20 for one visit or for helping you with a document. Factory workers earned about $41 a week then so spending half a week's pay on an interpreter meant going without something else, like food, paying your rent or some other basic essential. The quality of a family's life could spiral downwards if other solutions were not found. Sema and her brother were part of the solution.

A mountain of problems was always waiting to be resolved: wrenching a bond back from a real estate agent; helping a family get a bank loan, locate work or exchange goods at stores — the toaster that refused to pop, the radio that stayed mute and the shoes that fell apart. And Sema was more often successful than not.

'It was strange, but because my English was fairly limited I always gave very straightforward versions of what was being said. If, for instance, they swore at the person I accompanied, saying, "Tell him to bugger off!" I would say just that in Turkish. You never got a censored message with me — no creative interpreting for diplomatic reasons!' she said. 'No inhibitions and no embarrassment!

'People often used the semi-professional or 'pocket-money' interpreters, as we called them, but they were expensive. Only the banks had official interpreters. We never charged anything. My brother and I had been well drilled by our parents and we refused even little gifts of lollies.'

Sema, now in her mid thirties, is small with dark brown hair. She has intelligent, laughing eyes and a vivacious way of talking. She is friendly, but elusive. Several times when passing through Melbourne I failed dismally to capture her story before she finally resigned herself to my doggedness.

Sema's parents were very moderate in their religious beliefs and practices, but with Islamic and cultural values so intertwined it was hard to distinguish what was religious and what was national culture, she said. Their status rested partly on their ability to help community members. What she and her brother did contributed to this end, although it was never mentioned. At that time, she said, the Turkish community was very closely knit — 'not like today with all the different political and religious factions and organisations.'

Perhaps that is the way of guest workers the world over. When you see yourself as transitory, a passer-by, everything you save for and yearn for lies behind you. Once it is clear that you are a real immigrant and here to stay, you start trying to re-create what was important to you in your past — even down to sociopolitical, religious and other ties.

Sema went on: 'Here was I, a child interpreter, a ten-year-old kid doing the best I could. I don't think my English was so crash hot. Still, it sounded wonderful to people who couldn't speak a word, and everyone seemed to have this over-inflated opinion of my abilities.' I thought I detected a note of satisfaction.

One of her great success stories had to do with a rental bond. In those days it was common for two families to share a house; in this case one family wanted to move out and asked for their share of the bond back. The landlord refused to budge and the $20-interpreter proved unsuccessful. So Sema was brought in.

'The usual drama began, with the threats and the swear-words. "Bugger off!" the landlord yelled. "I'm not giving you anything!"

'I repeated this, and the enraged Turkish response. On and on it went! Eventually the landlord got so fed up he gave them the $120 back — anything to get rid of us, I suppose.'

Perhaps the landlord finally felt ashamed of swearing in front of a ten-year-old child, or perhaps he had finally seen the funny side of it all. *How do you translate 'bugger off!' into Turkish, I wondered.*

'One day a woman came to our house wanting someone to go with her to the hospital. We had only been in Australia for three or four months. "Take your brother? Oh no!" she said. "Woman problem."'

So off they went together, little Sema and the woman who needed her help, to the Royal Women's Hospital. 'I was looking forward to the tram ride, it felt like an excursion to me; the sun was shining and here I was away from parental supervision. I felt pretty important of course — an adult needed my help!

'A male doctor took the woman into a cubicle. Years later I realised he had given her a gynaecological examination, but what did I know then at ten? I remember to this day that when the woman emerged from the cubicle, her face was scarlet and she refused to look at me.'

It was the worst possible humiliation for the woman to have exposed herself to a male doctor. And to make it worse, a ten-year-old girl had witnessed her shame. In her own country a midwife would have handled this matter without a man in sight. What would her husband say?

'Of course I didn't know what was happening behind the curtain,' said Sema. 'I was innocent and naive. I thought it was the usual hospital business — listening to her chest, telling her to cough. But the woman must have thought I knew what was happening. Only years later did I remember and make the connection.'

Twenty-five years have passed, but she still recalls what the doctor said to her. 'Now I am going to give her this cream and she must use it before she and her husband ...' The doctor used words totally foreign to Sema, they meant nothing to her. 'I'm sorry,' Sema blurted out. 'I don't know what you are saying.'

He sighed and said it another way but again she shook her head, puzzled. What did these big words mean? He pulled his chair closer to her, and turned her chair around so that they were sitting eye to eye. Picking up a notepad, he began drawing little pictures to help her pass on his message to the patient, who sat there mute, still as red as a beet, twisting her hands in her lap while she studied the floor.

'Before she goes to sleep, with her husband ... she must use the cream' — and he pointed indicating exactly where he meant — 'down there'. He had used his entire repertoire — crudely drawn diagrams, mime and pidgin English.

Sema finally understood — from a ten-year-old perspective, that is — what was going on. Her face flushed, her ears and neck felt hot. She sensed that this was taboo. A strange man was telling her things she wasn't supposed to know about. 'Guilt, embarrassment, and fear — I felt all of those things. But most of all I sensed that my dignity had been assaulted and that I lay exposed. My childhood, my innocence was gone and I wasn't even a woman. I had lost something. An excited, happy little girl had gone on a great adventure to the hospital. Even in the waiting room I'd been all bubbly, full of self-importance.' But once she understood and felt the terrible shame, just like the woman, it became a horrible experience.

The doctor appeared in a good mood as he walked them out. Patting Sema on the shoulder, he looked down at her, 'Now when you grow up — when you finish school — you come back here and work as an interpreter for me. You were a very good girl.' She continued looking down at the floor.

On the way home Sema recalled not speaking to the woman. 'I said what I had to say, not looking anyone in the face. I just kept looking down at my feet. I never discussed this episode with my mother. I remember telling her, though, that I didn't want to interpret for women's business any more. And I never did. She never asked me why — maybe she guessed.

'Having to work all the time as an interpreter for adults, I had to grow up very quickly,' Sema said. 'Even today, when other people talk about their teenage years I've got nothing to say. Between the years of ten and sixteen I missed out on childhood. And there were many other children like me.'

The usually sunny, good-natured Sema became angry as she relived this once more. Her body tensed and she unconsciously conveyed something of the resentment she tried to swallow all those years ago. 'I got to where I am now on my own, studying part time at night, doing it the hard way. Sometimes I think I could have done much more with my life if I'd been able to do better at school or at least go on; but the interpreting consumed so many hours, it seemed to eat up my life. I was the eldest and was expected to pull my weight around the house as well. I've been juggling a hundred and one things since I was ten, with never a break.

'I feel as if there is a huge hole in my life — as if something is missing. I left school at fourteen. My parents believed school was a bad influence on girls. Even though they weren't practising Muslims in the full sense, they still had all the cultural baggage. I stayed home for two years, desperate to get out of the house and work. I was married off very young at sixteen, but it didn't last; I remarried years later.'

Sema sighed deeply and at last seemed to relax. 'My second husband has been my greatest friend and support. At last I'm happily married; I've completed my Bachelor of Economics degree and I'm thinking of going on. You know, sometimes I feel this urge to go on as if I'm still trying to make up for what I think I've missed.'

Isparta in southern Turkey is famous for its carpets and rose perfume. Fresh cool air from the Taurus mountains wafts over the inland town, whose carpet makers were once famous for their distinctive rose motifs.

Fatma comes from a family of traditional carpet makers. Generation after generation followed this ancient craft. Carpet making meant everything in the world to both sides of her family — it was their life. Uncle Hamid raised sheep to ensure that only the best wool would be used in the carpets' pile; his sons grew the cotton for the base; their wives and daughters spun the yarn which they would hand on to Aunt Hadiya or to cousin Aydin and his helpers to dye in delicate shades of ivory, pink and light blue. Fatma's mother faithfully re-created the beautiful floral designs for the small company of weavers to follow, while her father, as head of the family, with a son on either side, called out the number of knots of each colour as master weavers, or *ustad*, had done for centuries: 'One blue, two pink, three blue ...' Another uncle ran the family carpet shop and waited on customers, some of them shop owners from cities nearby, unrolling carpet after carpet and serving endless cups of coffee as they spent the afternoon making their choice.

Buying a carpet was a serious business in Turkey. Traditionally a girl was expected to have a special carpet with a rose design — *gul* is the Persian word meaning rose — for her wedding. In Isparta, girls started learning how to weave at the age of five or six so they could make their own carpet by the time they married. Boys were given carpets too, to mark the biggest events in their lives: their circumcision, the start of military service and their wedding day. The traditional motifs had special meanings: the tree of life, birds and dragons stood for the continuity of the soul and the human desire for immortality, while the rose represented the garden of Eden. Women also used carpet motifs to express feelings which custom prohibited them from declaring aloud or even whispering. A tombstone on a *kilim*, for example, means 'I'd die if I ever had to part from my beloved', Fatma told me.

Carpet weaving in the old days was a prosperous small business with a secure income, but modern ways and their erosion of tradition changed all that. Fatma's family went bankrupt and were forced to move to Izmir. Then, after her older brother died in the 1974 war in Cyprus, Fatma's parents prepared to move again. The family of carpet makers now put the roses of Isparta far, far behind them and joined the stream of migrants leaving Turkey for Australia. 'One day we were in Ankara, the next day in Sydney. We stayed a few weeks at the migrant hostel there and have only bad memories of the place. We were served pork for a long time before we discovered what we were eating!'

From Sydney they moved to Wollongong, an industrial centre to the south, where Fatma's father got a job at the BHP steelworks. From weaving rose carpets to a hot, noisy blast furnace — it seemed in some ways like being catapulted from heaven to hell.

After a time the family moved again, to Melbourne, where they lived in a high-rise housing estate in North Carlton for ten years, and where her father worked at the Ford car factory.

School was confusing. 'Back in Turkey, students helped one another, yet here everyone looked after themselves and there was a strong competitive streak which made me uncomfortable. No discipline, no respect for the teacher ... In Turkey we might have forty students in a room, yet there would not be a sound. Education was the biggest thing in your life and teachers were respected as much as your parents. Here teachers ignored kids kissing or carrying on in class, while in Turkey it was boys on one side, girls on the other!

'I counted myself lucky because my parents had mixed with non-Muslims in the city and did not stop me from making new friends. I was doubly fortunate because my mother worked only part time, teaching Turkish from home. We didn't become "latch-key" kids. Most Turkish families were in debt, so both parents were forced to work, usually on assembly lines.'

Some children hardly ever saw their parents. If they were both on shift work they would be leaving for work when the children were coming home from school. 'Kids were running away from home because parents wanted them to be Turkish and all around them they saw this Australian freedom,' Fatma remembers. 'Adolescents left at home all day to look after their brothers and sisters found the pressure intolerable.'

Four children Fatma knew, the eldest eleven and the youngest two years old stayed home on their own day and night during the week, terrified of opening the door. It was not unusual to hear of children being sent back to Turkey to be brought up by grandparents. This often led to more problems later because of the weakening of filial bonds of respect and obedience. But gradually things settled down. Children started to do well at school after they grew used to the taunts of 'Wog! Wog!' and to 'Being treated like morons by teachers.' There were opportunities in Australia — but at a price.

Parents, especially fathers, felt ashamed. Suddenly they were reliant on little children. They saw their authority and dignity disappearing as their children adapted to the new country more successfully than they — a shameful reversing of roles. A Turkish-trained psychiatrist once explained to me: 'The experience is similar to undergoing a second childhood, but this time the "adults" are children.'

'Slowly it dawned on us,' said Fatma, 'that we were the second generation of Turks in Australia. This made a very big impact on my family's thinking. We started to urge other families to keep their children at school, especially their daughters. I remember that we went from house to house trying to persuade people we knew; my parents felt strongly that this was the solution. If you were fifteen in those days, you automatically started working in a factory.'

Fatma is especially fond of her brother Zeynel; 'My mentor' she calls him. 'He was never too tired to help me with my maths, even after working overtime at the factory;

in Turkey he had finished high school. I remember him telling everyone who asked, why I still remained at school. "My sister will not work in a factory like me. She will have education and a better place."'

Fatma interpreted and translated for her parents just as Selma did. 'Most of my generation did this,' she says quite simply. There are no emotional scars.

Turkish parents paid a heavy price for their children's prosperity in the new land. They wove their dreams into a family carpet with their children as the centrepiece of their lives. But not all Turkish-born children were as lucky as Fatma, who graduated from university with a degree in accountancy and now has a steady career and no marriage plans as yet. There were casualties on both sides: some children as well as parents became lost and bypassed the caravanserai of dreams.

3

The boy from Bandung

Hundreds of years before the birth of the Prophet of Islam, Arab traders plied the sea and overland routes between the Red Sea and China. In their wake other merchants followed, crossing vast distances, defying danger and embracing the new. When Islam sprang up in what is today Saudi Arabia, these traders carried the new faith with them, and there grew a Muslim world of trade and commerce unrivalled in its day, linking the Sublime Porte of Turkey, the Persian courts of Baghdad and the Mughal palaces of India.

It is written that 'wealth does not come to the man who waits in his own bazaar haggling over a few dinars'. Those who dream of vast wealth must hazard the risks of the greater marketplace. During the fourteenth century there emerged in the Indian Ocean region two mighty ports controlled by Muslim rulers which drew traders as surely as sweet nectar draws the bee: Cambay, in Gujerat, India, whose ruling class had converted to Islam; and Malacca, on the Malay peninsula, which in the centuries ahead would attract the envy and enmity of the Portuguese. It was the custom for merchants travelling from Cairo, Mecca, Aden and the ports of the Persian Gulf to rendezvous at Cambay on their way to Malacca. And so Islam entered the Malay peninsula and the Indonesian archipelago, where shrewd rulers perceived it as a political instrument of potential value. The traders returned laden with nutmeg, cloves, mace, sandalwood, seed pearls and silk, leaving behind their money, trade goods and religion.

According to that inveterate traveller Marco Polo, Perlak, in Sumatra, had just become Muslim around 1292. By the early fifteenth century Islam had spread as far as Malacca and the northern ports of Java, which were in the final stages of their struggle against the declining Hindu–Buddhist central empire of Majapahit. Conversion is perhaps not the right word to describe how Islam came to Java. The change was a more gradual, syncretic process, in which yet another layer of culture was applied to an ancient civilisation. Today Indonesia is the largest Muslim country in the world, with a population of more than a hundred and eighty million people.

Indonesian–Australian relations are still developing. Our nearest Muslim neighbour is a country with a proud nationalistic spirit honed through the hardships of a three-hundred-year history of colonialism that ended less than fifty years ago.

'What shall we talk about?' Dede Sujatna wanted to know. He seemed wary and who could blame him. I had descended rather abruptly. He was a polite man — I was stubborn — and it didn't take long to persuade him.

Dede Sujatna is a senior academic at a Perth university. Trying to guess his age was difficult, yet I thought he must be older than he looked — a serene, cheerful man, dark brown hair combed away from his face, always neatly dressed and, by reputation, popular with his students. From past observations I believed him to be a very private man. Whatever his age, his memories were crystal clear: there was no warm nostalgia to burrow through. His story, which he told evenly, impartially, might have happened only yesterday, rather than fifty years before.

Dede had grown up in Indonesia during the time of

Dutch colonisation. Christianity was then the religion of 'the Dutch masters', and the prosperous Chinese middle class were mainly Confucian, Taoist or Buddhist. Islam, he told me, was regarded by the ruling elite as the religion of the underclass, the ignorant, 'the country bumpkins'.

Yet Christianity held little attraction for the vast majority of Indonesians and conversion to Christianity was rare. The Dutch, wanting to avoid armed conflict, were wise enough to confine missionary activities to remote regions in the eastern parts of the archipelago. Islam was, and remained, an important symbol of resistance to the colonial caste system, which was the antithesis of Islam's spirit of equality.

'I was about nine or ten when the Dutch surrendered to the Japanese in 1942, so I didn't notice much about politics during the colonial period. I wasn't aware of discrimination, but of course my parents were. Indonesians could not swim in the same swimming pools as whites, we could only swim in the rivers. We encountered many of the same things as black and coloured South Africans did under apartheid — the social clubs and park benches for whites only, the "No dogs and natives" signs at certain beaches.' His voice is calm, matter-of-fact, without a trace of bitterness.

Because Dede's father was a civil servant, he was permitted to attend a Dutch school — an obvious privilege. The family lived in Bandung, the administrative capital, known in its day as the Paris of Java. It was a beautiful city, high in the mountains, with cool, shady boulevards, clement weather and beautiful European-style mansions. Dede has good memories of his childhood. But his young eyes did not see the enormous social and economic gaps between the rulers and the ruled. Whites lived in spacious houses with neat gardens, waited on by numerous servants. Indonesians lived in kampongs — clusters of traditional houses which in the cities were more like hovels — crowded, with inadequate sanitation and insufficient drinking water.

When the Japanese seized Indonesia in the Second World War, the Dutch were imprisoned in the camps, humiliated and forced to do the work their servants had once performed. 'Then I began to realise that the Dutch were a different race from us and were now at the bottom of the ladder — crushed and oppressed too. New masters had appeared who were much crueller than the Dutch.

'At first we admired the Japanese. It seemed incredible — brown men defeating white men! Later, when our islands were stripped of everything to supply the Japanese war machine and we were starving, we saw things in a different light. Every Friday morning we missed school and were sent on a scrap metal hunt. It wasn't much fun because we had to search in all the filthy places — rubbish dumps and sewers — looking for metal to be sent back to Japan and used for the war effort. Still I didn't mind missing Friday prayers at the mosque for I was a child, and my faith, my *iman*, was small.'

Under the Japanese, school assemblies took on a military tone. The pupils would line up facing north-east towards Tokyo and bow to the Japanese flag and emperor. A quick smile crossed Dede's face as he remembered that time. 'When I prayed I faced Mecca, and at school we lined up and faced Tokyo!

'I confess that as a small boy I loved to watch the military parades — like all little boys I suppose — when the Japanese army marched in full regalia down the road; flags flying, straight lines, shiny buttons and boots, rifles on their shoulders and officers with their swords — to me they looked glorious. I admired this show without realising what stood behind it all.'

Javanese men were conscripted into working for the Japanese. *Prajurit ekonomi* (economic soldiers) was preferred to the term *romusha* or coolie. But by whatever name, the reality was forced labour, under dreadful conditions. Many Javanese — perhaps three hundred thousand — were sent to toil overseas. At the end of the war, only seventy thousand returned.

When Dede was about twelve, his parents became ill and, lacking decent food or medical attention, they both died. With his three younger brothers, he went to live with his elderly aunt, a childless widow, illiterate and poor. Every day was a struggle. By now the war was over and Indonesia was in revolutionary turmoil as the Dutch tried to retrieve their former power. When they occupied Bandung Dede, his aunt and brothers, and others from the kampong were forced to flee. 'The Dutch were expanding their territory all the time, so we kept moving, trying to get further away from the city, until finally we stopped — somewhere in the jungle — and built huts.' There they stayed for three and a half years. They ate anything they could find — grasshoppers, flying foxes, snakes. Finding water was always a problem. Only the most devout fasted during the holy month of Ramazan, although they all continued their prayers. The hardships he faced led Dede to rediscover his faith for himself.

'At fourteen I was still not old enough to hold a gun. You could not join the resistance army anyway until you were about seventeen. The men scrounged old Japanese weapons and anything we could steal or capture from the Dutch. I am talking about guerrilla warfare.'

Why had everyone left their kampongs? Dede explained that Indonesians didn't want to be seen as collaborating with the Dutch. They didn't want to live with the Dutch; they made their choice — living with the Dutch made you a traitor to the nation.

During those years in the jungle, the only schooling Dede and the other children received was from the village *ulemma* or scholars, who taught them Arabic, how to understand the Qur'an and how to pray. In 1949, on the declaration of Indonesian independence, Dede returned to the fourth grade, no longer a child, but resuming his role as a primary school pupil as he had missed four years of formal schooling. Instruction was now in Indonesian, not Dutch. 'Now I entered my education phase,' he told me. 'I had to support my aunty and my brothers.' For the last two years of primary school, where there were no fees, he managed to scrape by. To put himself through high school, 'I mixed mortar at a local Dutch cemetery which my boss — an Indonesian — was contracted to build. I worked in the mornings and went to high school in the afternoons.'

Dede gives the impression of having been a loner who had to put adolescent fancies behind him: his years as the family breadwinner matured him early. Unlike many of his schoolmates, he had, 'No girlfriends, no motor scooters, no radio. I was a poor boy who mixed mortar in the cemetery — who would go out with me? How I wished I had money for the cinema, a soft drink or ice-cream. But everything I had went to support the family.'

After graduating from high school, Dede went to teachers' college for three years. There he received a small wage. But he was still a poor boy with not enough clothes and one pair of shoes; most of his money was still handed over to his aunt. His life changed dramatically, however, when he won a Colombo Plan scholarship to New Zealand in 1960. The poor unsophisticated boy from Bandung was off to Wellington!

'Oh! New Zealand was a paradise! I felt like a real person studying at Victoria University for two years.' Almost for the first time in his account, the emotion escapes. For the moment, financial burdens were forgotten. Dede's Indonesian salary went to his aunt and the scholarship looked after his needs in New Zealand. When he returned to Indonesia, people looked up to him. He even found a girlfriend. 'My wife was my first, and my only girlfriend.'

In 1968, after additional part-time tertiary study, Dede

applied for two university positions in Australia, and was offered both. The Perth job finally snared him and his first lecturer's salary was $4800. By now he was married with two children, but for the first three months he lived alone, lonely and depressed, in a hotel room. Perth seemed little more than a seaside resort. Where were all the people? He finally located a house in West Perth for $20 a week, so that his family could come. Twenty-five years ago, they were the first Indonesian family in Western Australia.

'Now, from mixing the mortar in the Dutch cemetery, here I am in my nice air-conditioned office in front of my computer looking out at the university campus. I certainly can't complain. My family has done well. I have two homes, Australia and Indonesia, which I go back to every two or three years. I still have responsibilities for my relatives there. I thank Allah all the time in my prayers.'

Islam in Indonesia in the mid nineties had its own special quality. While there was a religious revival in Indonesia after independence, it was different from those in the Middle East and Malaysia — Dede describes it as strictly Indonesian: a moderate movement, still adhering closely to the fundamentals of Islam — the Qur'an and the Hadith — but studied and interpreted in a rational, scholarly way, emphasising consensus. 'An intellectual movement,' Dede called it. 'Our Islam allows for modern technology and a place in the modern world. We believe in the fundamentals of Islam, but we are not what the West calls "fundamentalists". Every Muslim group non-Muslims disapprove of automatically receives this label.'

Many Muslim men and women around Australia would agree with Dede. But while some react with irritation, exasperation or bitterness, Dede expressed only regret and disappointment that the country of his birth and the country he had adopted did not see eye to eye on some things near to his heart.

The years passed and Dede and I lost contact with each other, but in the wake of the Bali blasts on 12 October 2002 I was moved to speak to him once more. He has retired from academic life and now spends most of his time doing volunteer work with the local Indonesian community in Perth; he has hopes that they can build their own mosque very soon.

Clearly he is devastated by the Bali violence; like other Muslims he cannot accept that this was carried out by Indonesian Muslims; at first he does not want to believe it for this is not the moderate Islam he knows so well, that he stills claims for Indonesia. He grieves for Australia and he grieves for Indonesia.

And in spite of what we read in the newspapers and read into the photos of smiling assassins, Islam in Indonesia remains overwhelmingly moderate. The hardline Islamic groups form a small minority in a country where eighty-seven per cent of a population of two hundred and twenty million follow Islam; while a minority have shown their capacity for violence and street politics, only Jemaah Islamiyah (JI), at the time of writing, is suspected of terrorism.

The overwhelming majority of Indonesians support religious neutrality and do not want to become an Islamic state. Moderate Muslims still dominate political, social and religious life in their country. Indonesia's political culture played out through rallies and violent demonstrations is only a small part of the country's tradition. Fundamentalists, from any religion around the world, fear modernity and the threat of secularism above all else. The vast majority of Indonesian Muslims do not. Being a Muslim in Indonesia is not synonymous with being a terrorist.

4

Mountains and mullahs

'Strong vinegar only eats into its own urn,' is an old Albanian saying. The meaning is simple: 'If you become too bitter in life, you will only damage yourself.' Shaip Lutfi reminded himself of this when, each morning, he awoke immersed in clouds of thick, black depression which threatened to choke him before the day had even begun. Six months before, and exactly one week after his sixteenth birthday, he had left Albania far behind and fled to become part of the flotsam and jetsam of London's émigré underworld of the 1960s.

Albanians are an ancient people, a mountain people, who, like the Basques and the Welsh, have throughout history used their terrain to resist invaders and preserve their ways. After each conquest, each loss, the Illyrians, or 'free people', as they were known until the 1880s, withdrew into their mountains — home of some of the highest peaks in Europe — and focused on maintaining their ethnic identity and language. But there have also been compelling reasons to leave. The land is as hard as its history, the soil of poor quality, the terrain rugged, and Albanian families traditionally large. Many Albanians educated in Turkey under the Ottoman Empire bettered their lot by serving in the Turkish army or the administration. In the nineteenth century many more went to the United States, Canada and, eventually, Australia.

Albanians became Muslims when their country was annexed by the Ottoman Turks in the fifteenth century. In the valleys and the mountains, the two main strands of Islam, the Sunni and the Shi'a, both found a place. Sufi mysticism also became woven into the character of Albanian Islam. The old Sufi order Bektashi, or Bejtenxhi, is still strong today. And Shaip, so I learnt, had special links with it, as well as with the ancient, pre-Islamic tribes called Toska and Gega.

'My mother was a Sunni Muslim and a Bektashi, and she was also from the Toska tribe. This led to the odd argument between my parents, and I know my Sunni father, from the Gega tribe — who are stricter Muslims, I've been told — would have preferred greater control over his wife. But her Bektashi, Sufi ways were her means of evading this, almost like her protection against incursions into her soul and spirit.'

I thought it unlikely anyway that a woman who had fought in the Resistance during the Second World War would return meekly to the role of a wife, unquestioningly obedient to her husband, but I kept this to myself.

Shaip was of medium height, but his wiry build made him seem smaller. He had a mountain people's tribal face, his features craggy and irregular. He was intelligent and voluble, with a quick, darting mind.

'My father was the local postmaster in our small town as well as the *muezzin* in our mosque who called the faithful to prayer. He would accompany the imam on special occasions like funerals and boys' circumcisions. He was thirteen years older than my mother, whom he met when they were both in the Resistance, and they married after the war. Father was already married at the time, and his wife refused to accept a second wife and so they were divorced, although he looked after both families and we were all very close — I remember his first wife as a second mother to me.'

Albanian partisans fought against two enemies: the Italian fascists and the Nazis. His village was just seven kilometres from the border separating Albania, which had been annexed by the Italians, from the German-occupied areas of Yugoslavia. Before he was born, Shaip's village lay in Albania. After the war it became part of the Republic of Macedonia in Yugoslavia. His father, as local postmaster, was well placed during the war to collect intelligence, passing it on to partisan leaders in the mountains. His mother was responsible for collecting caches of arms and munitions, which she often hid in her family's cellar. The Albanian resistance movement has been largely overlooked in the chronicles of European war histories, but guerrilla warfare was a way of life and everyone was aware of the constant danger. Men and women fought as equals, and 'The acts of heroism by women were the equal of anything the men did,' Shaip said. 'About seventy per cent of Albania was Muslim and most of the women fighting were Muslim, so a lot of ordinary women, like my mother, fought hard and desperately — expecting and receiving no mercy.

'My father's life also hung by a thread on many occasions. In 1942 he intercepted a communiqué from the German high command to the Italian high command about an Orthodox priest they had captured who was supposed to be a Communist. The Communists were the leaders of the Albanian Resistance and received short shrift when captured — a bullet in the head if they were lucky. Well, the Germans were going to hand him over to the Italians in Tirana, the capital. Unless it could be proven that he was definitely not a Communist, he wasn't going to last long! My father discovered that about five thousand signatures on a petition vouching that the priest was not a Communist might save his life. So he hastily collected them, sent them to the capital in time and the priest was released.'

A year later, his father found himself arrested and facing death. 'I have learnt,' said Shaip, 'that the world is a very strange place indeed and hope is the one thing in life you must not squander.' Someone of the Orthodox community had decided it was score-settling time against Muslims. Memories of the Ottoman Empire were easily stirred and old resentments fanned. By now the German forces were restricted to outlying villages; most of the area was under partisan control. 'They arrested my father, and while he and dozens of others were being led to their execution, an incredible chain of events happened; even today I still shake my head in amazement! The humble priest whose life he had saved only a year before turned out to be the Archbishop of the Orthodox Church in Macedonia. And his son turned out to be a Communist who was also a regional leader of the Yugoslav secret police. Together they saved my father's life!' Shaip believed that more than coincidence lay behind these events, which taught him never to judge people on the basis of ethnicity or religion.

'What kind of sixteen-year-old boy,' I asked Shaip, 'leaves his parents, his country, his friends, to blindly run away to nowhere?'

'The kind who finds himself discriminated against at every turn; the kind who has absolutely no future. And who, when he turns seventeen, will find himself doing military service for two years and is terrified that he will one day find himself shooting and killing his cousins and uncles, who, by sheer accident of history [the postwar re-drawing of borders] are in Albania, on the opposite side of the Yugoslav border from where he lives.

'I lost a community,' he said. 'Even on our side of the border Albanians were moving. A year after I was born, in 1949, the government gave us the choice of going to Turkey. Many seized the chance, leaving their houses behind to be resettled by Croatians and Serbians.'

At fifteen, as part of his pre-military training, Shaip had had a taste of army life. He feared military service as if it was the plague. And so he ran away. Slowly he made his way through Austria to Germany to the United Kingdom, where he was issued with a refugee pass and registered as an alien. For the next two years he struggled to survive.

'London was a twilight realm for émigrés, refugees, aliens — call us what you like.' Shaip described an international underground of outsiders linked by despair. Spaniards, many of them homosexuals forced to flee because of dictator Franco's purges, milled around like lost souls. There were Syrians, Lebanese, Palestinians — young people from all over the world.

It was not hard to imagine the life of the grey youth of Europe as they exchanged their stories and tips by which to survive: the endless cups of coffee and the smoke-filled haunts; the chess games; the poetry; and the philosophical discussions about the era.

'My obsession at this time, the thought I kept coming back to all the time, was that if I died at that moment, not a single person would know who I was.'

Once a month he was obliged to report to the Home Office in London, which served as his only link with the real world. Fifty pounds in a savings account kept him from being deported. 'I worked really hard to make the £50 and I never, ever withdrew it, although believe me there were times when I was hungry — very hungry. I was averaging a meal a day and often went without. Most cafés and restaurants paid us a pittance — £6 a week and a daily meal when the proper wage was £22. But how could we protest? We were grateful to get it!

'What kept me sane was my reading.' During this period he discovered his talent for languages, and taught himself French, Dutch and Swedish, as well as English.

Shaip was thrilled when he learnt he might be able to migrate to Australia, where he had an aunt in Melbourne. But first he had to survive the interview at Australia House.

'The official sat there at his desk with this extremely thick file in front of him. It was all about me! At one stage he pulled out a photograph of me riding my bicycle when I was thirteen! How on earth had he got that? It really floored me! They had either done their homework very well or else their intelligence networks were excellent.'

'What were they concerned about?' I asked.

'They were always worried about Communist connections in those days. Because my parents had been in the Resistance, they suspected a Communist background. It was well known that the Albanian Resistance movement had been largely run by Communists. While this was true, non-Communists were also recruited; no one cared what your religion was then, as long as you believed in the path of Resistance!'

He left the interview believing his chances of getting to Australia were doomed, but a week later he received notice that he would be allowed to immigrate on an assisted passage.

'You were one of the lucky ones — a ten-pound passage?'

He corrected me gently. 'It was eleven pounds something, and I should know because I counted every penny, not because by nature I count my pennies, but because I was so poor.'

My book was about Muslims, travellers from a hundred and more different countries, all with a common thread linking them. My conversation with Shaip had been limited to the political and secular, and I wondered about his ties to Islam.

'The Muslim part of me was gradually diluted through a

set of historical and political circumstances,' he said. 'We were a minority in a newly constructed secular state — Yugoslavia — where officially there was little time for religion and where, in fact, traditional life needed to be stamped out if the nation was to progress — or so our leaders told us. To get into high school or the university, it was almost a precondition that you not be a Muslim.' At least in his area.

'Perhaps it might have been different — no, I'm sure it would have been different if I'd been born on the other side of the border in Albania, where Muslims were not a minority.

'Today I am only a nominal Muslim. I don't go to the mosque and I have lost the ritual, but my core values are all Islamic: respect for human life, respect for other individuals and a concern for justice and fairness. Being Muslim is a part of my identity and that is where it remains,' he said with dignity.

There are relatives in Albania Shaip wishes he could see again after more than twenty-five years away. He was reunited with his parents some years ago when they visited Australia, and is seriously thinking of returning for a visit, but he says he risks being arrested, even after all these years. For having avoided national service he faces a minimum of five years and maximum of ten years in jail — sentences slapped on him in absentia. He also leaves me to understand that life was made very hard for his parents because of what he did.

Most of Victoria's Albanian immigrants entered Australia in small silent waves from the 1920s. 'They are a quiet community with a low profile ... they have reacted to oppression in their homeland by what I call retreating to the mountains of the mind,' Shaip says. 'Over the years they have received very little government funding.' The Albanian mosque is in Drummond Street, Carlton, but many non-Albanians attend as well. He describes the Albanians as an ageing community, disparate and isolated, although they relate well to other Muslim groups, especially the Turkish community. Shaip continues to work with his community today.

To prove that he was not embittered — like the strong vinegar in the old proverb — Shaip decided to entertain me with a selection of jokes and funny stories. He reminded me, with a broad smile, 'Even the imam shall dance to the people's music.'

> An illiterate peasant asked an imam to read his letter to him, as was the custom for those who could neither read nor write. 'What makes you think that I can read?' said the imam, who was new to the village.
>
> 'But you are a man of the cloth!' said the peasant.
>
> 'Well, here's my turban and here's my cloak — you read it!'

Many such humorous tales came to Albania from the Ottoman Empire, which may in turn have received them from somewhere else. The eccentric and foolish Mullah Nasrudin, a bumbling 'religious scholar' who is anything but scholarly, crops up a lot. Humour of this sort is a clever device — a wonderful outlet for religious and social dissent. Its barbs are not directed against core teachings of Islam and certainly never against God, the Qur'an or the Prophet. They are directed against the face of religion as it appears in the village — the mullah. Their target is the religious establishment; its effect to undermine the power of that establishment.

Practically all Muslim countries have their own stories reflecting the national character. All of these stories are created by people living in societies dominated by imams, shaykhs, maulavi and other religious figures. However, while many of these religious figures are scholars educated in eminent institutions, some, like our Mullah Nasrudin, are definitely not!

> Nasrudin Hodja felt very hungry as he walked down the road, carrying two cooked turkeys under his arm, on his way to a religious feast at the house of some colleagues. Suddenly he could no longer bear the pangs of hunger or ignore his rumbling stomach so he stopped and tore off one of the turkey legs and devoured it. But how would he explain the missing leg to his friends? Sure enough, one of them noticed something was amiss, whereupon Nasrudin declared: 'Well of course it is a well-known fact, and God himself has decreed, that once every forty years there will be a turkey born with only three legs.'

Like a magician leaving his best act until last, Shaip revealed how, during his first year in Australia in 1969, he drew a black marble in the national service ballot. Through a bizarre set of circumstances Shaip, the newly arrived non-citizen, found himself conscripted and facing the possibility of a tour of duty in Vietnam, fighting in that unpopular war. How had his immigration file ended up with the Department of National Service? Bureaucratic bungling? Shaip remained suspicious of government officials and the military so he had no wish to draw attention to himself by confronting the department, and no one he trusted could advise him. Was history repeating itself?

'My suitcases were packed in case I had to leave once more. But then,' he said, 'I failed my medical.'

II

Ramadan in Melbourne

I carry these memories with me as I carry my arm or my body.

Hanan al-Shaykh, *The Story of Zahra.*

5

Fading fast in Lygon Street

I left Perth on the midnight flight — the infamous 'red-eye special' that only the foolhardy or the desperate ever take. When I landed three thousand kilometres away, the clocks at Tullamarine Airport told me that it was 7am, not 4am as my recalcitrant body kept trying to assert. It was the first day of Ramadan. Melbourne Muslims had started fasting at sunrise, two hours before, while I had been flying, semi-comatose, somewhere over South Australia.

The question bothering me was whether I should fast or not. Technically, as a traveller journeying more than twenty kilometres, I was exempt. But no, I had stubbornly resolved, I would start my fast on Day 1 of Ramadan. Besides, surely the travel exemption was meant for medieval travellers, centuries ago, alone in the desert or journeying in a caravan of donkeys and camels — not for a spoilt modern passenger sitting in an air-conditioned jet!

Still, it was a rocky first day of Ramadan as I disembarked dazed, jet-lagged and dehydrated. I was house-sitting for old friends in North Carlton and after settling in, though still feeling dazed and jet-lagged, I decided to stock up on food (already food was becoming a priority). What better place than nearby Lygon Street? This was a big mistake.

Everyone in Lygon Street seemed to be sitting at a sidewalk café. If they weren't eating or drinking, they were buying food, ordering food, recommending food, selling food, displaying food or discussing food. The smell of cooking attacked my nostrils. Shop windows displayed epicurean delights and succulent morsels from faraway places. Lygon Street was full of restaurants and coffee houses — everyone knew this; but never before had I appreciated just how many there were! Lygon Street was a village of consumers and cooks, gourmets and gluttons, I noticed morosely. Ambushed at high noon, I had already begun to regret my decision to fly and fast. The whole world seemed to be eating except for me. I felt dizzy and unwell, and longed for sunset so that I could make my *futoor*, or break my fast, with a cool glass of water. I fled — but not before berating myself for my frailty in lusting after sun-dried tomatoes, Italian goat cheese and 'the best pizzas in town'.

The first day of Ramadan is always the hardest. It's a big adjustment for the body to make; to consume nothing — neither food nor drink — between sunrise and sunset for thirty days. It is also a huge psychological struggle in a society which makes no concessions in terms of either rhythm or lifestyle to those who choose to fast. Converts to Islam often experience difficulties the first time they fast. They have not been part of a family of fasters, linked to a large community of fasters, in a society of fasters, where everyone waits in anticipation for the end of Ramadan and celebrates Eid ul-Fitr with great joy and gusto. Often they find themselves fasting alone, perhaps as the only Muslim in their household.

A Muslim I met one day in Geelong tried to explain this sensation. 'I try to go to the mosque every evening, but I want to be fair to my non-Muslim wife and kids and still be part of their lives,' he said. 'I like praying at the mosque for all the religious reasons, but I also need to be with other

Muslims or the isolation becomes too much during Ramadan and it's harder for me to keep up the discipline of fasting.' Faith and dedication often have to compensate.

Muslims are generally loath to exempt themselves from fasting, even on the lawful grounds of an illness requiring medication. I was returning to the community of fasters after many years. My reasons were clear: I would spend the month of Ramadan interviewing and visiting Melbourne Muslims, and it would be shameful to do this without fasting myself; fasting would be good for my self-discipline, and it was a gesture of solidarity for Bosnian Muslims. A symbolic denial of food would obviously not provide a political solution for Bosnia, but it did ease my personal sense of frustration.

Ramadan is all about striving or doing battle against your *nafs*, your innate human desires or 'the enemy within'. *Sawm*, Arabic for fasting, means much more than abstaining from food and drink, cigarettes and sexual intercourse between certain hours, nor is it done for show. It's a private arrangement between you and your God. Observing Ramadan through prayer and fasting is one of the Five Pillars of Islam, which inwardly support and reinforce one's faith. It is a struggle against indiscipline, consumerism, greed, anger, hatred, self-righteousness, false pride, slander and other human vices. It is an attitude of mind; a time to take stock of personal weaknesses, a kind of self-appraisal often spoken of as the greater *jihad*, or battle. *Sawm* should not be forced or undertaken just because others are fasting — everything in Islam depends on your intention, or *niyyat*. If you secretly break your fast, only you and God will know; so it becomes a test of faith for a full month every year.

Rashid was a Bangladeshi of enormous patience and logical mind, happy to argue any fine theological point with me. Trained in Islamic law, he was a shaykh, or religious scholar, about as different from Shaip's beloved nutty Mullah Nasrudin as night from day.

'The devoutness and piety of Muslims are measured by how they observe the Five Pillars, no matter where they live,' Rashid said. 'Muslim country or non-Muslim country — there is no difference, there are no excuses!'

It was night-time, and we had just finished our meal after a day's fasting. Rashid's wife was sitting with us, resting quietly. I didn't think she understood much of what we were saying, but we smiled a lot at each other to make up for our lack of conversation.

'What about some more curry?' Rashid gestured and his wife looked up, all set to disappear into the kitchen to prepare another batch of *parathas* for another round of eating.

'Observance of ritual ... Isn't this what we mean by calling someone a practising Muslim?' For some time now I had been interested in the labels people use to describe themselves — and others.

'In some contexts, yes,' he replied enigmatically.

The labels always confused me, and on occasion irritated me. There were practising Muslims, devout Muslims and pious Muslims. Others described themselves as pragmatic or 'part-time' Muslims. I also came across some who announced, 'Yes, I'm Muslim, but non-practising.' Among the latter, I sometimes noticed an air of defiance, sometimes nonchalance or embarrassment. The Muslims I met in Melbourne were always willing to label themselves — except for the devout, which is perhaps the way of the truly pious.

In Islamic countries overseas, community pressure may be placed on individuals to fast: perhaps your mother-in-law expects it, your husband, your wife or your boss, or even your government. But to a large extent, individuals expect it of themselves. Australian Muslims who do not pray and who do not attend the mosque regularly, or are lax about other practices, are still likely to observe Ramadan, either fully or partially. The part-timers will ensure that they compensate or atone for this in the appropriate way.

Nevertheless, there are those who do fast and those who don't. So when I was making arrangements to meet people, certain delicate moments arose when both sides were trying to judge whether one or the other was fasting. Some people found it too difficult to work in the middle of summer while fasting and might only fast on weekends; some were exempt on religious grounds because they were elderly, sick or pregnant. Some found that their workplace could not or would not accommodate their needs, making fasting extra difficult. Others felt conspicuous and isolated and had problems dealing with this. Then there were the nominal, or 'statistical' Muslims who, while not denying their religion, chose not to fast at all. There were also large numbers of Muslims who fasted throughout the thirty days, uncomplaining and spiritually uplifted by their actions. I wanted to meet them all, but I only had thirty days ...

Muslims have different degrees of attachment to Islam, although this usually remains hidden to outsiders who sometimes behave as if Muslims are perpetually frozen in prayer. Of course, there are Muslims who insist on communicating nothing but the religious aspects of their lives, as if they are hardly touched by the day-to-day problems of mere mortals, so perhaps both sides are to blame for this particular apparition of the 'ice-age' Muslim.

The Muslims I talked to for this book exhibited the full gamut of cultural, traditional and individual expressions of Islam, all linked together by the basic principles of the faith

— a kind of 'unity in diversity'. And the more people I met, the clearer it became that it was the individual's standpoint which determined his or her degree of 'Islamicness'.

I talked to Brian, a university researcher, about trends in current Islamic research. Many religious writers wanted to emphasise unity, not diversity. They disapproved of research which focused on un-Islamic cultural and behavioural patterns at the expense of the overarching body of faith and practice in which all Muslims shared.

Brian was excited about future generations of Australian-born Muslims. He spoke as if a new age was about to descend. My feelings were more reserved. I doubted that the evolution of an Australian Muslim identity, and the diminution of traditional and cultural practices from around the Muslim world that this entailed, were just around the corner.

I asked Melbourne Muslims their views on the thorny question of Muslim identity. 'You're either a Muslim or you're not! There's no halfway!' said an elderly, devout Turkish Muslim with a long history of community involvement. He had little time for 'half-hearted Muslims', he growled. 'My father believes in the golden age of Islam, when our religion was pure. He follows the way of the Sunna in the tradition of the Prophet Muhammad (may peace be upon Him),' said the son of a middle-aged Muslim who spent time at the mosque each day. Other orthodox Muslims described this man's father as 'very strict'; a few used the word 'fanatical'. 'I'm a pragmatic Muslim,' said a thirty-year-old Lebanese social worker. 'I practise what I can; I guess we lead a pure Muslim life. We don't eat pork or drink alcohol, our moral and ethical outlook is Islamic and my daughter goes to an Islamic school. In a way I'm not a strict practising Muslim, I guess, because I don't do the rituals by the book.' This woman wanted her daughter to mix with non-Muslims but still retain her language and tradition. Others remarked, 'Emotionally I am Muslim and I still carry my name, but really I'm nominal only'; 'I try to fast each year, it's about all I do now, and I go to the mosque at Eid time'; 'I would describe him as a secular Muslim, I think, probably too much western education, but still a Muslim of the heart.'

Clearly, there were different degrees of faith, or *iman*. The devout held strongly to the seven articles of Islamic belief and the Five Pillars of Islamic practice. At the other end of the spectrum was the 'minimalist Muslim' who did not always fast or pray, and whose understanding of some details of the faith might be shaky, but who accepted the validity of Islamic beliefs and practice. Of course, 'minimalists' were expected not to 'loiter indefinitely', but eventually to advance to the higher stages of commitment.

Snaking their way in and out of everyone's lives, in ways they were not even aware of, were influences like education, upbringing, personal experiences and the sly intrusion of cultural traditions.

Famida, a postgraduate student from India whom I met through Brian, touched delicately on the tendency of some Muslims to be judgemental. 'People cannot see into your heart; they can't weigh up your actions, so they usually measure your commitment by watching to see if you observe the externals — the ritual. Do you pray, read the Qur'an, fast and so on.' Her comments reminded me of those of a young liberal Muslim from the United Kingdom whom I'd once heard on the radio. He had said that for purists it was not just a question of 'believing' in God, but rather 'how you believed'. Often the concern with 'how you believe' becomes exaggerated for those who are part of a minority in a non-Muslim country. But even in Muslim countries, the ultra-orthodox, sometimes identified as fundamentalists, seem to be preoccupied with 'how you believe' questions.

Hussein Hasan's office had all the marks of a proper bureaucrat: in-trays, out-trays and pending trays; pens, letter openers and files piled high. He was fastidiously dressed in a suit and a striped, button-down shirt, and sported a thick Zapata moustache. He works in education, mainly doing research. Friends and colleagues say he is good at his job. The day I spoke to him he was not fasting. He candidly admitted that altogether he would probably fast for two weeks each Ramadan. 'Eid for me is much more than good food and friendship; it is a deeply religious experience. Although I don't fast all the time, I know what I must do to make up for this.' He supports many causes both overseas (Bosnia, Somalia, Afghanistan) and local (Turkish schools in Melbourne, Turkish people needing help).

Hussein was ten years old when his Turkish–Cypriot parents took him from Melbourne to live in Ankara, the Turkish capital. Settling here in 1948 had been a slow process, painful and laborious. Now, in 1962, they were uprooting themselves a second time.

'My parents took us back because they became worried that one day we might be indistinguishable from other Australian children. They felt our traditions, language and values were disappearing, and they refused to accept this as a consequence of migrating. Remember, this was the early 1960s: the Turkish community was small, with few mosques or schools.'

Fortunately for Hussein, he did not have to endure the traumatic separation from parents and siblings which some Turkish children went through. Instead it was the best of times for young Hussein. 'At first I only mixed with the American boys at school, but as my Turkish improved I became part of a Turkish gang of kids.'

Hussein's parents had told him Ramadan stories from their own childhood, but 'Those recollections meant little to me. Sure, we had always observed it as a family in Australia. But now for the first time I was part of a community of believers, a community of fasters. It was a very special feeling that I still recall with wonder. It was a sensation that never quite manifested itself again for me here.

'Everything revolved around fasting in Turkey, and children were especially cherished — that is the only word I can find for it. Everybody in my gang fasted and we were very careful with our language and behaviour.' He smiled. 'We would admonish one another: "Don't do that, it's Ramadan!" or "Hey! You've broken your fast by doing that." You could break your fast by pushing someone in anger, losing your temper or being irritable because you felt hungry.'

He vividly recalled the charitable side of fasting. 'Giving alms to poor people made me aware that not everyone was as fortunate as my family and that we must all share.' He also remembered the ending of feuds and fights. 'My father led by example. I was told that now was the time to forgive my enemies.'

When he returned with his family to Australia in his teens, Hussein continued to fast. Australians didn't understand why he wasn't allowed to drink or eat — let alone why he shouldn't even *think* of eating. Fasting became a strain at school, especially in the hot summers, so he would do as many days as he could until it became an extreme effort.

'I treat Islam as a personal way of life. That is how I've always seen it and that is how I practise it. I had a wonderful religious teacher in Australia — his name was Dr Kazi, a Pakistani academic. I probably made his life miserable with my never-ending questions and challenges, but he taught me about the philosophical view of Islam, the visionary side. Because of his patience, his influence, I have remained within Islam when I might have strayed. I have taken the philosophy of the religion and adapted it to my lifestyle.'

Like the vast majority of Muslims who have immigrated to Australia, Hussein is critical of the mass media. 'The media want visuals. They are surprised when they hear that I'm a Muslim. I don't fit the stereotype.' But he is also critical of Muslims who never leave their own circle.

Yet it seems to me that this issue is not as straightforward as it appears. Differences in language, lifestyle and family values set up barriers. Social integration, or even minimal contact with non-Muslims, becomes problematic for many. Among non-Muslims this leads to resentment — 'they don't mix, or they think they're better than us!' For some Muslims it is not language that erects barriers so much as an extreme discomfort at the drinking that seems to accompany so much social intercourse. While some Muslims unperturbedly drink their non-alcoholic beverages, there are many who would simply rather not be in an atmosphere characterised by varying stages of inebriation. Alcohol is *haram*, or forbidden, in Islam, and some Muslims feel that it is hypocritical to participate in social events where alcohol is the key to 'having a good time'. The very few Muslims who do drink, usually do so privately and not in front of other Muslims — they become 'closet drinkers', their drinking something to be hidden.

On a different tack, if you are a Muslim who only eats *halal* meat and *halal* products, how do you continually explain this to friends who want to go to 'normal' restaurants?

Hussein's seven-year-old son was going to the mosque with his father for the first time ever to mark Eid ul-Fitr. 'He is now of an age to understand fasting, so perhaps in a few years he can do a mini-fast of half a day to see how he goes.'

I asked Hussein how one went about selecting a mosque in Melbourne, where there were so many to choose from — about twenty-five, I'd been told. I knew that language was an important factor. People often prefer going to a mosque where the *qtbar*, or sermon, is in their own language. The prayers, of course, are always in Arabic, which, as the language of the Qur'an, God's own spoken revelation, holds a pre-eminent place in Islam. Commonsense told me that location might also be a consideration. But since there were several Turkish mosques in Melbourne, I wondered if anything else (politics, for instance, I thought but didn't say) influenced people's choice of a mosque.

'For me, the quality of the sermon is important,' said Hussein. 'Our imam at the mosque I attend communicates a global view of issues; he talks a lot about family values and children, your obligations to your family and to your new country, Australia. It's a small mosque and there is a good sense of camaraderie. Our imam is interesting; what he talks about is topical — there are no fire-and-brimstone absurdities, and I like the intimacy and the warmth.'

As I travel around Australia listening to people's stories, there seems little that I can do to repay my 'characters' for their time and patience. Occasionally I am able to bring them up to date with what is happening in the Muslim world elsewhere. By way of thanks, I was able to tell Hussein about my conversation the previous day with Moira Rayner, who at the time was Victoria's Commissioner of Equal Opportunity.

'Most Muslim groups are spectacularly naive about how to get their stories across or get their stories corrected,' she claimed. 'Someone writes a preachy, angry eight-page letter to the editor complaining about some article, for example, and then can't see why it isn't published!' Moira was well aware of the problems such groups faced. 'If you belong to a minority culture and you are being vilified in the press, or Islam is being vilified, you have to make a big effort to get good-news stories into the papers and become a bit more sophisticated in your strategies. You really have to work at your marketing. You need to chop down the myths about oppressed women, Rushdie, the *fatwa* and the dreaded fundamentalists.'

'What would you talk about instead?'

'Promoting family values is good,' she answered. 'How Islam looks after its dependants and its old and vulnerable would go a million miles, and from what you've told me, you need to push the charitable and good works side. No one knows about them!'

'So,' interrupted Hussein, a little testily (after all he had been very patient), 'Muslims are gross amateurs when it comes to publicising their activities? She may be right, but I don't think confronting the militant images which capture the "prime time" of people's minds is quite that easy.'

6

The cannons of Ramadan

Rokaya Nabulsi is a poet who lives in Greensborough, twenty-five kilometres from central Melbourne. She is a softly spoken woman who chooses her words as carefully as if they are precious stones, her graceful hand movements underlining the lyrical rhythm of her speech. My own entrance was hurried and apologetic. I was an hour late having become very lost in the hilly Greensborough area. I was feeling tired and a little irritable, but Rokaya's serenity helped me to unwind as we sat together and she talked about her life in Jordan and Australia.

Rokaya immigrated with her husband and two small children in 1971, after the civil war in Jordan. Her first Australian Ramadan, in rural Gippsland, was one she would never forget, she told me. In Gippsland she lost her baby of four and a half months through cot death. Working in a factory, testing telephone cables, she would break her fast alone with just an apple and then resume her work. She and her husband worked in different parts of the factory. Fasting in isolation is sad; you can easily forget the significance and become homesick and melancholy.

'My first Ramadan here was not a happy one,' said Rokaya. 'My memories were too fresh; I could still hear my parents' and brothers' and sisters' voices calling goodbye. I tried to pretend for my husband and children's sake, but I do not believe they were deceived.' In 1971 she was the only Arabic-speaking woman in Gippsland, and she and her husband do not recall any other Muslims. 'In Australia you must make compromises during Ramadan. How can I compare fasting in Jordan with fasting in Australia? The whole community is not fasting; the laughter is not as loud; the happiness rests with your own small family; excitement does not touch you wherever you go. But most of all, when I recall the atmosphere or the thrill of Ramadan in Jordan, I think I miss the cannons.'

'Cannons?' I was startled. Cannon fire meant only one thing to me — war, and of course, Jordan has suffered its share of wars. 'No! No!' Rokaya laughed. 'Not those cannons — the cannons of Ramadan!'

For much of her life she had lived in Amman, the capital of Jordan. There it was the custom — as it is in other Middle Eastern countries and Egypt as well, I am told — for two cannons to be fired each day during Ramadan: one in the morning for the last meal before dawn, called *suhoor,* which is followed by the *fajr* prayer, and a second cannon at sunset, signalling the breaking of the fast — *futoor* or *iftar* — which is followed by the *maghreb* prayer. In Amman, after the first cannon is fired — 'It is not a big cannon,' Rokaya assured me — 'the *misaharati,* the man responsible for waking you before dawn, comes to your street. It is a personal thing, where he stands before your house singing out your name and beating his drum. "Oh, wake up, Farouk! It is a beautiful morning! Do not miss your *suhoor* ... Oh, wake up, Farouk! Rouse your family, the sun will soon be rising. Time to eat and pray." Sometimes in small towns a parade of young boys follows him for part of the way, until they get too hungry or too tired. You never see this man's face until Eid ul-Fitr, when Ramadan is over and he comes to collect his *aidiyya,* a small present of money for the service he has performed.'

The town of Amman is built on seven hills and from a distance, Rokaya says, these hills and the buildings on them all have a strange quality about them, making them stand out against the sky. Every sunset as a child, she could see the silhouette of the boy whose job it was to fire the sunset cannon. 'He would reach out carefully and light the cannon's long wick and then run back quickly out of danger. There was never more than one cannon shot, it was too noisy.'

Eid in Jordan was the day of presents. In her youth, they were simple things — a pair of new shoes, a new outfit — not like today, Rokaya said, when 'Parents spend so much time and money gratifying each whim, each daily fancy.' 'Morning time at Eid is for visiting the cemeteries where your dead relatives lie and for giving *sadaqa*, or alms, to the poor.' For the three days after Eid you have short visits from relatives and must make return visits as well; it is essential to cover your whole extended family.

'Today in Jordan, both men and women go to the mosque on Eid day, but in my time women did not go. After all these years of being a Muslim, I recently discovered that it was written in the Qur'an that both men and women should go to the mosque. In Melbourne more women go to the mosque now than before. Today in Jordan there are so many changes from my youth. Some of them are very important and some are small. Often it is the small differences that you remember, that act like a key to the memory. When you open the door you may not recall as much as you hoped, but all the old feelings are there; they do not change. When I look at a piece of chocolate, I remember as a child eating chickpeas and walnuts covered in sugar — we never had chocolate. My husband, when he was young, lived on a sultana farm where they grew the sweetest, plumpest sultana grapes in the world — according to him. One of the downstairs rooms was kept as a storeroom for the sultanas — a little treasure house filled almost to the ceiling with mouth-watering sultanas. Every morning, as he came down the stairs from his room, he would reach in through the top window, stuff his pocket full of sultanas and go off to school. A sultana farm is like a wine farm without the wine.'

Over the years, family celebrations in Australia began to fill Rokaya's early emptiness. 'This builds up the excitement that I used to miss. Although we are not related, Jordanian and other Arabic-speaking families visit one another and it is an intimate feeling because we have seen our children grow up together. Last night we came home at 5.30 in the morning. We were with friends and we sang and read verses from the Qur'an. Making *suhoor* together with a larger group gives you a larger portion of happiness.'

We talk about the adjustments you need to make in Australia, the compromises made because the differences in social context are too strong to ignore. Second and third generation Muslims, unless they return to their parents' homeland, seldom fully appreciate the mood Rokaya spoke of; the atmospheric partnership between excitement and devoutness.

'Everywhere you go the feeling is electric: crowds of men and women strolling about in the evenings, special songs usually sung by men for making *futoor* and the *muezzins*' stirring calls to prayer echoing from the minarets. Daily routines are also changed to accommodate the extra demands fasting makes on your mind and body. In Jordan school lessons are shorter — thirty minutes instead of forty-five. Adults start work later, finish earlier and take a nap in the afternoon — unless you are a woman with many household responsibilities and small children.

'Someone told me that in Saudi Arabia they hold their business meetings at night and the shops stay open. If this is so then I do not approve. It is wrong to reverse night and day; it is also wrong to fast all day and feast all night.'

I reflect how memories grow more intense after one leaves one's homeland. Memories belong in the past, but unless they are given a place in the present you remain half a person, a shadow in the wings. Remembering the Ramadans that were brings you alive again, but is also painful, for they can never be relived. Your children create their own memories, but yours may yet live on because you pass them down, in fragmented snatches, as best you can, hoping that the recipients will somehow relive them for you, even if only in their imaginations.

Over the next few hours, Rokaya talks about her poetry and her dreams. She draws me back through the years and we pass from Ramadan to other celebrations; from one caravanserai to another time and place in her life before she became a traveller and a poet. Travellers are a nostalgic band, and perhaps Muslim travellers are more nostalgic than is sometimes good for them. But Rokaya's nostalgia was bathed in sweetness with no signs of regret.

Her father was a very big man. All his life he wore a dark brown beard, short and neatly trimmed, as was the fashion. It was his habit to stroke his beard when deep in thought; his eyes would narrow and he would gaze ahead, lost in a world of religious books and obscure legal points which his family never understood but which represented the wealth of his private world.

'He was a *qadi*, an Islamic judge, who performed marriages and religious divorces, and dealt with wills. That is why we moved around Jordan so much. We children could always tell when there was a divorce case before him because he would try so hard to reconcile the couple, working right up to the very last minute until all hope was gone. It seemed to us that he would be very sad for days afterwards. My mother would make his favourite sweets, and we would try to draw him into our childish games hoping to ease the pain. We knew divorces made him unhappy, although these matters were never discussed in our hearing.

'Muslim people in Jordan do not often make wills on paper. All such matters are dealt with according to Islamic law. But a man can write a will to dispose of the one-third of his property that he is permitted to give away outside his immediate family, should he so wish. So there were times when my father would be involved in matters of inheritance. He would always closely scrutinise any documents and question witnesses to ensure that the family, especially the wife and daughters, received their proper due under Islamic law. But once I remember him hurrying home in his black suit, his stiff white *umamah* on his head and his long black robe swirling behind him, to tell us all about the missing money he had discovered.

'"*Al'ham dulillah* — Praise God!" he cried triumphantly. "There it was!" A large sum of money had gone missing from a property recently sold by the deceased just before his death. The dead man's four children searched everywhere. The court was on the point of saying, "So be it," but my father insisted it be found for the sake of the children and he searched for it himself. He thought, "Where would I hide this money if it belonged to me?" And he found it — in the man's walking-stick! He unscrewed the heavy brass top and there it was, tucked cleverly inside.

'Cases of elopement were also kept hidden from us. "Not in front of the children," my father would whisper to my mother, and they would disappear into the small room he used as a study. Naturally we still knew what was going on. It helped us understand why he was so strict with us, because in some towns where we were stationed a lot of elopements seemed to happen. Sometimes young people would fall in love and circumvent their parents' wishes for an arranged marriage — this was more prevalent in country towns, where boys and girls seemed to mix more. It happens in Melbourne too, and sometimes in Jordan a Muslim boy and girl will run away if they cannot get their way. In both countries it is a disgrace terrible beyond imagining, and the wounds do not heal until a grandchild comes into the world. Sometimes they never heal. Families in Jordan to whom this happens feel the dishonour like an enormous weight on their heads. Of course an elopement between a Muslim boy and a Christian girl can be a tragedy in Jordan. It is not approved by the Christian communities, although it is permitted among Muslims. But never, never can it happen between a Muslim girl and a Christian boy unless he converts first.

'Civil disputes between Muslims and Christians happen sometimes in the countryside. I remember how my father went and visited the priest at Christmas during one dispute, to wish him well at his holy time of the year. Everyone was surprised, but he said that we should all be more tolerant. The next year at Eid ul-Fitr, the priest visited us!

'But I promised to tell you more about fasting in Jordan! You see, whenever I think back on Jordan I remember my mother, who, *Al'ham dulillah,* is still alive, and my father, God bless him, who died ten years ago. When the news came of his death, I wrote a poem. For me there was emptiness — the air had died and I could hear the cries of my brothers and sisters even though they were far away. Ramadan is the time to remember our loved ones, so please let me tell you a little story about him. It is a story which says everything about him.

'My parents had twelve children — nine girls and three boys — all born at home with the help of a midwife. My mother would sob because she had borne yet another daughter. Sons were traditionally preferred, and her sister-in-law's children were all boys. I remember my mother's tears after the ninth daughter, my latest little sister, was born.

'"What are you crying for? Look at this wonderful gift from Allah!" my father laughed. He always made sure that my mother had a proper rest on that first night after each baby was born. The newborn baby would sleep in his bed; he would hold it in his arms and think of the special name he had chosen. While my mother was in labour, he would try to read, and whatever name or word he was reading at the last minute — they were always Islamic books of some kind — this name he would select. He would also whisper the call to prayer, the *azan*, softly in the right ear of the new baby so that the first words it heard should be the name of God: "*Allahu Akbar* — God is Most Great."'

Rokaya is a popular Arabic name, particularly for parents who like to name their daughters after the wives or daughters of the Prophet. Rokaya was the Prophet's second daughter, whose mother, Khadijah, was Muhammad's first and only wife until her death. A remarkable woman, older than her husband, she had been his employer before their marriage. Khadijah was the first person to embrace Islam; thus, as the Moroccan sociologist Fatima Mernissi says, somewhat romantically, 'Islam began in the arms of a woman.' Perhaps Rokaya's father was reading about the Prophet's second daughter, by his beloved wife Khadijah, when the midwife told him that his latest child had greeted the world.

7

The Alexandrian quartet

'We warn you, Hanifa, they are a very fiery couple. They're wonderful friends of ours, but if you want a peaceful evening after *futoor*, please visit us on another night. We welcome you to our home at any time — it's your decision, my dear. But take care: your head will turn from side to side, like someone watching a tennis match.'

The 'invitation' was disconcerting. I wondered whether there was another reason for Dr Anice Morsy's equivocal offer. We had known one another since the 1980s when he was a commissioner at the Victorian Ethnic Affairs Commission and I was a public servant there in the heyday of ethnic affairs, so we were old friends. Ignoring his warning, I decided to brazen it out. Whatever he meant by 'lively discussion', it might be a chance to feel the pulse of Muslim life in Melbourne quicken. 'I'll be there after sunset, *Insha'Allah* (God willing),' I said. Poor Anice! Trying to steer me away from his friends had only aroused my curiosity.

Omar and Laila were a 'mixed' couple, meaning in this case that he was Egyptian and she was Lebanese — as were Anice and Najat. We were sitting around the dining table praising Najat's array of delicacies. Some were made especially for Ramadan, like her marvellous *kamar el din*, translated as 'the moon of the religion', and another Lebanese favourite: cheese halwa made from unsalted cheese, semolina and rose water. Like a proper host from the Middle East, Najat assured us that the meal was poorly prepared and unworthy of us. Of course, this was not to be taken literally, but such remarks emphasised the hosts' humility and modesty. Hospitality is a stringent duty throughout the Middle East and both hosts and guests have roles to fulfil. 'Give the guest food to eat even though you yourself are starving,' is an old Arabic saying. Both Anice and Najat took this injunction seriously and were generous and warm hosts.

Anice was a jocular man, good humoured and gregarious with twinkling eyes, a neat moustache and curly grey hair. I could count on the fingers of one hand the number of Arabic-speaking men I had met who went without a moustache of some sort. Recently retired, Anice had worked for many years in the Health Department in the field of preventative health. He collected committees like some people collect stamps; two of his main interests were the Ethnic Affairs Police Liaison Committee and the Australian Arabic Chamber of Commerce. Najat was quieter, much more reflective and slightly less at ease in speaking English. She was a journalist with fifteen years experience in the Arabic-language media and had published several books in Arabic. She and Anice spoke Egyptian at home. Anice had honed his English in Australian work environments and tended to take the lead in our talks. Najat listened closely to everything that was said, correcting any errors, misconceptions or flights of fancy that she noted. Her quiet demeanour masked a determined spirit that went to the heart of any dispute. In many ways she acted as the conscience of the group.

Laila's face was lean and expressive and when she spoke it came alive; her whole body seemed to take part in the conversation. With her red henna rinse, western clothes and jangling bracelets, she reminded me of photos and movies I had seen in the 1960s and early 1970s of smart

Egyptian women, out in public in brightly coloured sleeveless dresses with a French air about them, red lipstick and nails, huge rings and delicate gold chains around their necks. From what I have heard, there is little of this look to be seen on the streets in Egyptian cities nowadays, although one can never be sure what is hiding under the *chadoor* (veil) and *abeya* (long cloak) or at home in the privacy of one's own four walls.

With Omar I had to watch and wait. He was a little portly with a receding hairline, dark brooding eyes and a perfectly sculptured nose. He directed most of his comments through Anice.

All four were in their early sixties and were now retired, although each one's life was crammed full of committee meetings and community projects. They had originally met as young married couples in the beautiful city of Alexandria on the Mediterranean coast, two hundred kilometres from Cairo.

Our conversation was mainly in English for my benefit, with people breaking into Egyptian or Lebanese when they chose. We talked a little about the book I was trying to write and how difficult it sometimes was to coax people to speak openly rather than tell me what they thought they should tell me or what they imagined I wanted to hear — 'impression management', I called it. I often suspected they were on their best behaviour. From Anice's earlier warning, I expected no such reservations from tonight's gathering.

'I take permission from my husband first, of course,' Laila began. 'But I lived in Egypt for eight years after I was married, and if you want to hear something interesting, ask me how spoilt Egyptian men are and how this happens.' Asking for her husband's permission was a courtesy which sat rather oddly with the aggressive tone of the rest of her sentence.

Anice chuckled. He knew what was coming. Omar was

not hearing this for the first time either and had darted a quick 'don't go ahead with this' look at his wife. She ignored him.

'Egyptian sons are horribly spoilt; spoilt to extremes by their mothers and waited upon by their poor sisters. "Keep quiet! Your brother is studying," a mother will say to her daughter. "Go and get tea for him." This, even when the daughter is at university too! The mother makes life so easy for the son. And the father, of course, gives him more credit for what he does than all the girls in the world! So when he gets married he wants a mother again, not a wife! This is what is worrying me. I notice that when a man wants to emigrate, or leave the house, or get married, he cries because he thinks he'll be too far away from his mother.'

This was too much for Omar. 'No, no, Laila! You are not telling the truth! This is not how it is.' He looked to Anice for support, who rolled his eyes roguishly but wisely stayed out of the fray. 'You, Laila, are Lebanese. The Lebanese are migrants by nature; half the population is in the country and the other half outside it. We Egyptians are different. Remember, Anice, when we were young men, what a big event it was to leave your home?'

'Yes, what you are saying is true,' said Anice. 'I remember when I was going to my first appointment as a district medical officer and had to go away for two weeks to a town only three hours from Cairo by train. My mother was crying, my sisters spent two days packing my bag, and everyone came to see me off at the train — twelve people all weeping and wailing very loudly. Australians would think we were all going to a funeral. You could not imagine such a public scene!'

Najat interjected, 'You told me that every evening your mother would cry at the dinner table because, "Anice is not eating what we are eating now," or "My *habibi* — my darling — is not eating his favourite sweet; think of him all alone!" And he is not the only boy in the family — there are three sons and three daughters!'

Anice wriggled a little in embarrassment. Omar had won the allegiance of his straying confederate back again.

Now that the lines had been drawn — wives versus husbands — Laila warmed to her subject. 'That is nothing, Najat — nothing, I tell you! You know we got married twice, first the civil ceremony in Egypt and then the Islamic wedding in Lebanon for my parents. Then in Lebanon we had the cons ... what do you call it?'

'Consummation,' said Anice,ever the gentleman and not prepared to take advantage of a woman's difficulty with words.

Omar shot him a look that plainly said, 'Whose side are you on anyway?'

'The first day of our honeymoon in the most beautiful spot in Lebanon, I wake up and hear Omar crying. He is writing a letter to his mother!' Laila disclosed, hands over her eyes and shaking her head.

'Homesickness is a terrible thing,' muttered Omar.

'On the morning of your honeymoon?' Laila laughed.

'He wanted his mother to see him so happy with his wife,' Anice tried to smooth things over. 'Why don't you tell the story of how you met?'

Everyone moved to the lounge room and settled down for what promised to be a 'bumpy ride'. Omar sat down by himself in a velvet chair, arms folded, his back to the wall, already under siege.

'He met me on a training course in Egypt. Thirty of us from fourteen different Arab countries had this workshop, you call it now, on community development. Egyptians, you know, cannot understand other Arabic dialects, only the Egyptian dialect, but the others there — Lebanese, Syrians, Iraqis and so on — we talked easily to one another and also understood Egyptian.'

'That is because of Egyptian films, television and radio — everywhere you find them outside Egypt in the Arab world,' ventured Omar.

'It was a love marriage,' continued Laila, ignoring Omar's interjection, 'but he didn't like me at first. He thought I was too *aneeda*, too stubborn.'

'I called her "Miss Authoritarian". You were not helpful, Laila — uncooperative and very bossy. It was a stormy start.'

Laila did not bother denying any of this — it was of little importance to her now. She stared at her nails, waiting to resume centre stage.

'Later we started writing letters,' Omar went on. 'They got hotter and hotter — but not in the western sense.'

'Real love letters, written in the language of love — Arabic.' Now and then Laila let her cynical side drop. 'But I don't forget that on our honeymoon, he missed his mother!'

'And now the immigration story!' commanded Anice. It was a ritual with these old friends that every time they came together they would turn back the clock almost twenty-five years.

'After marriage, migration was the most important decision,' said Najat. Her mind drifted to the time when she and Laila had spent week after week, day after day, trying to persuade their husbands to emigrate to Canada or the United States or Australia. They pleaded, they cajoled, they never let up. Omar had been the last to surrender. Laila had threatened and challenged his manhood and sense of honour until he finally gave in.

'Go on, why don't you blame me!' A dramatic wail from Laila, more theatrical than anything else. This was also part of the ritual.

'You are Lebanese; it is a tradition for your people to emigrate. But, yes, you were certainly the driving force, Laila,' conceded Omar.

'At least you didn't turn up in Australia wearing a three-piece suit and an overcoat in March,' said Anice, and they all laughed.

Australia was the first country to reply to their applications, so Anice and Najat arrived in 1969. Omar and Laila arrived a year later. They chose Melbourne because according to the Bank of New South Wales (now Westpac) pamphlets at the Australian Embassy in Cairo, Melbourne's weather was closest to that of Alexandria. 'Later I found that it is actually Perth which has the similar climate.'

Anice started teaching at Sunshine Technical School. In his very first week, one of his students approached him.

'Sir, when you came to Australia what did you do with your camel?'

Anice knew it was a genuine question, not an attempt to be humorous or derisive. 'Which one do you mean?' he asked her. 'My taxi camel or the private camel? How do you think we could park our camels in Cairo with a population of ten million — you'd have a pyramid of you know what! No, my dear, you see camels in Hollywood movies, but not in the heart of Cairo.'

'You are too understanding,' said Laila. 'I am never patient with stupid questions. When I started first at the office ... all the questions! "Where do you come from?" "What is your religion?" I get fed up! One day I tell them I am Catholic; next day I say I am Jewish. It's not their business to ask me what I am. If they ask a rude question, I give a rude answer.'

Nobody in the room doubted her for a minute.

The conversation turned to fasting. Anice admitted that this year he had started fasting a day early, on Monday — in time with Egypt and Jordan — not on the Tuesday, as we officially did in Australia. The Islamic calendar is based on the lunar system rather than the solar, so the dates of festivals vary from year to year.

'If you can see the new moon with your naked eye or through a telescope then you start fasting the next day. But I heard it on the BBC news about Egypt and Jordan starting.

'In Egypt,' Anice continued, 'a religious authority goes to the highest peak and if he can see the new moon, then fasting begins the next day. If he doesn't see it but learns that it has been sighted in a nearby Muslim country, then he can also say fasting begins the next day. It is hard to see the new moon here; I only saw it myself on the third or fourth day. Unless you rely on astronomy you cannot really say. I don't think it hurts anyone if I start one day earlier than everyone else in Australia; it's not a big deal.'

I had heard of different interpretations of the start of Ramadan clashing. Even the famous Moon-sighting Committee under the aegis of the Australian Federation of Islamic Councils, which is supposed to officially decree the beginning and end of Ramadan, doesn't seem able to reach consensus easily. This means that Australia's different Muslim organisations, most of which are formed along lines of ethnicity and nationality, often disagree on this important point.

The Moon-sighting Committee might decree that Sunday will be day one. Everyone seems to agree, 'Yes we will accept this ...' and then, lo and behold some eminent figure or another 'defects' and everyone stampedes. One group will hold day one on a Friday, a rival group on a Saturday, with the followers of the Moon-sighting Committee abiding by the original Sunday decree. This then has a flow-on effect with the grand festival of Eid ul-Fitr being held on different days as well.

Try as it might, the Moon-sighting Committee at present does not seem to work. With its splendid astronomical name and earnest membership, it is supposed to put an end to the wrangling and arguments among Australia's various Muslim congregations and religious 'experts'. My sympathy lay squarely with the 'Moonies', but some of the Muslim converts who spoke to me alluded to 'a madness in the air', and shook their heads in bemusement, and sometimes in desperation, at the lack of unity and what they saw as the signs of a fiendish, Muslim Monty Python at work.

I could see that Anice, Laila and Omar were about to become embroiled in another skirmish over the ins and outs, the rights and wrongs, of when to start fasting, so I tried to change the subject. 'Anice, what does fasting do to the body?'

'First, remember that if it becomes a terrible hardship for you there is an escape; you can feed a hungry person. A diabetic should definitely not fast. To pregnant women I say, "Take my fast for you, but don't hurt yourself and don't hurt the child."' Najat explained, 'If the woman is afraid God will punish her for not fasting, Anice reassures her by saying, "If I am not telling you the truth, may God punish *me* by taking the credit I have earned by my fast and give it to you instead."'

'There are other exemptions,' Anice went on. 'Women are exempt during their menstruation, not so much because they are "unclean" as because they are weaker from loss of blood.'

When he was still working, Anice had made sure that his fasting didn't affect his productivity, 'So the bosses could never be critical. They couldn't believe I could do without food and drink. Then I was a smoker too, a heavy one. How could I last without a cigarette, they wondered.'

'But after all, Anice, you only had to last until sunset,' I put in. After sunset, the festivities begin.

'You hear it on the radio and television, day in and day out, the shaykhs talk about it in the mosques, telling people not to overeat,' Anice shrugged. 'The body suffers if there is over-indulging. Too many Egyptians overeat at night during Ramadan. Many think it is a time of gratification — though I can only talk about Egypt.'

'You are supposed to feel with the poor who are hungry, not become a glutton,' was Najat's succinct way of putting it.

Anice was animated, for this was a favourite subject of his. 'If you look at the amount of money the Egyptian government pays to subsidise costly foods like figs, apricots, pistachio nuts, dates, almonds — all imported and paid for with hard currency — and sweets from Lebanon, Syria and Iraq, clearly the Egyptian people are not disciplining themselves!'

'Is overeating in Ramadan *haram*, then?'

'I think *haram* is a bit too strong,' Omar answered.

'Some people in the Middle East even drink alcohol after fasting all day!' said Laila. 'That is double *haram*!' Since alcohol is always forbidden, drinking it during Ramadan seemed twice as bad to her.

'That is long ago,' objected Omar, 'not these days!'

Laila was quite vehement. 'There is a lot of all-night partying, I mean eating all night and sleeping all day.'

'I'll tell you something else,' said Anice. 'We tell Australian businessmen not to try making business deals in the Arab world during Ramadan. Often men do not turn up to work until 10 am and are gone by 2 pm.' He was quite wound up by now.

Anice and Omar, Najat and Laila took turns telling me about the tensions which emerged in some households. Smokers in particular often became 'fidgety' during Ramadan and tempers flared. Children had to keep quiet while the men slept. Husbands and wives argued when the wife wanted to buy the expensive imported foods her neighbour served but which they couldn't afford. There were new Eid outfits to be bought, and the kids would beg for Eidi money. Less well-off families sometimes went into debt. It all sounded very much like Christmas on Bankcard!

'Women in Egypt have to be extra tough,' said Laila. 'While the men — husbands, sons — can sleep in the daytime, women must fast and at the same time cook, shop, feed the children — no sleep for them!'

'Our men are a little bit spoilt,' Anice admitted sheepishly.

I noted there was no such concession from Omar.

'What is the difference between something *haram* and something else which breaks your fast?' I asked.

'Well,' Anice led the way, as usual, 'having sex with your wife in the daytime is not *haram* but it definitely breaks your fast; wearing perfume is the same. You also break your fast if you look at women with lust ... looking once is all right, but not a second time.' Everyone laughed. 'Some say that brushing your teeth is permissible, but very strict Muslims might say no. There are some so strict that they try to avoid swallowing their own saliva; I disagree with that.'

'Islam is really reasonable,' Omar said. 'I believe it all depends on your intention, your *niyyat*. If, for example, I pick up a cigarette, light it without thinking and inhale, and then think, "What am I doing?" and throw it away, clearly I did not intend to break the fast, so I can continue.'

Because I had known Anice for so long, I felt I could ask him, 'How good a Muslim do you think you are?'

'I try as much as I can, considering the situation I am living in here. But I am worried that our knowledge of Islam in Australia may be declining, in spite of the mosques going up. In Middle Eastern countries there are neighbourhood mosques and you don't spend all your time driving to one. Regular attendance is so easy. There are also a lot of religious programs on the radio, discussing this Hadith or that Qur'anic interpretation. It is much harder to be a devout Muslim in a land where you are in a minority, and very hard if you are not a reading kind of person.'

When he and Najat first arrived in 1969, few Australians knew about Islam. 'But I am not a coward Muslim, I thought, hiding my Islam; I wanted to be a courageous Muslim, declaring what I was. Omar felt the same, didn't you?'

Omar nodded.

'I tell them, "I'm a Muslim, you have to take me as I am,"' he swept his hands dismissively. I sensed he was trying to bluff me, but I couldn't be sure.

Anice went on to tell me about an argument he had had with an imam on a recent trip back to Egypt. 'He told me that emigration was *haram* unless you were a refugee from a land where your life was in danger and you could no longer practise Islam — Somalia or Bosnia, he meant. I was very angry with him. "You have no virtue," I told him. "You are living in a Muslim country. Come with me and see where I live. That is a real test!" I go to this imam because I expect him to be more knowledgeable than me on religion and religious law, but he does not represent the shadow of God on earth. No imam can tell me, like a priest could, "You are not a Muslim, you are a *kafir* — an infidel." He can't tell me, "You can't come to the mosque!" He can't excommunicate me. He may remind me of my obligations but he can be contradicted.'

Do not put your finger in a scorpion's nest if you cannot stand the sting.

I had observed none of us women was wearing a head scarf of any kind. Laila, who seemed to be dozing, woke up immediately. 'I am against wearing it, and especially in Australia!' she said. 'Women do not get jobs because of it.'

'Yes,' agreed Najat quietly.

'I do not see it in the Qur'an,' continued Laila. 'Modesty of men and women is there. I don't think that it fulfils any purpose, and I don't agree with it, not in Australia anyway.'

Clearly I had touched a raw nerve. I knew of women who had started wearing the *hijab* for the first time after they reached a certain age — in their forties or fifties. Was someone in her household hinting that it was time for Laila …?

'But it is in the Sunna,' Omar protested, 'the Prophet's (peace be upon Him) own tradition.'

'The Qur'an tells us — men and women — to cover our heads in the mosque,' intervened Anice.

'Yes,' responded Laila, 'but it doesn't tell me to wear it outside in the street. You know very well that that is simply custom.' Chin in the air, she looked at Najat, who signalled her agreement.

Najat looked at the men sternly, 'I prefer that men behave themselves, it is better than covering the beauty of women.'

'It is part of the Sunna,' repeated Omar. 'Women must not flaunt their beauty, they must not be exhibitionists' — this was greeted by a raucous laugh from Laila — 'and a woman's hair is part of her beauty. But I do not call a woman who does not wear the *hijab* a non-Muslim and you two should not call those who do backward.'

'I want better education for women,' snapped Laila. 'They should demand their education and learn the true meaning of modesty; not spend so much time worrying about a piece of material on their head.'

The men were exasperated. 'You must not look down on these women, they are good devout women.'

'You two miss the point,' said Laila. 'We are not looking down; we are not pointing the finger. We only say it is not …'

'Mandatory,' finished Najat.

'Why get so excited about the *hijab* anyway? Why not get excited about the right to work? Besides, if you wear the *hijab* in the Middle East it makes you invisible, but here in Australia it attracts attention. That is not the purpose.' Laila and Najat were not foundation members of the Arab Women's Solidarity Foundation for nothing!

There is another old Arab saying: 'A woman first holds her husband with a pretty face, then by his stomach, and lastly with the help of a *sheb-sheb*, or wooden slipper.' I wondered if Laila and Najat might soon give thought to wielding the *sheb-sheb*. Omar, I am sure, would swear that Laila, his beloved 'scorpion' was already an expert.

8

El Sadeaq

The hour before sunset is total chaos in the old districts of Cairo; huge crowds of people join a mad, wanton rush to be with their families in time to break fast. Cars speed by, some even lurching onto the kerbs and along the pavements in desperation, people try frantically to stop taxis, others dash on foot across roads or hang precariously from jam-packed buses. The noise is deafening; horns bleat insistently, the tinny screech of bicycle bells fuels headaches, overwrought people yell at anyone who crosses their path, shopkeepers bellow at passing shoppers in a final effort to sell their wares, radios blare. The overall effect is of a vast crowd of 'refugees' retreating in panic before an advancing army.

Everyone has been out shopping — caught again in that last-minute stampede between small kiosks and in narrow laneways. Fears mount that the Ramadan cannon will go off any second. Here you stand with seconds ticking away, and it will take you another fifteen minutes at least to reach sanctuary! Yesterday you swore to forgo this madness. Yet unbelievably, in this city of more than fourteen million people, almost everyone reaches home in time for *futoor.* The streets become still; people bunkered away out of sight as if the pre-sunset rush had never happened. Surely this qualifies as a modern-day miracle!

Television goes off the air for half an hour while families

pray and eat together. There are special programs, not all of them religious; entertainment shows, soap operas, dramas and special quiz shows. People savour their release and the streets of Cairo fill with a happy throng until the early hours of the morning as everyone visits friends after sitting with their families. Mosques turn on coloured lights and shaykhs recite the Qur'an all night long in special covered tents set up in public squares. Often singers and dancers perform for hand-clapping crowds.

After Cairo, Melbourne's rush hour seems positively placid. Of the city's total population of about three million — about one-fifth of Cairo's — only about sixty thousand are Muslims. People are orderly and in no unusual hurry as they make their way home by bus, tram, train or car. Some Muslims work through their lunch hour so they can leave work early. In Melbourne, as in Egypt, they prefer to make their *futoor* or *iftar* with their family or, if they belong to one, with their religious organisation or mosque congregation. On weekends especially, mosque associations and societies organise special evenings and prayers, so that if you want to be part of a larger gathering, as many people do during this special month, you can. But during the week, many have to make their own festivities and without family and relatives on hand, this is difficult. Muslims who have never observed Ramadan overseas, even those who have listened carefully to their parents' tales, are not in a position to make comparisons, and their Eid is generally the wonderful time it should be. But for those who have experienced the throb of a whole society acting as one, and the energy and emotion this generates — in Cairo, Lahore, Kuala Lumpur — Ramadan and Eid in Australia are never quite the same.

From her wing-backed recliner rocker, Wafia commands her domain with good humour and patience. On a good night she catches about four hours sleep. Occasionally she has the dark, under-eye smudges of the chronic diabetic. But on days when she has kept stress at bay and her blood sugar level is under control, her soft round face, firm mouth and bright eyes survey her world like a benevolent general's, and she motivates her family troops to go out and conquer the world. Manoeuvring with agility, she transfers to her wheelchair and reaches for the telephone. Wafia makes about twenty phone calls a day; these, together with her fax machine and the 'agents' who drop in and out, give her an impressive intelligence network. A former social worker and maths teacher, she now runs her own consultancy on cross-cultural communication and is president of the Arabic-Speaking Welfare Workers' Association.

She and her husband Hossam hardly ever mention the nightmarish ten months she spent in hospital. She went in for a diabetes-related complaint, but there she contracted golden staph and her body system collapsed. She then withstood nine operations in two months as doctors and nurses tried to save her leg.

Wafia and Hossam have a gigantic circle of friends — an outer circle of two hundred and an intimate circle of fifty from the El Sadeaq society. Added to this are non-Muslim friends from different backgrounds; Wafia's colleagues, and her daughters' workmates. The coming and going, laughter and teasing, blow like gusts of wind through the household. Wafia and Hossam have three daughters — Aya, twenty-two, Marwa, twenty-three and Mona, sixteen. I considered myself lucky to be staying with the family for a week.

'*Haram,* Mum! Don't look! Dad, close your eyes!' the girls sang out as a television commercial flashed on showing a boy and girl trying on jeans and kissing. Teasing their parents was a family joke. 'Some people say that you're not supposed to watch kissing or anything sexy on television, especially if you've been on *haj* to Mecca,' said Marwa.

Wafia and Hossam are not the kind of people who like to wear their religion like a badge for all to see. Among those who do so, however, debate rages endlessly over what is or is not *haram*. Activities from watching television to wearing jeans are stigmatised. Other Muslims, however, believe that labelling every second thing *haram* is ridiculous and ultimately degrades its true meaning.

Wafia's daughters were no different from other young women their age: their interests ranged from work and school studies to fashion, music and movies, and their social lives. They wore fashionable clothes and presented quite a dazzling picture with their dark eyes and long curly black hair. Hair products littered their bathroom: gels, sprays, shampoos, conditioners, brushes and combs on every surface. Life in the fifties with a ponytail was much simpler, I thought.

Marwa confided that years ago many Egyptian–Australian parents were mainly concerned with finding an Egyptian boy for their daughters, even at the expense of compatibility. 'There were a few marriage breakdowns which led to divorce; everyone learnt the hard way. Our mum keeps insisting that she's not arranging anything, she's not pushing us into anything, "Just providing the opportunities," as she puts it,' said Marwa with a grin.

'That's true,' agreed Aya. 'We're under no pressure at all. In our age group there's a shortage of Egyptian–Australian boys, but for Mona's generation there's no "crisis", if you like to think of it that way. Anyway, at the moment we're far too busy to settle down.'

The current trend was to find a partner in Egypt, although some young women had married Anglo-Australians, who were required to convert because Islam does not allow Muslim women to marry non-Muslims.

'Their new fathers-in-law keep an eye on them to make sure they haven't converted for marriage purposes only!' said Wafia. 'I think they're doing a good deed by acting as surrogate fathers. I certainly don't see it as manipulative. After all, there is nothing wrong with seeing your own religion as the best.'

'When are you going to move out?' the girls were often asked by non-Muslim friends, who accused them of leading sheltered lives. 'We are under no pressure to leave home,' they would reply, 'and we're lucky that we don't want to.'

Their astute parents had ensured that by not placing harsh insistence on one side, there was no rejection or rebellion on the other.

Sadeaq means true or sincere in Arabic. El Sadeaq — the faithful friend — was a name given to the great Caliph Abu Bakr, who succeeded the Prophet. The El Sadeaq Society in Melbourne has a community centre and a small mosque for its mainly Egyptian members. Over the years vast amounts of time and energy have gone into making it what it is today — a giant surrogate family embracing Egyptians of all ages, to whom it offers a range of activities: religious, educational, recreational and social. El Sadeaq also employs a full-time imam who leads prayers, gives scholarly religious advice and counsels those in need, as well as participating in women's and young people's activities. A bureaucrat told me, 'They're more modern in outlook than some other Islamic groups.' Others used terms like reasonable, liberal, flexible and, inevitably, 'non-fundamentalist'. All of this surprises El Sadeaq members, who see themselves as ordinary practising Muslims.

So how did it all begin?

'When we first arrived we dealt with basic survival

needs like accommodation, jobs and so on,' Wafia recalled. 'But as we prospered, and especially after some of us returned to Egypt for the first time and saw the changes, the differences, we started to think more about what we were doing to our kids in Australia.'

Hossam said, 'We knew we had done the right thing economically — our lives were much better, there were good futures ahead for our girls. But as you grow older you start to think of other values, not just dollars. I noticed on my first trip back to Cairo that there was more emphasis on religious matters and less blatant copying of the West than I remembered. We started to worry, and so did some of our friends.' Hossam was a retired high school teacher whose mild authority was always present, but never dominant, in this household of women.

What was going to happen to the next generation, the group of friends wondered. 'Already the kids were beginning to forget their language and their past — in other words, their identity.'

In Egypt, religious education was funded and provided by the government. The group realised that in Australia, parents would have to assume this role or suffer the consequences: children losing filial respect, moving out of home, questioning traditions and hiding their religion from their peers. It was not a matter of staying Egyptian — sensible parents could not expect this from children born in Australia. Perhaps what they wanted was an Egyptian–Australian identity for them. But if this was to happen, the children must retain their language — Arabic, the language of the Qur'an. So the parents returned to Islam in a way that they might not have done in Egypt, and assumed responsibility for their children's total spiritual wellbeing. They founded the El Sadeaq society to provide what neither the state nor society could: religious education for their children. It was hard at first. Syllabuses had to be compiled, materials trialled. Fortunately in the Egyptian community there were plenty of professional teachers and former administrators.

Since those early days, the society's functions have multiplied, and now that many of their children have grown up, crafty parents see El Sadeaq as offering them a network of friends and even potential marriage partners. Thus the society takes on yet another characteristic of an extended family. 'While we used to kid ourselves that the society was only for the children,' said Wafia, 'it is going to be invaluable for all of us as we grow older. We will grow old together, just like a family with blood ties.'

Some Egyptians, of course, preferred to stay outside the 'family', happy with the privacy of their lives and the opportunity to stretch themselves in a way that wasn't possible in Egypt. They didn't want to reinvent customs they had left behind.

'We don't have "privacy" as westerners know it,' said Wafia. 'It is not a precious commodity with us. In the end everyone depends on others. Some will jump to the conclusion that the individual becomes less important in our tradition. Not so! But the individual cannot survive without the group.'

No sanctions are placed on those who leave the El Sadeaq family. Wafia said that some Egyptians had participated for only a few months, left and not been seen or heard from again. Others only participated during major festivals.

'Finding the right shaykh or imam for your mosque association must be a problem in Australia,' I said to Hossam and Mahmoud, a thin, grey-haired man in his late fifties who had dropped in to visit his old friends. Mahmoud was now retired and living in Queensland, but in his day he had been an active member of El Sadeaq.

'There are no Australian-trained imams at all. They all come from overseas — Lebanon, Egypt, Malaysia, Indonesia, Turkey.'

Hossam told me that the Egyptian government paid the salary of a shaykh to act as imam, counsellor and general adviser for the El Sadeaq mosque. I knew that the Turkish government also financed religious classes, but there were some important differences, Hossam said, 'El Sadeaq members are responsible for the shaykh's housing, and have the right of hiring and firing.' Hiring a suitable imam or shaykh for an Australian mosque is a tall order. Certain qualities are essential if religious leaders are going to 'fill the bill' so to speak, in Australia. Hossam explained, 'Ideally — of course this is only my opinion — he should be fluent in English, familiar with Australian culture and migrant problems, understand our minority-group status and be sympathetic to women's and youth issues. Of course, religious knowledge goes without saying. Sometimes they don't work out and we have to send them back.' My mind pictured a bulky, wriggling parcel stamped 'Return to sender'.

The power that many communities had to hire and fire meant that often the unfortunate shaykh had many masters to please. 'But most shaykhs and their families enjoy living in Australia,' Hossam said. 'I think they try hard to please the committees they more or less work for. Their situation is very different from that in Egypt or other countries where the government controls their appointments.'

Shaykhs were originally learned men only; their roles did not become professionalised until about fifty years ago. Today they are paid by the government in Muslim countries and earn extra money from attending funerals, anniversaries of deaths of family members, and so on. There are a host of reasons for calling on a shaykh today.

Perhaps someone has passed an exam and the celebration calls for a recitation of the Qur'an or perhaps a couple want to make an offering for a son ... the list goes on.

In Egypt, shaykhs are trained by other shaykhs and there is even a government department that handles this. Some Egyptian–Australians tended to be critical of this control, I found. 'You shouldn't have a public servant paid for by the government as a religious leader,' argued Hossam. 'Go back to the earlier days of Islam, when it was voluntary and men did not make a livelihood from religion.'

Hossam would like to see Australian-trained imams performing religious functions voluntarily and Australian-trained professionals from the local community employed as youth workers, teachers and social workers.

I wanted to know more about the shaykh El Sadeaq had just brought out from Cairo for Ramadan. I would be meeting him in a few days. 'Is he a reciter or an interpreter of the Qur'an?' (Egyptian shaykhs tend to specialise in a particular area.)

'I believe he is famous for his voice; he was trained to read and recite aloud,' Hossam replied. 'It's an old El Sadeaq custom. Each year we invite such a shaykh for the thirty days of Ramadan and everyone shares the expenses.'

I offered them a shaykh story from my own collection, one related to me some time before by an old friend.

'A visiting shaykh was asked why women were not encouraged in Egypt to attend the mosque for their prayers. The shaykh answered, "Well, it is obviously because women are unstable; they get emotional and they cry. It is far too disturbing to have them present in the mosque." Naturally the women were furious and demanded that their husbands set him right. The men, however, were more philosophical. "We brought him over for his voice," they said, "not for his religious knowledge," and the women continued going to the mosque as before.'

Khalfan and Huda were giving a dinner in honour of the visiting shaykh. He dined like a splendid *wazir*, with everyone passing on the choicest pieces from the banquet plates. A strict code of etiquette was in place, but as a special guest, I, too, was welcomed with inordinate warmth and courtesy. One dish after another was pressed on me, as a visitor from interstate. Regular and familiar guests like Wafia and Hossam came next, and the host family served themselves last.

Every night the shaykh, as the visiting dignitary, dined with a new family. Obviously he was saving his voice for the Qur'anic recitation, for he spoke not a word at the table, his eyes fixed steadily on his plate as he concentrated on his food and made sure that his robes and his flowing white beard remained spotless. Then again, perhaps he was unused to men and women eating together. He also led the *maghreb*, or evening prayer, in the family room. The men prayed in front, the women behind. The teenage boys were a sight in their back-to-front baseball caps, T-shirts and baggy trousers. One minute they were laughing and teasing one another, talking about the latest rock video; the next minute, as the prayers started, they dropped everything and started praying with their fathers as naturally as breathing in and out. One little nine-year-old bumped his head on a wooden shelf as he moved from one position to the next. All his mates were reduced to stifled laughter. No one shushed them or seemed angry.

After the shaykh had read in his sonorous and remarkably beautiful voice, I suddenly became aware that the tapestry hanging right above his head depicted a group of nymphs in their usual state of undress! I was stunned!

Islam forbids depictions of the human face or figure, whether in paintings, sculpture, hangings or carpets. And here we had nudity as well!

When I asked about it, Huda blithely announced that the tapestry had been on the wall when they bought the house. There goes another stereotype, I thought. This was an orthodox household, with our hostess in *hijab*, but the risqué scene had disturbed not a soul — certainly not the elderly, short-sighted shaykh.

Neamat's shopping bags were bursting with dried fruit: apricots, prunes, sultanas, figs and dates. Tonight at home she would make the popular syrup, *khoshaf*, used traditionally in the Middle East to break fast. I wasn't very fond of this drink — it is too sweet for my taste — but I usually found it impossible to refuse without giving offence.

Neamat had dropped in to see if Wafia needed anything. The outward signs indicated a traditional, orthodox woman. She seemed quiet and modest in her plain customary garb. But after six children and nineteen years at home, this so-called 'traditional woman' had decided, two years ago, to hone her English skills and return to tertiary education.

Her husband, a supervisor at Australia Post, wasn't happy about it at first, but after she got a part-time job as a community worker with the Anti-Cancer Council he became more helpful around the house. These days he is proud of her achievements, bragging to his friends, but reminding them never to let her know.

'Of course he still insists that I neglect him,' said Neamat. 'But friends are not blind — they can see that he and the children don't suffer. He didn't believe I could do it and I made sure nothing changed for him. But still he tells people he suffered and sacrificed a lot.'

The interview is 'limping along'. Neamat remains guarded and is obviously not at ease with me, in spite of Wafia's reassuring presence and even though we are under her roof. It is only after I say in mock exasperation, 'Neamat, I am not with Immigration or the CIA!' that the ice is broken and we start to talk informally.

'I tell you a funny story,' she said. 'It's the opposite of what people think about how we in Egypt marry. I married at nineteen against my father's wishes — married because I wanted, I definitely wanted to. My poor father, he wanted his girls to finish their education. That was almost a must in Egypt in the 1970s — education for girls was really valued.'

Her father had insisted she should be a doctor, but she wanted to marry and have lots of children. She knew that a number of suitors had been seeking her hand, but her father was adamant — she was too young to marry and must finish her studies. And so he sent them all away, refusing all those anxious young men with sweaty palms who came knocking on the door. 'Don't send them away. You should ask me first!' Neamat cried to her shocked father. How dare his younger daughter challenge him under his own roof, or any roof for that matter! This was the first of many such altercations between them. Both were intransigent, both equally stubborn. Finally, as a last resort, Neamat determined to arrange matters herself.

She first met her future husband at a girlfriend's house. The proprieties were observed and she was never alone at any time with him, nor did they directly address each other. 'I didn't believe in love. I just felt comfortable in his presence. He was a man I could trust; he was looking at me as a person, not an object.' All of this was divined by eye contact alone. Neamat told her mother, 'This is a good man.' Her poor father was in the dark until the very last minute. Through her mother, by now an accomplice, Neamat arranged for the cakes to be prepared. Then her mother tentatively announced, 'There is someone who is interested in your daughter who wants to meet you. Please, you have nothing to lose, just look and listen to him.' So her father was wheedled and cajoled, and finally persuaded — much to the relief of the rest of the family and their neighbours, who had had to endure constant shouting matches. Neamat was obviously determined to have her way. So they were married and Neamat came to Australia with her husband, who had only been in Egypt on holiday. After they were engaged and alone together for the first time (with her giggling sisters spying on them), the first words she blurted out to him were, 'How many children do you want? I want a lot!'

III

Lakemba country

*It is when you realise you're not going back, you want this place to open up a little so that one can live with a little respect and dignity, if Allah wishes (*Insha'Allah*). If a Catholic goes to mass on Sunday and carries out the orders of the Pope, they are called devout. We practise our religion and people here abuse us for it. We are fundamentalists — fanatics!*

The Northern Crescent, BBC film (1991).

9

Bed and breakfast in Lakemba

> Muslim writer (female) from Perth needs accommodation urgently from mid May until Eid ul-Adha. Prepared to pay very good rental. House, flat or independent bed-sitter, Lakemba area, near Haldon St and public transport.

No book on Muslims in Australia worth its salt, I decided, could ignore the Muslim heartland of Lakemba, Sydney. Muslims living there have the reputation of being staunch and devout; if that is so, this would show me a degree of orthodoxy, on both an individual and a communal plane, that I had not experienced elsewhere in Australia. I found the idea of observing Eid ul-Adha, the Festival of Sacrifices, among the Lakemba believers, hard to resist.

Finding a comfortable place to stay in a congenial atmosphere was not difficult — over the years I had developed a circle of friends in Sydney. My problem lay in finding a place of my own, where I would not be 'adopted' or become the spoilt darling of traditional Muslim hospitality — always generous, always overwhelming. I needed an independent nest where I could observe and participate on a purely selfish level, bothering no one. Staying with any of my Muslim friends under these terms might give offence, and besides, the six weeks I planned to stay was far too long for any friendship to remain intact.

Hence the need to subject myself to the perils of open advertising in the *Muslim Times*.

I spent some time pondering over the exact wording. What I planned was strange for a Muslim woman: leaving my husband and home in Perth and looking for temporary accommodation three thousand kilometres away. Any misleading impression that I might have marital problems must be avoided at all costs — hence the reference to my Perth base. Using the word 'writer' rather than 'researcher' might also reassure those who liked their privacy. A strictly orthodox male-headed household would be taboo for me — an unaccompanied, unrelated female stranger. What I needed was a house with a lone woman whose husband was absent overseas, perhaps away on *haj*, or who was separated or divorced. If I offered a good rent under these circumstances, I might be considered a financial asset rather than a cultural liability. Establishing my religious and ethnic credentials — which for some locals would be of more interest than my professional background — could be done over the telephone once I had received a response.

Three weeks later, on a dark, rainy Friday night, I found myself standing with tape-recorder, laptop computer and suitcase outside a small house in Punchbowl Road, Lakemba. I was looking forward to meeting my new landlady, Denise. I knew very little about her — only that she was an English convert to Islam, divorced by her husband and patiently waiting out her *iddha*, the three-month minimum waiting period necessary before a divorce is considered final and a woman can remarry.

Her telephone call had been brief. She had asked if I minded a dog — this had completely thrown me off balance! A dog, from my experience, was almost unheard-of in praying households and considered *haram* and *najis*, impure, by most Muslims. While it is permissible to keep dogs outside as working animals, looking after livestock, hunting or acting as guard dogs, they are not supposed to be indoors. When a Muslim has been licked by a dog he is required to wash seven times before he can pray. In a household where adults and children pray five times a day, this would mean a never-ending cycle of ablutions. Although the Qur'an does not forbid dogs and urges kindness towards all animals, certain Hadith clearly dictate that dogs are not permitted except under certain circumstances. But some Muslims who rely more on the Qur'an than the Prophet's traditions argue that keeping a well-looked-after dog as a pet, in this day and age, is not harmful. Denise was a woman living alone, I reminded myself, and no doubt kept the dog for protection.

The door was opened by a woman dressed in a black *nikab* — a long garment and veil which together covers the wearer's body and face or, if adjusted, allows her eyes to show. One hand was holding a telephone, the other restraining an enormous English sheepdog. I was suddenly face to face with the kind of image often seen on television: images of women shrouded in black, holding placards with 'Kill Rushdie' and 'Down with America', images that frequently dominate Australian perceptions of Muslim women.

As soon as the taxi driver left Denise unveiled herself, replacing the *nikab* with the more conventional *hijab*, or headscarf. My landlady was in her late twenties, statuesque and pale skinned, with wide trusting grey eyes. Her scarf prevented me from determining her hair colour but gave her an air of tranquillity that I later came to realise was deceptive.

By now I felt a little disoriented. First of all, Punchbowl Road seemed to be an extremely busy four-lane highway with cars and trucks roaring by. Then the sight of my hostess dressed in *nikab* had been a little unsettling —

Denise had described herself to me as being 'fairly relaxed religiously'. And the dog was enormous and clearly very much at home inside the house! *Haram*! *haram*! I thought. My confusion increased when I was shown my room and found a baseball bat lying on the bed — Denise explained that she'd had a break-in the week before. But the room was larger than I had expected, with an old desk in one corner and a single bed with a doona-style cover. There was no wardrobe, but we overcame this by placing a broomstick between two picture rails and, anyway, there was a chest of drawers I could use. Overall it reminded me of shabby student digs in the 1960s, but it was clean and Denise had put herself out to find me a desk.

The house consisted of two bedrooms, a kitchen-cum-open lounge room and a bathroom; the floor coverings were linoleum and the furniture was sparse. In the sitting room was a black vinyl lounge, draped rather oddly with red satin bed sheets. The house was drafty and I was glad I had packed my electric blanket. Denise had also kindly given me a small heater for my room. But the location for my purposes was superb — just around the corner from the mosque, with the main shopping street and train station only five minutes away. At last I was among the true believers in the heart of Lakemba!

'We converts must do everything right,' Denise complained. 'The born Muslim can make mistakes.' The way of the convert, at least in the early stages, seemed difficult. Denise grappled with a whole range of issues ranging from theological points about the hereafter to the sometimes baffling Hadith injunctions. These govern everything a Muslim does: how to dress, what to eat, how to behave. Islam leaves its followers in little doubt about what is *halal* (permissible) or *haram* by laying down a strict moral and ethical order. It is a complete way of life, not something you put on and take off at will. Denise was struggling earnestly with these to the best of her ability, but there seemed to be monumental obstacles along her path, usually put there by well-meaning Muslim friends — some of them converts like herself and others born Muslims. She was flooded with advice, often contradictory, mostly well-intentioned, but often culturally rather than religiously based.

As we sat talking over a cup of tea on that first night, I learnt that one of the early problems for a convert is trying to make sense of what is *haram*. In Denise's world, her Muslim girlfriends were the arbiters of what was properly Islamic and what was not. Denise suspected that sometimes they were right and sometimes they made mistakes, but she seemed to lack the will or the confidence to resolve her dilemma.

'How can I know? What do you think?' she asked plaintively. She had had little formal education, having left school at fourteen. She told me she worked in a factory packaging biscuits; before that she had been unemployed for a time. She said little about her family except that they were far away, and vaguely hinted at some dark familial turbulence in the past.

Having been told television was *haram*, she had recently sold her set. Her red and black satin sheets were also *haram* and had been relegated to chair covers, being glimpsed by a strange male without her *nikab* on was *haram*, so opening the door to the pizza delivery man was an intricate exercise — almost like an obstacle race. She had to peer through the door, fling on her *nikab* and adjust her veil so that it completely covered her face, find her purse, throw open the door and hope that the pizza was still warm! Yes, she knew that having Snooky the dog inside was *haram*, but the Muslim sisters had decided her need for protection was a legitimate extension of the circumstances under which the Hadith allows dogs. Apparently the sisters could be swayed from time to time, but they were usually fairly strict in their pronouncements. (I wonder if they realised that the 'guard dog' carried out his duties from inside and was cosseted and permitted to sleep outside her bedroom. And I suspected Snooky sneaked in to join his mistress once I retired.)

Denise's circle of Muslim women friends believed it was their duty to come down hard on new Muslims or Muslims who strayed from the true path, and in Denise — with her eagerness to embrace Islam and follow the way of the truly devout — they had found a willing victim. This was a theme we returned to again and again during my stay: the problems encountered by new Muslims keen to learn and naively assuming that born Muslims must know everything. I learnt from Denise how confusing it could become for a single woman sifting through the mountain of advice she received — in her case from young women who were totally convinced that they were one hundred per cent right and who, in the main, did not take kindly to doubt or disagreement. Social control is a butterfly net trying to snare those who will not conform, but in a community like Lakemba, and for someone alone, it can also offer security and even a surrogate family.

Local beliefs and customs, mainly of Middle Eastern origin, are often at the root of the advice converts receive; some of them are clearly village beliefs and superstitions with no basis in Islam. Superstitions such as the 'evil eye', laying curses, love talismans and so on run rife among certain Arabic-speaking women whose Islamic education has been limited. But this was small consolation for a woman like Denise with little formal education, not given to reading heavy tomes on religion and easily influenced by peer pressure.

Denise is right. The process of becoming a Muslim is

much tougher for converts than for young children of Muslim parents, who have the advantage of being gradually and gently socialised into the Islamic way in their early years, and who generally receive considerable forgiveness and tolerance for their mistakes from parents and other adults. Children grow up with parental role models, with the opportunity to evolve into a more religiously knowledgeable adult — time is on their side.

Converts have to become perfect Muslims in a less patient, less forgiving environment. Unlike children brought up in a particular ethnic culture, converts in their religious infancy receive their nourishment from many different cultural traditions, which they must somehow assimilate with their own early learning experiences. Born Muslims and converts sometimes forget this. 'We have no cultural background,' I have been told by many a convert around Australia, 'and have no inhibitions in looking for the truth.' While this may be so, it continually astounds me that Anglo-Australian converts believe that they have no cultural values or traditions of their own. Perhaps they are too busy warding off the strong cultural practices found among many Arabic-speaking Muslims that dominate Islam in Australia and elsewhere.

Many converts end up trying desperately to cling to 'the text' — usually the Qur'an and the Hadith — in an attempt to find their way through the cultural mazes to the essential heart of Islam which they originally found so appealing. Shedding cultural practices can become a full-time occupation for well-educated female converts to Islam — women on a voyage of self-discovery who have converted for purely religious and philosophical reasons, not because their husbands are Muslims or their partners converted, or because of some obvious emotional need. Several such women have organised support groups for those converts experiencing a form of culture shock and needing advice.

'Once we have the education to discriminate, we can cut out the cultural distraction,' said one woman. 'I admit to looking sceptically now at everything. I remember being told that you must shave your hair before you read the Qur'an. I'm glad I found out in time that it's just not true! It was being mixed up with another practice. There were others like me, so in our group, if we were uncertain about a Qur'anic interpretation we'd ask one or more of the shaykhs; we found they usually have the best knowledge.'

The same discreet approach is often applied to sectarian issues. Whereas born Muslims know whether they are Sunni or Shi'a and which school of religious law they follow, most converts find the choice confusing, preferring to opt out of the debates and stay neutral. 'I am a "straight-out Muslim", with no labels attached,' they say.

But for Denise, Islam was the sum of right and wrong behaviours which she absorbed from her new peers. In spite of her religious bewilderment, she was cheerful, disarming, garrulous and very much divorced. As I would learn in the weeks to come, she was a woman of contradictions — mainly caused by her short and fast introduction to a new set of rules and her open, friendly personality, which had caused not a few cross-cultural communication problems. The demeanour she assumed, the clothes she wore, her language, were all at odds with a lively, engaging personality quite at ease in the company of men. Denise made friends with the opposite sex easily and spontaneously. Clearly it took a great act of will to change her behaviour, deportment and body language, forcing them all into line with the internal changes that Islam had made to her life, pummelling them into a more obedient shape in contrast to her earlier permissiveness, or 'English behaviour', as she quaintly called it.

10

Little Tripoli

The next morning was one of those delightful late autumn days when the sun's touch warms rather than scorches and there is no sign of rain. I had slept, or rather slipped, all over the bed, unused as I was to satin sheets, and I resolved to ask Denise for a plain cotton sheet in exchange for the exotic black one she had given me. This morning I saw her without *hijab*; her light brown hair was in a ponytail and she had on a loose tracksuit. Later in the day, when she returned from visiting friends, she was wearing a cream *nikab* with full veil; once more she had regained her mystique. With Denise, I sensed a touch of the theatrical — a slight suggestion of play-acting — in her costume changes.

But now it was time to see more of Lakemba, especially Haldon Street, described by friends as Little Lebanon or Little Tripoli, perhaps because so many Muslims living there came from the region around Tripoli in northern Lebanon. My route along Wangee Road led me past bungalow-style houses and blocks of flats side by side; Lakemba's residential mix is matched by its cultural mix — Arabic speakers, Indians, Vietnamese, Pacific Islanders, and an older generation of Anglo-Australians. Lakemba is an old suburb which developed after the railway opened in 1909. I walked past the famous Imam Ali Mosque, better known as the Lakemba Mosque, whose high-profile imam, Shaykh Taj-Din al-Hilali, was away on *haj*. The mosque is an impressive building with its creamy brick facade and tall minaret. At the end of the month it would be the focus of the Eid ul-Adha celebrations and draw thousands of worshippers.

Haldon Street was full of shoppers, mainly husbands and wives loaded down with plastic bags on a busy Saturday morning. I was immediately struck by the number of Muslim women wearing what was later described to me as the 'Lakemba uniform'. Basically this consists of an ankle-length, dark-coloured, loose-fitting buttoned coat, worn with a white or cream-coloured *hijab*. It is a style often seen in parts of Lebanon and Jordan. There were also more colourful clothes worn by Indian or Pakistani women, who tend to prefer the national dress of *shalwar kameez*. Now and then I also glimpsed the austere *nikab* favoured by extremely devout women when outside the house.

Haldon Street may be the only street of its kind in Australia — one where a Muslim woman feels conspicuous for not 'covering', regardless of how modestly she is dressed.

Slowly, I began to realise that the way a woman dressed in Lakemba sent out clear messages to other Muslims, as well as non-Muslims, about her modesty, her piety, how she wished others to see her and perhaps, in a few instances, even her obedience to her husband. Dress had a multiple function beyond the original idea of protecting a woman from the gaze of men. Above all it sent a strong signal that the wearer was (or wished to be seen as), a 'practising Muslim'.

The subject of clothing and covering followed me like a persistent shadow in Lakemba, whereas in Melbourne it had appeared less intrusive. *Hijab* seemed to be the norm and excited no curious stares or rude remarks; cultural diversity had made a place for itself in Lakemba, or so it seemed.

Shopping proceeds at a leisurely pace along Haldon Street. Friends greet one another, laughing and joking, exchanging the latest news outside Sunny's Delite Emporium, Radwan's Pharmacy, Al Noor Men's Hairdresser. There is not the compulsion to finish as quickly as possible and be on your way that dominates the shopping habits of the multitudes pushing trolleys along sterile supermarket aisles. In Haldon Street are shops which have re-created as best they can the atmosphere of shopping in Tripoli and other Lebanese towns and villages. Many of the shops have Arabic names, and Muslims from beyond Lakemba come here specially to buy the olives, oil, breads, nuts and dried fruits. You enter a shop in Haldon Street and marvel at the emporium of culinary wonders from the kitchens and markets of the Middle East — barrels of olives, mountains of dried fruit — and laugh as your tongue stumbles over the unfamiliar Arabic brand names. The aromas of coffee, spices, and herbs like *zatar*, a mouth-watering, magical topping of oregano and sesame seeds (to which I would become badly addicted) tantalise your nostrils, re-creating an atmosphere of bazaars and traders, of feasts and far away places.

People in Lakemba treat shopping as a social event and stand talking with all the friends they meet in the aisles and on the footpaths. Arabic speakers — whether Muslim or non-Muslim — are renowned for their lack of reticence. Putting it plainly, they talk loudly ('even in the mosque,' as other Muslims tell me in soft, shocked voices). The rich, flowing sounds of Arabic fill the shops and streets. There are also Vietnamese and Indian establishments with their own delicacies next to shops selling taro and sweet potato to people from the Pacific Islands — all to be found in little Haldon Street.

Over the years Lakemba, like other working-class suburbs such as Auburn, Marrickville and Bankstown, has provided cheap accommodation with relatively good access to the city by bus and train. Groups have settled close to each other, established their social networks and support systems, built their clubs, schools and mosques. Today there are about ten thousand Muslims living in and around Lakemba in the Canterbury local government area. Most are Arabic speakers who immigrated during Lebanon's civil war, often semi-educated, without much English, and now unemployed because of the economic downturn.

Making friends with female Muslim shopkeepers was effortless, even on day one. Local businesswomen were curious, wanting to know what I was up to and why I had travelled all the way from Perth to Lakemba of all places! As an unknown, unaccompanied Muslim woman, I wisely refrained from striking up conversations with male shopkeepers. I would later ask other people to introduce me or to offer their names by way of introduction. For although I was no *hijabi* — a term used by some young women to describe fellow wearers of the *hijab* — my Pakistani ancestry was obvious and I modified my behaviour accordingly. For the next six weeks I would be a regular visitor to local shops, making daily purchases and catching up on the local gossip. In a small, close-knit community like Lakemba, intelligence networks are always at work, and purveyors of local scandals and domestic secrets unveil rumours, gossip, news of all kinds — some true and some undoubtedly false — to eager buyers. You got value for your dollar when you shopped in Lakemba.

'These young students from overseas! If only their poor parents knew what they got up to! They drink over here, you know!'

'Her mother-in-law threw her out of the house — her husband is too weak to do anything about it and his mother threatened to bring a curse down on his head.'

'Poor child, she's not well in the head — very nervous — so they're going to send her home to visit the shrines and see if the local shaykh can heal her.'

'I don't care what you say, but repeating *Bismillah* [in the name of God] over Kentucky Fried Chicken or a McDonald's burger doesn't make it *halal*!'

At least once a day I passed by Radwan's Pharmacy, not daring to enter until one day a local identity came to my aid, someone whose name melted away any suspicion about this strange woman who, it was whispered, sometimes plucked a tape-recorder from inside her capacious bag! Now my patience was rewarded and I officially met Radwan El Metsalem.

'Is he better?' were the first English words Radwan ever learnt to say. The second phrase he mastered was, 'He is still the same,' the answer he heard from the doctor and nurses day in, day out, until his brother died two months later.

Radwan, who I guessed was in his early thirties had immigrated to Australia as a fourteen-year-old — one of the worst ages for anyone to leave their home, he told me — with his parents, one sister and two brothers. His three older brothers were already here. Nine days after their arrival in Sydney, one of his brothers had an ultimately fatal accident driving down from Queensland to meet them. Each day the family visited the hospital, unable to speak English, totally mystified by the unfamiliar medical system. It was here that Radwan learnt his first few sad words of English.

The interview with Radwan took place at the back of his pharmacy under difficult circumstances. Customers would enter the shop every few minutes needing his personal attention and we were getting nowhere very fast, until at last his assistant took over and Radwan allowed himself a break. Inside the shop, Arabic was the language of power, authority and transaction. 'There've been times when an English-speaking customer comes in and I automatically talk to him in Lebanese,' he laughed.

The atmosphere of Radwan's shop struck me as different from that of other chemist shops. The people coming in to have their prescriptions filled, people whom I supposed to be sick or ailing seemed, with few exceptions, cheerful and talkative and very interested in one another's health. Radwan's pharmacy was much more than a dispensary for medicines, ointments and other potions.

'My customers often give advice to each other. Someone comes in with diabetes and a prescription from the doctor and before I know it the person waiting next to him is telling him about some natural cure — what leaves to use, how long to boil them and when to drink the tea. They freely exchange all sorts of local herbal remedies. Our people have a lot of faith in herbal cures,' he informed me. Little did he know that he was talking to the daughter of a herbalist.

Radwan was cheerful and good humoured, a young man with a light, expressive voice who used expansive hand gestures to reinforce whatever point he was making.

'I've always wanted to be a pharmacist since I was a little boy in Lebanon,' he confided. 'It fascinated me when I was young. If you visit Lebanon today, you will find old remedies hand in hand with modern pharmaceuticals, and both are well respected. You find these little traditional *atori,* or medicine places, more like kiosks, on the streets. They mix medicines for you while you wait, crush the almond leaves or make up the salve ... maybe offer a little hashish if you are wounded and in bad pain.'

The roles of pharmacists in Lebanon and in Australia are very different. 'People in Lebanon call them "half a doctor" and patients go to them and describe their symptoms and ask their advice. Doctors are expensive there and more difficult to come by,' Radwan said. 'So people think, "I might as well go to the pharmacist." In Australia, Lebanese people expect the same. Maybe the doctor hasn't enough time for them, or maybe they want to check up on what he's given them. So they come by for a chat and some advice.'

Mental health issues affecting immigrant women had always held particular interest for me. I asked Radwan if such problems were kept at arm's length by some people in migrant communities. He said that a stigma was indeed attached to mental illness: less educated people were afraid of such 'ailments'. They would use phrases like 'God forbid ...' and recite prayers to ward off what they saw as an unnatural affliction.

I knew that in Lebanon and elsewhere in the Middle East, some uneducated people invested the local shaykhs, whom they believed were closer to God, with the power to cure illness. Cures could range from the medicinal to the supernatural and included prayers, charms and folk remedies. Shaykhs who were reputed to be good healers attracted crowds of people seeking remedies for anything — colds and cancer, backaches and boils, and the age-old ailments like unrequited love, the evil eye and possession by *djinn*, not forgetting, of course, the malicious and malignant wishes of those who envied you for your beautiful son, your hair, your health or your wealth!

Leaving the sensitive area of mental illness and 'folk Islam' behind us, I asked Radwan if he had ever thought of moving away from Lakemba, perhaps to a more affluent suburb.

'Never!' It was clear he was surprised I had even asked. 'I feel so close to this area. I went to Punchbowl Boys High School, which was pretty horrible in those days and very racist.' (He went on to tell me anecdotes the like of which every boy of Lebanese, Greek, Italian, Vietnamese or Aboriginal background knows so well and can never bury.) 'I even came back here with my wife after we got married.'

That was after he had completed his studies and established his business. What did he think of parents who encouraged their sons to think about settling down when they were eighteen or nineteen? 'I don't agree with this custom,' he said, 'but you see, parents want to keep the boys out of mischief. Bringing up your children properly in Australia is a challenge, and at least in Lakemba you know your children will have Muslim friends.'

'Keeping boys out of mischief.' Even learned shaykhs had difficulties with young men. Some problems were the same the world over — only the solutions were different now and then.

Every Muslim needs *halal* meat and I had found one of the best *halal* butchers. The proprietors were Anis Kahil and his son Khaled. After complimenting Anis on the quality of his meat and its presentation, I learnt that Lebanon and Turkey were well known for their expert butchers. In the Kahil family the trade had been handed down from father to son for three generations, as was often the way in societies where families and clans were also self-sustaining economic units.

Anis Kahil had the look of a man who had worked hard all his life. He was slight, with greying hair and tough gnarled hands. Khaled stood next to his father, tall and well built, a picture of robust health, with curly black hair, a neat moustache and confident bearing. Undoubtedly he was the kind of son Anis had dreamt of; one who would find his way in this new land, negotiate a path through the quicksands of the English language and improve his position with education, yet still remain true to his father's ways, retaining his language, his religion and strong bonds of filial respect and obedience.

'Twenty-three years,' said Anis. Turning to his son, he spoke three or four sentences in Lebanese, obviously instructing him to convey his exact meaning.

'My father has worked in Australia for twenty-three years and has never once been on the dole. He gets upset when he hears Lebanese called dole bludgers. He works a thirteen- or fourteen-hour day. There are thousands like him,' Khaled said proudly.

That night I visited their home for dinner and listened to father and son rhapsodise about the Lebanese lifestyle. During the course of our noisy, laughter-filled and frequently interrupted family discussion, with Khaled — who is a computer science graduate — sometimes acting as interpreter, they drove home just how boring Australia could be socially.

'Here in Australia,' said Khaled, 'your daily rhythm and your routine are prescribed, set out for you: ten minutes for morning and afternoon tea, forty-five minutes for lunch, come home, television and then to sleep.' The whole family joined him in a chorus of agreement. 'It's tedious and repetitious!' he said. The room seemed to swell in accord, with exclamations rising and falling to indicate how strange and unfriendly it all seemed.

'Boring!' said Khaled's new Syrian brother-in-law, a very recent, homesick arrival.

'In Lebanon you don't know what is going to happen that day.' Khaled was not speaking of political or military matters but of business. 'You could sell nothing in a day — or you could sell millions! I'm a million per cent — not one hundred per cent — a million per cent sure that if you walked down a back street in Australia at seven o'clock at night, you'd almost die of fear — it's very, very lonely. In Lebanon it takes you an hour to walk down a street that would normally only take ten minutes. You need one hour because every few minutes someone greets you, asks about your day, insists that you come in for a coffee. "How are you?" they call. Everybody knows each other because it's so small.

'There the kids finish school at two o'clock and the family sits down together for one big meal at lunch, at night the men smoke the *nargeelah*, the hubble-bubble water pipe, and the talking, storytelling and visiting are never ending.'

The old social customs from the past — how hard was it to transplant them to sprawling suburbia?

'The social life in Lebanon is better for the women,' Anis said.

'Dad says the women have the *subhiyat*, or women's gathering, during the day. After they have done the housework in the morning, they visit one another, sing and dance at each other's houses, drink coffee, eat cakes and come home before their husbands.' Men socialised at one another's homes but also patronised the coffee houses, which were a way of life for men and out of the reach of women.

Khaled's mother agreed that life in Australia, with only television to replace the fun of strolling or visiting cafés with crowds of others late at night, was dull. With six children to look after she had had some horrible times, she said, isolated at home without her big noisy extended family of grandparents, parents, brother and sisters, uncles and aunts. In Australia you might not even know your neighbour's name.

The Kahils' memories of Lebanon are strong and deep, but Anis Kahil loves Australia too. 'Australia is one of the best countries in the world!' he says. 'In this country we are given all our human rights: we can build a mosque if we want to — sure, people can say, "No you can't," if they want, that is their right too, but the law is not automatically against us and if our claims are seen as legitimate, it is on our side.' Anis Kahil believes that, 'You need a heart big enough to love two countries if you are an immigrant; it shouldn't be a case of choosing one over the other. It's like having two children; your heart must be big enough to love them both.'

11

The rope of Allah

'If you don't want to be a practising Muslim, you don't live in Lakemba.' My new friend Sameena Hussain addressed me very seriously as we sat together in her lounge room. I was about to receive my first lesson in the ways of Lakemba and why some Muslims decide to live there. Sameena is an Indian Muslim who has lived in Australia for nearly fifteen years and she had agreed to be my guide. She was recommended to me as one of the gatekeepers to local affairs and one who, as an active and practising Muslim, knew all about the organisational side of Lakemba. Initially Sameena had been wary of my motives and had quietly checked me out before agreeing to meet. Lakemba culture is by nature suspicious — sometimes for very good reason.

'Letting your hair down' can be taken literally in strict Muslim households. Once inside her own four walls a woman can remove her head cover and relax, alone, with other women or with her family and relatives. I quickly noticed that this was a 'shoeless household' and removed my shoes inside the passage. This is not the custom in all Muslim households, but it is certainly the Lakemba way. While it is not mandatory, shoes are not worn — often for reasons of hygiene — in many households where people may pray, sit and eat their meals on carpeted floors.

Sameena was in her early thirties, with an expressive,

slightly worried-looking, smooth brown face; luminous, heavy-lidded, black-brown eyes, and masses of glossy black hair. I sensed that she felt passionately about many things. The house was quiet for the moment. Everyone else — Sameena's husband, her four children, her sister and a nephew — was out for the day. It was her day off from work at a childcare centre and I was anxious to make the most of this chance to be indoctrinated into the mores of Lakemba.

'Quality of life is more important to a practising Muslim than standard of living,' Sameena began. 'By quality of life we mean the religious life. This is an important reason for people to live here. They can live near the mosque, go to prayers, join in all the different religious and educational activities. If you need them, the support systems are all here — you are part of a real community, not just one family.'

'Lakemba seems like a village to me,' I said, 'a village where everybody knows everyone else; where there are different circles with different leaders and different undercurrents and tensions at play, a village where you may find yourself cast out if you infringe the rules or fail to conform.' I had reached this conclusion on the basis of my early observations and the comments of Muslim friends who had once lived in Lakemba: 'Lakemba is suffocating — we had to get out.' 'We still visit friends in Lakemba, but to us it was like a prison!'

'It's a dumping ground — when you arrive, you ask the taxi *wallah* at the airport where the mosque is and he drives you straight to Lakemba!'

'There are very judgemental Muslims in Lakemba ... take care!'

It was a bold way to open our discussion. Sameena, not having expected a confrontation, struggled to keep a straight face and collapsed in giggles. 'All right,' she conceded with good grace, 'I admit there are critics, people who leave after a while because it doesn't suit them or because they're not ready to be one hundred per cent Muslim; but there are a lot who stay, who'll pay $20,000 extra for a house here just to be near the mosque and other practising Muslims.' Her eyes shining, she leaned forward in her chair, anxious to convince me of the merits of living in the circle of true believers.

'Parents want their children to be closer to an Islamic environment,' she continued. 'They are scared of losing them. Muslims in Lakemba are like a fortress, a stronghold for Islam against un-Islamic influences. We are told, "You Muslims are one body and if one part of the body aches, the whole body should feel the pain." Those of us living in Lakemba represent that one body. And being with other Muslims reminds people of their duties, "enjoining what is good and forbidding what is evil",' she paraphrased from the Qur'an.

'So living near the mosque means being part of one large Muslim community — the *ummah* — where you don't fall by the way, and if you happen to stray, someone can bring you back to the path?'

Sameena nods yes. She is pleased with me after all — my first lesson has gone well.

For many Muslims like Sameena, living near the mosque is in itself an act of faith and provides a safe harbour for social and cultural contact and more. To the truly devout, mosques symbolise the core of their religious and psychological identity. When Muslims perceive themselves as being under siege in a non-Muslim land, a mosque gives them focus and drive. To build a mosque, many will donate inordinate amounts of money, give of their time and labour in endless rounds of fundraising, and fight legal battles for what in mainstream Australia is an unpopular cause. They are not alone in feeling besieged.

Non-Muslims often view the arrival of large groups of Muslims in their neighbourhoods with apprehension, as was dramatically shown in the Campbelltown Mosque dispute in 1991, which brought out the ugly underbelly of religious bigotry. This bitter wrangle with the local council over an application to build a mosque was a lesson for Muslims elsewhere. While the mosque was built and the scars have long since healed, the dispute involved costly litigation and painful divisions within the wider community.

One of Sameena's favourite sayings is, 'The rope of Allah.' It is from the Qur'an, Sura III, verse 103 (The Family of Imran): 'And hold fast, all together, to the rope of God (which God stretches out for you), and be not divided among yourselves'.

The lines evoke an image of people struggling in deep water to whom a Benevolent Providence extends a strong and unbreakable rope of rescue. If everyone holds fast to the rope of Allah their mutual support adds to the chance of collective safety. This conveys the important message of the unity of the *ummah*, or believers.

Lakemba offers this security in numbers. It's an enclave where Muslims can find safety, support and help; where they can join together with like-minded people and become part of 'the many', the *ummah*. Shoring up one's religious identity when one is part of a minority can become a full-time occupation, especially in a society with at times conflicting values — especially family values. The fortress metaphor used by Sameena expresses the view of many Muslims in Lakemba, who see themselves embroiled in a battle against *kafir* ways. Australian popular culture and its effects on their children are something they dread.

But what Sameena saw as the essence of Lakemba, standing shoulder to shoulder in a modern *jihad* as one united body dedicated to the way of Allah, unswerving in its devotion, is exactly what other Muslims living outside the 'fortress' find unsettling. Many are indignant at what they interpret as a 'holier than thou' approach — at the subtle pressure and sometimes direct confrontation brought to bear on those perceived to be 'straying'. Those branded as less practising or less devout, become critical in turn. Many non-Arabic-speaking Muslims from outside Lakemba, often well educated and well read, have little patience with what they see as over zealousness or even fanaticism.

Lakemba is not the smooth, placid pond it may at first seem. As in most small communities there are rival groups and rival leaders, and power struggles are not uncommon. But Sameena did not reveal this to me. It was only after another two weeks of endless cups of coffee and Lebanese sweets that the other players strutting the Lakemba stage became evident. By then I had managed to unearth some 'village secrets' for myself. The day-to-day lives of most people passed uneventfully, as in average suburban life; the majority went to work, attended mosque on Fridays, took part in annual festivals and participated in some local religious activity or another. But among unemployed men (and the jobless figures were high) more time could be spent at the mosque, and organisational politics and factional disputes became grist to the gossip mill — an ongoing soap opera providing fuel for endless discussion.

To these men the mosque is a wonderful solace, a balm to wounded pride and their feelings of shame and alienation. They have been made redundant and are dependent on small children to interpret for them; they sense that the respect once accorded them as heads of the family is disappearing — everything is failing them — but the mosque is there and God is there.

Leaders in Lakemba, whether religious or secular, must — as must leaders everywhere — deliver the goods if they want to stay in power. What is deemed to be beneficial varies. It may be a government grant to build a cultural centre, funds for a training program or English classes — the list is endless. Wooing politicians and bureaucrats and being wooed in return is expected of leaders. The constant rounds of receptions, openings, launches, consultations and visits; the speeches and votes of thanks; the long lines of people — usually men — anxious to gain the ear of the guest of honour for a quick bit of lobbying, have meaning beyond the ritual. It is a two-way process, in which allies and votes are secured, rumours quashed or floated, and opinions and needs voiced. The hosts see themselves as being listened to, and they bask in the reflected honour when their society president or council executive or shaykh is shown respect. Leaders have then 'delivered the goods' and have a better chance of retaining the grassroots support of their local communities, particularly important at annual election time.

In 1975 Gough Whitlam, then prime minister, laid the Lakemba mosque's foundation stone; former New South Wales premier Nick Greiner made a dramatic entry by helicopter one Ramadan, and Paul Keating as prime minister also made an official visit. (A local joke making the rounds in Lakemba during the 1993 federal election had it that Keating had 'blown the Muslim vote' because of his financial interest in a piggery — *haram*!)

Everyone I met told me that Lakemba had undergone a transformation over the past ten years. There is an energy there and a strong community spirit that occasionally makes one wonder what the suburb was like before, and how Australian-born old-timers have felt seeing their neighbourhood transformed.

Esme certainly remembered. With little embarrassment, she told me about her own anti-Arab feelings when she lived in Arncliffe. In the early 1980s, when the famous Al-

Zahra Shi'a mosque was being built there, she and her first husband sold their house, packed up and left in disgust. Esme is a good sport and readily described her resentment. 'All those Arabs hanging around talking that strange lingo, knocking out the leadlight windows — we felt the place was deteriorating, so we sold up.' Her crystal ball failed to reveal that eight years later she would marry one of 'those Arabs', and eventually become a 'dangerous' Muslim herself, living close to the Lakemba mosque where she came to know Denise.

Most of Lakemba's contemporary history needs to be patched together like some giant jigsaw puzzle. Which particular piece of history interests you? Whose version do you believe? Are you more interested in the history of social movements or are you a follower of the 'Great Man' theory of history? I myself am interested in change — social and religious change.

Zainab and Hadia, whom I met one day in the women's section of the mosque, reminisced about the Lakemba they remembered from the 1980s. Hadia, soft voiced, quiet and confident in her movements, was a Lebanese Australian. Zainab was a plump, jovial Anglo-Australian convert who had difficulty sitting still and whose telephone never seemed to stop ringing. Along with the sweet Lebanese coffee came large helpings of candour.

'I remember the way it was,' began Hadia, 'when my husband and I arrived from Lebanon in 1976. We were in shock. We didn't know how to cope — we had never lived in a non-Muslim country before and had no idea what to expect. Allah forgive me, I was so frightened that I stopped wearing my own clothes, stopped covering, because when I looked in the mirror I looked all wrong for Australia — I was ashamed.'

Even in the early 1980s, few women wore the *hijab* in Lakemba. Within six or seven years however, all of this would change. The transformation is remarkable! Despite mutterings from an insecure old guard, Australia's once monocultural outlook has been irrevocably changed. Muslims show no signs of not belonging in Lakemba. They own the pavements, they stand outside the shops and schools waiting to pick up their children. Arabic is heard in the streets, the shops, the banks, and hard looks and nasty words are far and few between. As I walked around Lakemba in 1994, the pride and sense of belonging were abundantly evident. Fear of being accosted or otherwise singled out for being different seems to have gone — for good, I hope.

In the early 1980s many Arabic-speaking migrant women made a conscious decision to learn more about their own religion. It was all they had to fall back on at a time of acute psychological pain. When other Australian women asked them questions about Islam, their ignorance was highlighted. Most of them had very little religious education — indeed, very little education at all. Now a wave of self-teaching spread.

'At the same time ... or was it earlier ...' said Zainab, 'we convert women were also organising a support group to extend our poor knowledge of Islam — it was really an exciting time! I've always thought, Hadia' — and she gave a sly wink — 'that it must have been the convert women who forced you Muslim-born women to get off your backsides and get organised.' She turned to me with a broad grin, 'Obviously they weren't going to be beaten by a bunch of converts! They'd rather die than admit it, but their pride was hurt.'

Hadia refused to be drawn, but entered the game by rolling her eyes and saying to me in a stage whisper, 'These converts ... so much to learn.'

I was relieved to witness this exchange. Until then I had heard talk of a certain coolness between converts and other

Muslims: 'They were giving us hell!' is the way one convert had described it. 'Communication problems' was a mild description for some of the early dust-ups I had heard about. 'Psychological difference' was another way of looking at it; a phrase diplomatically used by Muslims who respected converts for studying Islam's tenets deeply and making them operational in their daily living. Some saw born Muslims — those who inherited their religion — as too complacent and often lazy, especially in contrast to the zeal and passion of the convert.

I told Hadia and Zainab that Lakemba struck me as being like a big village. 'Yes, it's close like a village,' agreed Hadia, 'with all the gossip and closeness of village life — it's hard to keep a secret in Lakemba!' she giggled.

'It's hard to be independent!' came Zainab's barb. 'What I find so funny is that all of this happens in a working-class suburb twenty minutes from the heart of Sydney.' For a moment she became serious. 'Let's not get too carried away with the village image. People choose to live here, after all. For some it's great; others can't wait to get away. Both sides get vitriolic about their choices. It's all very petty, very un-Islamic if you ask me, spending so much time criticising each other,' she said drily, folding her arms as if distancing herself from it all.

As a diversion, I showed the rough diagram I'd made of the various groups I'd detected and the undercurrents I'd unearthed so far. Curiosity overcame them both and they bent their heads over my chart. Luckily it passed muster, except for two or three omissions, and together we developed a revised outline.

We confined ourselves to local Lakemba groups. There were a host of different *dawa* (religious awareness) groups, convert support groups, youth groups, *tafsir* (Qur'an discussion) groups, large groups that met at the mosque, small groups that met in houses or in an empty room above a coffee shop. Forming another category were the official governing bodies and agencies which competed for grants and favour from the state and federal governments. Both women agreed that the arrival of Shaykh Taj as imam of the Lakemba mosque in the mid 1980s had opened up Muslim women's lives in a new way and given them greater access to the mosque. Even those who disagreed with the imam (and there were many) and saw him as part of the Lakemba 'culture of control' were unstinting in their admiration for what he had done to empower Muslim women — in a religious sense, I hasten to add. He had set up regular Arabic classes and Qur'an discussion groups, and founded and nurtured the Muslim Women's Association of Lakemba, among many other accomplishments.

But not everyone approved of his endorsement of women's religious education. Some local alliances expressed a dislike of the shaykh's activities as they fear educated women, able to read the Qur'an and the Hadith, might start to question some of the customary practices and cultural traditions that confine their lives. From time to time major and minor power struggles of one kind or another seem to bubble like a spring out of the Lakemba ground.

The level of superstition and religious ignorance in less religiously educated Lakemba circles was a source of worry to the two women. Hadia showed me a little gold talisman her mother in Lebanon had given her as protection against the evil eye. I was fascinated. I stared at it trying to fathom what lay behind this bizarre blue gaze fringed with black eyelashes. It stared fixedly back at me, as if it sensed my disbelief in its magical powers. Belief in the evil eye goes back centuries. It is based on the notion that some individuals have the power to kill or bewitch with a glance. To ward off such looks, people in many cultures, especially around the Middle East and the

Mediterranean, use replicas of eyes to frighten off the evil — so the thinking goes — even when their owners are asleep or otherwise preoccupied. The belief that blue eyes are somehow fiercer may date back to the time of the blue-eyed, northern European crusaders.

My second visit to Sameena's home gave me the chance to ask for her version of the revival in women's learning in Lakemba. Zainab and Hadia had described it as a turning point. What did she think? I had struck gold! Sameena talked about the trend animatedly; for her it was not an occurrence of the past but was still going on. Clearly, the revival of women's learning had happened in different groups at different times over a period of about ten years. While for some it had ended, for others like Sameena it continued to burn brightly.

'This revival, if you like to call it that,' she said, 'is driven by women, mainly those women who feel there is something to be gained by living in one large Islamic community, who value the support systems and the networks that offers. It is incredible just how ignorant most of us have been about the foundations and inner workings of Islam. Now, practically every Muslim household in Lakemba has at least one woman who is involved in some activity, usually to do with educating herself. Men have had it all the time!' For the first time I was seeing Sameena as the crusading women's advocate, passionate about what women have achieved and the opportunities yet to come. 'Men have had access to the mosques, the prayers, the meeting places, the conferences — they have controlled all of this, while we have been on the outside, looking in. We have stayed at home!' A familiar cry of women everywhere.

So how were women educating themselves? What sorts of women's groups were there?

'Groups come and groups go,' Sameena answered. 'My own *dawa* group has been running for five years now and is still growing. About eighty women come regularly. We use the *shura* method where the format is prescribed. Readings from the Hadith are done by women nominated at the men's *dawa* group earlier in the week,' she said.

I was curious about this *shura* method and learned that it is a style emphasising consultation and consensus. No one person makes an authoritative decision; the group decides. It is time consuming but democratic.

I was confused until it dawned on me that Sameena was describing a process used by 'the men'; 'the men' were the ones using the *shura* method. They decided which selection would be read by the women, and which women would do the reading in Arabic. There seemed little opportunity for discussion. I was sure that I had overlooked something in Sameena's explanation, something that instinctively I decided not to probe further with her at this time. In the weeks ahead it would become clearer to me just why her group is so different to others that I had come across in Lakemba and elsewhere in Australia. But one thing was clear, her group disallowed individual interpretation of the Qur'an or the Hadith. Sameena supported the *shura* method because she believed it eradicated the petty squabbles many Lakemba women's groups used to get bogged down in when they made their own decisions.

My mentor was adept at juggling the seemingly irreconcilable: on the one hand she proudly described the 'women-driven' religious revival in Lakemba and the opportunity it had given women to enter the men's domain, yet she saw no inconsistency between this and a situation in which the men made all the decisions for the women, even down to what text they would read. Rather than confront Sameena with this contradiction, I changed the subject.

'Leather socks!' I blurted out. Sameena looked at me strangely. 'The leather socks story,' I repeated, trying to prod her memory. Years before, I had been told, heated debate had arisen in a certain women's group over whether women needed to wear socks when praying. One woman insisted dogmatically that God did not listen to prayers unless the person praying had socks on. She claimed that this was the 'way of the Sunna' in the Prophet's time, when women reportedly wore leather socks, and argued that there was a Hadith supporting this. No one could persuade her otherwise; she brooked no dissent and would not discuss the matter any further. What frightened the others, who were mainly new to Islam, was not so much the sock theory but her intensity, her closed mind and apparent unwillingness to listen to anyone else's ideas. A few weeks later the group quietly disintegrated, as if its spirit had been broken.

Sameena did not recall the story. 'It was before my time,' she said, staring at the floor. We did not discuss it again.

12

Sheherazade and her suitors

By now Denise and I were growing more at ease with each other and had settled into a comfortable routine of separate but amiable coexistence. Her life followed simple routines — work, dog, religious studies and her lifeline, the telephone. Weekends were the time for visiting. Evenings were spent chatting on the telephone with her girlfriends in marathon sessions lasting up to an hour at a time. At night she read the Qur'an, performed her final prayer and retired early. Denise did her best to pray five times daily as required, and performed one *salat* at her workplace; neither her prayers nor her dress disturbed anyone where she worked.

Her friends were all young, married women who'd converted originally to please their husbands; their men were taxi drivers, which explained why they could spend so much time on the phone at night. Many of them seemed unhappy, with endless domestic crises to be resolved and imagined slights to be smoothed over. They had a penchant, too, for 'religious' discussions of (in my impatient eyes at least) a trivial nature, usually on minute matters of ritual, or the ongoing pursuit to identify and root out what was *haram*. Their concerns were of the kind that can preoccupy women forced to, or choosing to, stay at home — women with too much time on their hands, few resources and limited personal freedom. Few among the circle seemed able to leave their homes without their husband's approval and were expressly forbidden to attend Qur'an study classes.

I did not try to hide my amazement. This was unlike anything I had ever encountered before. Was it because they were isolated Anglo-Australian women with no relatives to intercede and stop this oppressive nonsense? Was it their own vulnerability, or some strange acquiescence on their part in playing the role, as they understood it, of obedient Muslim wives? Denise not so long ago had been in a similar situation yet was unable to explain the pattern of events that led to this domestic tyranny.

The behaviour of Denise's friends seemed almost like a 'before' picture of Muslim women. Zainab and Sameena's stories, in contrast, showed the 'after' transformation of women increasingly knowledgeable and aware of their Islamic rights as well as duties. I realised that Denise, Zainab and Sameena moved in different circles, but it was more than that. I needed a more detached explanation.

On past trips to Sydney I had met Silma Ihram, an articulate, educated and determined woman who almost twenty years before had become a Muslim during a long stay in Indonesia. Two years had passed since our last meeting but she was still the same: slim, with brown eyes, quick, energetic movements and rapid speech well suited to a mind that moved quickly, with no need to search for the right word or ponder a question for too long. She is well known for speaking the plain truth as she perceives it and translates words into deeds at the blink of an eye. This is a 'woman warrior' who would have marched shoulder to shoulder with the Sahaba (Companions of the Prophet), I think to myself.

Silma knew all the cliques in Lakemba and didn't mince words. 'Women are miles ahead of the men in Lakemba,' she said, 'but in some circles wives are held back by their husbands, especially if the men feel they are getting too far ahead — even in their religious education. It happens with born Muslims and converts alike. How I hate those terms,' she added vehemently.

Unlike Denise and her friends, Silma exercised control over her life. She identified strongly with Islam, but this had not turned her into a 'good', obedient Muslim housewife, for above all Silma was a woman of action. 'Men, in a sense, can hide their Islam, especially if they work with non-Muslims,' she went on. 'They appear strong, but at work Ali becomes Al, Jalal becomes Jim, Daoud is David and so on. Women are on the front-line — they look different with their *hijab* and modest clothes. So they make easy targets. "Where's your camel, luv?" or "Take that tea towel off your head!" are par for the course for Muslim women. And that's mild in comparison to the jostling, spitting and ugly abuse that we got when the Gulf War started in 1991.

'Because of their visibility, though, women found that non-Muslims also began asking them questions about Islam, questions which, much to their embarrassment, they couldn't answer. That's what triggered this wave of women's learning in Lakemba and elsewhere. Women had been made aware of their religious ignorance and wanted to do something about it. If we were to perform our *dawa,* our duty to teach others about Islam, we had to know the answers to some very sticky questions.' She drew a deep breath. 'Now some of the men, particularly those whose own Islam may be weak or who are less knowledgeable, feel threatened, and some of them try to sabotage these efforts. This is not difficult, as the women are often preoccupied with their traditional roles: they have children to bring up and are expected to breastfeed their babies for two years. Some men actually have more kids to keep their wives "out of trouble".'

'Does she cover?' During the first week of my stay, at least half a dozen of Denise's girlfriends asked if I was, in their terms, 'a practising Muslim'. Suspicion of outsiders is very much part of the Lakemba 'village' culture. If I did not cover or pray, I might contaminate Denise. Her answers obviously disappointed them and one day halfway through my visit, I received a phone call from her friend J, who reminded me ('it is my duty, sister') that I would burn in hell for my transgressions. I politely tried to steer off the subject but she continued remorselessly — she had the verve of the newly converted and the confident energy of her nineteen years behind her. After discovering that I was no 'religious virtuoso' we hung up on each other and parted company forever — I had made an enemy.

Denise later told me that J was quoting me as saying I did not believe in the Qur'an, and that she had branded me a *kafir* or unbeliever. This was a searing example of the Lakemba preoccupation with externals. Far more important, some believed, to judge a Muslim woman by whether she wore the *hijab* or not and whether she prayed five times a day, than by what was happening inside her head or by her actions. Critics of the 'Lakemba way' often mention this concern with the forms of observance rather than morality and ethics, calling it the 'ritual purity game'. Once again it is not simply a question of believing in God that concerns purists, but 'how' you worship God.

Was I already sinking into the Lakemba swamp of gossip and character assassination? I came to the conclusion that there was nothing to be gained by defending myself against J's attack, although I took pains to explain to Denise what had really happened.

In Muslim circles, a common way of assaulting someone's credibility is to call them a *kafir*. It is a slur used by converts and born Muslims alike, and in Lakemba I grew to hear it on almost a daily basis. There is a Hadith warning people to use this term with extreme caution or else, so it is written, it will rebound on the accuser should it be untrue. That didn't seem to worry these people. A local who asked not to be named told me, 'It is a major crime to call someone a kafir. It is more likely to be used to put down someone who is not a Muslim, or used in an insulting way to a fellow Muslim someone disagrees with either politically or religiously.' Sunnis sometimes insult other Sunnis by calling them Shi'as — members of the other major stream of Islam, which is in disagreement with the Sunni majority on certain practices and interpretations. A third insult is the Arabic word *almaynee* or *ilmani* which means western or scientifically educated. Three deadly insults lined up like sharp rocks to attack the credibility of people, or groups who dissent. What a relief it was to learn that really devout Muslims in Lakemba refused to use these terms!

One evening I asked Denise how she had found Islam, and this opened the floodgates of stories about her ex-husband. Apparently he was not very religious, as she put it, when they first met.

'I kept nagging him, "Why don't you go to the mosque? Why don't you pray like you're supposed to?" So he started and then he became friendly with this older man and that was the beginning of it all. The older bloke was Lebanese like my husband, but he was a Tablighi — do you know about them? The Jama'at Tablighi is a group who are really strict. They told my husband crazy things like, "Women only have half a brain" and he started behaving differently. He became very religious, was always in the mosque, and when his men friends came to the house he would make me sit in the toilet, even with my veil on!'

I reminded Denise that I was expressly in Lakemba to collect anecdotes and learn of people's experiences and that perhaps she should be more discreet in what she told me. Still, I made a mental note to look into the matter of the Tablighis and see what I could learn. I felt the need to undertake some local research, as Denise's explanations were sometimes hard to follow and this anecdote seemed quite bizarre. I listened fascinated as Denise, a working-class Sheherazade, continued her tale.

Her marriage was an Islamic one — of a kind — a so-called religious ceremony, but one not conducted by any registered marriage celebrant, or imam, or indeed anyone who abided strictly by Shari'ah law. Denise could recall neither witnesses nor any marriage contract. Under the Australian legal system the event would not have counted as a lawful marriage. Denise's experience illustrated the problems that may arise for some young women who 'marry' into Islam unprotected, naive and ignorant about the proper form of Islamic marriages.

A year or so after the ceremony, her husband decided to unilaterally divorce her and without letting her know, he made the arrangements. Everything he did was un-Islamic — even her marriage, from what she said, seemed to be a 'word of mouth' one, not the public event that Islam demands in order to prevent the very things that happened to Denise. Denise still appeared bewildered by it all and continued to show more resignation than the indignation one might have expected.

A few months before, I had spoken with Majeeda Bibi, an erudite Fijian woman, about Islamic marriages in Australia. From what Majeeda had told me, Denise's disaster fell into the category of 'shady marriages to Anglo converts'. Majeeda had been furious about these mockeries, as she called them. 'The man says it is enough that "I tell you" I have married you and "you tell me you have married me". At the time of the Prophet Muhammad (peace be upon Him), a marriage needed at least two witnesses on hand. It had to be public; this was one of the conditions to prevent a man from later denying parenthood. This was before an Islamic state had been formed. By the time we got such a state, with a legal system and judges, marriage had become formal and was recorded. The Islamic system of clerical recording was meticulous. These backyard "word of mouth" marriages are marriages under neither Australian law nor Islamic law.' Majeeda felt enormously sorry for Anglo-Australian women who underwent such marriages without knowing what they were getting into. Unfortunately, this described Denise's marriage to a T.

'I didn't know he was doing it wrong — not telling me,' Denise said. 'And then he said he had made a mistake and we weren't divorced after all — he didn't have the right number of witnesses or something — so he married me again — in the car park under the mosque. I sat in the car and one of his friends performed the wedding and then he divorced me properly.' All this had occurred before Ramadan, earlier in the year.

By now my head was spinning. Before talking to Majeeda, I would have been sceptical about Denise's claims. But now I had no reason to doubt her.

Even Denise's conversion had happened without her knowing. I discovered this when her friend Esme, the woman who had fled Arncliffe when the Al-Zahra Mosque was being built and who in one of life's little ironic jokes had later become a Muslim, was telling Denise and me about her wonderful Egyptian husband. She described her conversion at the mosque and her daughter's hysterical outburst when she had learnt of her 'defection'. 'The imam asked me if I was doing this freely, of my own will. I told him yes, that it was entirely my own decision, a genuine conversion. I said the *Shahada,* the declaration of faith — "There is no god but Allah and Muhammad is His Prophet" — and I was given a little certificate.'

Denise looked crestfallen. Nothing like this had happened to her. 'I was tricked. Some women told me to repeat something in Arabic — I didn't know what I was saying — and then they kissed me and told me I was a Muslim and that now my husband would be very happy with me. I only did it in my heart, for myself, last Ramadan.'

This seemed very much part of the 'willing victim' mantle which Denise wore with a certain aplomb. There were times when she seemed almost an accomplice to the personal disasters that had befallen her. But then again she was a woman alone, without relatives, 'a battler' who had worked all of her adult life and in spite of all the calamities that had taken place still possessed a sweetness and gullibility which, in most people, would have turned to bitterness and distrust long ago. She seemed unable to avoid all the dreadful things that had happened to her under the guise of Islam. Anything that people told her was 'Islamic' seemed to possess an irreversible magic for her.

Denise was counting the days to the end of her *iddha* waiting period; soon she would be able officially to receive suitors. The girlfriends were beginning to jockey for position, pushing their own choices, usually friends of their husbands. Matchmaking is a local industry in Lakemba and Islam accords no special merit to celibacy. The idea of staying single even for a short while had clearly not entered Denise's head. When I raised the possibility with her she nodded politely, but stared past me, dreaming some private dream of conjugal bliss.

She was quite explicit in her requirements: she wanted a practising Muslim husband who didn't want to stay in Australia and would take her with him back to Pakistan or Egypt or Morocco, where she could become part of his extended family. In readiness for her next marriage, she had compiled long lists of Islamic names and their meanings, and had narrowed the choice down to four or five. She would enter her new life with a new name.

Denise and I shared a secret. In the first week of my stay, she had started receiving suitors, one at a time, men she seemed to have met through her friends. Officially they were not courting her — after all her divorce would not be official for another three or four weeks. They arrived singly at the front door, to be greeted by Denise in full *nikab* with only her eyes enigmatically peering out. She would take their gifts of red roses or nuts into the kitchen and then proceed with her guest into her bedroom, where her 'Arabic reading lessons' took place. These men were not here to woo Denise or for any such frivolous reason; they were here to help her with her Arabic pronunciation!

No one told me, but I gathered that I must be the chaperone. The first visitor was Afzal, an Indian student doing a business course. He wasn't religiously inclined, which in Denise's eyes went against him. The second was Hassan, a tall and handsome Moroccan whose gift of pistachio nuts seemed more welcome than Afzal's red roses. By now I was embarrassed both for myself and for these young men. The only one at ease seemed to be Denise, who seemed blissfully unaware that what she was doing was full of contradictions. *Nikab* or no *nikab*, to be entertained by a 'not quite' divorced woman in her bedroom, no matter what the reason, no doubt caused a lot of confusion in these men's minds; or did they accept this kind of behaviour more readily from young Anglo converts? I felt obliged to point out the incongruity of a fully veiled young woman reading the Qur'an in her bedroom — yes, I realised the door was open — with an unrelated male who probably wanted to marry her!

'Gee! I never thought about it like that,' was Denise's guileless reply. 'I don't like using the lounge room because there's not much furniture.' She covered her face with her hand in embarrassment. 'I'll tell them to stay away; I thought it was all right if you were there. I've never let anyone come before. Stupid me! It's my old English ways again!'

Once again I had fallen into the trap of becoming more participant than observer. I was finding it impossible to keep the roles separate and remain coolly detached.

With this little discussion behind us, Denise brought me up to date on mating rituals. That very day she had met Yusuf, a tall, handsome, doe-eyed young Egyptian who owned a shop in Haldon Street. He had passed on the phone number of an older female cousin in case Denise was interested in finding out more about him — or marrying him. Yusuf's parents were back home in Cairo, which was why his cousin would have to act as proxy.

Love strikes quickly in Haldon Street, I thought to myself.

I wished that Denise could benefit from the informal matchmaking services of someone like Jamila Ahmad. Jamila changed her faith from Baptist to Muslim, but only after reading deeply and widely and having become convinced it was the right faith for her. The night that I spent at her family home was unusually quiet: the five children were off with their father at their weekly karate class. Jamila's speech was laconic and her observations on human foibles humorous without being too harsh. She had a passion for Arabian horses, which she bred on their semi-rural property ninety minutes from Sydney. Jamila had a fine collection of books on Arabian horses and told me all about the lyrical tributes used by Arab poets to describe them — epithets like 'daughters of the wind', which go back to before the time of the Prophet. 'The Prophet (peace be upon Him) was a great lover of horses,' Jamila told me. 'We learn about this from conversations recorded as Hadith. The horse, or *faras*, is said to be created from a handful of wind, made for pursuit and for flight — an animal that flies without wings.'

We turned to the subject of women converts. Jamila was

quite concerned about women in their late twenties and thirties who converted of their own accord without marrying into Islam. She described them as spiritually aware, independent, intelligent — and without partners. Their unusual status gave rise to a dilemma not experienced by most born Muslims. 'How can you meet a prospective partner? With Islam's rules on social segregation there is really no place where they can meet someone of the opposite sex. There is no family structure to help them or to check into the man's background. Many are isolated, with loose family ties or none at all, because of their conversion to Islam. Some families are unable to cope with the defection, or betrayal, as they see it.'

'What kind of Muslim husband do they want?'

'Well, certainly not lukewarm Muslims,' Jamila snorted derisively. 'Intelligent, financially independent, well-educated women are discriminating. What they are looking for are practising Muslim men with similar intelligence and interests.'

This seemed like a tall order to me. Finding out whether couples are compatible is made difficult by segregation rules, so in the past, Jamila and her husband had held gatherings to allow people to meet one another in a chaperoned environment, more than once if need be.

Singles bars, computer dating services, aerobics classes and discos were not going to attract your average practising Muslim, I thought. They don't drink, date or dance. It struck me that some 'discerning' women may never marry after all. If they had to forgo having children, they were paying a high price for their beliefs. New initiatives like marriage ads in the *Australasian Muslim Times* might help, but I remained a little sceptical:

> Educated Australian lady Muslim, 45, English-speaking only, studying Qur'an, seeks true-believing gentleman,

non-gambler, non-smoker, non-drinker only. Photo appreciated.

Devout but liberal Muslim man, 39, olive skin, brown eyes, non-chauvinist, honest, passionate, highly educated scientist. Seeking slim, intelligent lady, 25, to share and enjoy good things in life.

By now Denise had met about fifteen men, mainly through her friends. 'It's almost a full-time occupation,' she joked, 'now that I've come on the market.' Denise gave the impression that a horde of men was lining up waiting for the official start of the 'Denise Handicap' once her divorce was Islamically final. She was having a glorious time and surely only a begrudging spirit would reproach her after the difficulties she had endured.

'Why not take your time? Say you're just not ready.' The cultural norm I was familiar with was the Pakistani tradition of protracted negotiations between sets of parents.

Within a week Denise had made up her mind. The winner was Yusuf, the Egyptian, and although this had been intended as a pragmatic decision she was head over heels in love with him — even though he was not as 'practising' as she would like. She was already full of reasons why this was no longer important. If she had a good, practising Muslim husband, he might force her 'to do my religion for him as a sign of my obedience and not for Allah. But with Yusuf, I'll do Islam for me because I want to.' And he didn't want to stay in Australia; Yusuf was happy to go back to Egypt. Denise yearned for a family and rejected the notion of rearing children in Australia. Again I wondered about Denise's own family background.

First the bad news had to be broken to Afzal and Hassan — not an easy task as both had had high hopes. For another week they hung on tenaciously, phone call after phone call, until finally it became my job to answer the telephone and tell them Denise was not at home.

A trickier problem was how to break the news to the girlfriends. After all, she had found Yusuf herself, just by going into his shop one day, dressed in her *nikab*. They had started talking and things had progressed from there. *Let the unbelievers note! You can still flirt with a woman whose face you cannot see!* Three incidental meetings in his shop with the counter separating them and one formal visit to his cousins, and the decision had been made. Denise was right, the girls were bound to be disgruntled now that their selections had been bypassed. Sure enough, when she informed them of her marriage plans, all hell broke loose.

The girlfriends were furious. 'You'll regret this! What do you know about him? You shouldn't have been meeting him anyway', 'My husband says he's only after permanent residency', 'You've been deceiving us! We had good men only waiting until your *iddha* was over before they were introduced to you', 'My husband is very angry and I'm not allowed to visit you again'.

Poor Denise and poor Yusuf. In the next few days Yusuf's business boomed. A lot of 'new' customers came in, ostensibly to buy something, but really to inspect him, and he gamely ran the gauntlet of questions about his antecedents and other matters. This led to another avalanche of telephone calls. 'Did you know he's already married?', 'He's not a good Muslim, Denise, he doesn't pray and he only goes to the mosque on Eid', 'We warn you, you're making a mistake, 'You must marry for the sake of Islam ... He must be a praying Muslim!'

'Is it true that he's already married?' I asked her, trying not to show my amazement.

'Yes, he didn't try to hide it from me,' she retaliated, sensing another argument. 'He married for permanent residency. They were never properly — Islamically — married; it was a registry marriage only. She's Australian and she took off with the money he paid her, and now he can't find her to divorce her legally.'

For Denise and some others, the only marriage that counted was an Islamic one. In their eyes Yusuf had not really been married before. For many Muslim men, the prohibitions against premarital or extramarital sex are so strong and ingrained that what Yusuf appeared ready to do seemed the lesser of two evils. Living together without benefit of a Muslim ceremony, even one that seemed in some minds slightly dubious, was unthinkable.

'So you'll have an Islamic ceremony only; you won't be able to use a Muslim marriage celebrant to make it legal under the Australian Family Law Act, and register it, because that would make Yusuf a bigamist. Legally you will be in a de facto relationship.' It sounded awfully messy to me.

'I suppose so, but he'll marry me again when we go to Egypt. Under Shari'ah he can have more than one wife.' Only if he can take care of them equally, and if his first wife consents, I thought. Liberal Muslims, on the other hand, argue against polygamy.

By now I had met Yusuf. Denise's description of him was apt, as far as I could tell. He was tall and good looking, with soft, pleading eyes, in his late twenties or early thirties, with curly, dark-brown hair. His voice was low and husky and he wanted very much to marry Denise, he told me.

My role of mute observer had completely collapsed by now, so I pleaded with Denise to organise a watertight marriage contract — a kind of pre-nuptial agreement, which, unlike in the United States, is not yet legal in Australia. Muslims sometimes overcome this by lodging the contract with a lawyer as a kind of promissory note or financial agreement to the bride.

Once her *iddha* was over, Denise's engagement became

official, and she grew more and more preoccupied with figuring out the amount for her *mehr*, or dowry, which the groom must provide under Islamic law. This is always included in the marriage contract and would belong to the bride for her own use. Denise shunned jewellery. 'I'd rather have a set of religious books.' When she was asked on the Day of Judgement what present she had received, she would be able to say, 'I got a book to help me learn more about You and be closer to You and to love and fear You more.' Receiving jewellery would make her feel vain and 'Push me away from Allah. Allah doesn't like proud people.' While her piety was admirable, Yusuf's family insisted that she have jewellery, clothes and the customary sum of money.

I began to notice a change in her dress. The *nikab* had gone and she had taken to wearing a scarf with a long skirt and loose top. She no longer covered her face. She implied that she had worn the veil because in the past her husband had accused her of staring at men and if men smiled at her, well, she smiled back. 'It's an Australian habit,' she told me, shrugging her shoulders. 'Now, though, I don't feel protected like before,' she complained.

One morning we walked up Wangee Road on our way to the railway station. Along the way we passed men, obviously Muslims, and Denise went to great pains to render herself invisible by casting her eyes down and fairly ostentatiously walking around them. Ironically, but not surprisingly, far from making herself invisible by this extra-demure behaviour, this obvious shying away, she drew inordinate attention to herself. Was it all some elaborate game, part of a complicated courtship ritual she had made up, I wondered. I remembered the day her former brother-in-law had come to the door and she had answered it fully veiled. 'Why are you dressed like that?' he had asked, evidently astounded by the change.

One day not long after the engagement, Esme came to visit and the three of us had a long discussion about the attraction Muslim men hold for some Anglo-Australian women. 'My first husband was Australian and he dominated me completely,' Esme said. 'I was terribly unhappy and got to the point where I had to walk away to save myself. And then I went on a cruise and this little man turned up with his bubbly personality, so thoughtful and so generous. When we were back in Sydney we continued to meet and we started living together. But I could tell that he was troubled by our de facto relationship, so we got married at the mosque, both under Australian law and Islamically, because a Muslim marriage celebrant performed the ceremony. All he wants to do is make me happy. He's so different from Aussie men — he means what he says, we are real partners; he never tries to dominate me. My parents nearly died. They kept on saying, "Now he's going to ruin your life, he'll oppress you, you'll be a slave" — which is what the average Australian seems to think happens to Muslim wives. Now they just adore him.'

Esme had been inspired to become a Muslim by the model her husband set. 'There had to be something to this religion if it could produce such a good man. So I read books and asked a lot of questions and finally felt that I wanted to become a Muslim — there was never the slightest pressure on me.'

I asked her if it had been tough being a convert in the early stages.

'When you're at the mosque and all this stuff comes out of the loudspeakers in Arabic and you can't understand a word of it ... it's very confusing.' She had also found fasting very difficult. 'I tried, but I gave up after a week and only fasted on weekends then. It was just too hard. My husband said that you have to get accustomed to it.' The only real adjustments she had to make were getting used to 'Egyptian kitsch', as she called it, 'All that red velvet and chandeliers.' Her own tastes were much simpler, but she and her husband had reached a compromise: 'He toned down the red and gold and I brightened up my dull Aussie tastes.'

I asked Denise why she had never found a good Australian boy. 'I've always been fascinated by Muslim men and I don't like the Australian way of having a good time, with all the drinking and swearing that goes on. Aussies have no spiritual life — their attitudes and values are so different from Muslim men's.'

'Muslim men are not embarrassed about being religious,' agreed Esme. 'They are not ashamed to show their religion.' This had impressed her. 'In Anglican churches, most of the time you only see little old ladies. When you see Muslim men walking into the mosque, they look proud and strong; they live their religion, it's not superficial as it is with Christians. It features in their conversations and gives a strong focus to everything they do.'

Denise put it another way. 'A Muslim man sends out the message, "I'm a Muslim man. I'm really macho". But church men ... they seem really wussy and wimpish.' Although her marriage had been so unhappy, she had not turned away from Islam because of one bad experience. Islam had what she was looking for. 'It's there, I know it is,' she insisted urgently. 'I just have to find it. I have to work harder to find it and then everything will be all right.'

On her dressing-table was a photograph of Denise as a little girl, standing in front of a farmhouse with a cheeky grin on her face. Although she tried hard nowadays to capture the outward look of a dignified, serious-faced Muslim woman, there were still times when the mischievous little girl, who wanted to be loved by everyone, peeped out.

13

Eid ul-Adha

Even from a distance, the spirit of celebration overcame everyone. They flocked to the mosque on this day of days as if drawn by a magnet. As they drew nearer, their excitement escalated in response to the imam's rhythmic chanting — '*Allahu Akbar*, God is Most Great.' Today was Eid ul-Adha, the Festival of Sacrifice which commemorates a day of great historical and religious significance when the Prophet Ibrahim was called to sacrifice his son to God in a supreme act of faith and obedience.

People had been gathering since dawn. Local police turned up an hour later to block off the road. By 7 am Wangee Road was jammed with an excited, happy throng. People spilled into front gardens and onto balconies or perched on walls. All wanted to be together for Eid ul-Adha. The next day, newspapers reported that more than seven thousand people had attended the Lakemba mosque. Elsewhere in Sydney and around Australia crowds were gathering for the same celebration, but Lakemba claimed the largest gathering of believers in the country.

I was spellbound. From my vantage point opposite the mosque, I could see over people's heads. The scene was far different from anything I had imagined. Inside the mosque, the religious and political aspects of Lakemba life were unfolding. Dignitaries, community leaders and politicians were paying their respects (and being seen paying them), and there were dignified prayers and speeches. But outside it was a festival — an unofficial youth festival with wave after wave of laughing, chattering young people. The allure and sheer magnetism of the occasion were irresistible.

Eid ul-Adha is the second most important religious festival of the Muslim year, although there are some who rank it ahead of Eid ul-Fitr at the end of Ramadan. It is the kind of occasion when even the less devout and the less practising came with their families to pray and join in the communal celebrations. Nearly everyone in the Lakemba crowd had relatives or friends overseas who might at that very moment be circling the Ka'aba in Mecca as they completed their *haj*, for the festival coincides with the annual pilgrimage.

Flocks of young men stood around like peacocks or, from time to time, cruised a little, posed a little, and sent out their messages in non-verbal code. What resembled the old 1940s zoot suit — wide padded shoulders, long jackets and trousers — came in the most amazing hues: deep purples, brilliant emerald greens, mustard yellows and oleander pinks. Lebanese boys, with their modish hair styles and shiny shoes, displayed a style of formal dressing that I had not seen en masse for many a year — 'cool' was everywhere.

How could young women hope to compete? By contrast, the girls wore subdued clothes — their mothers had been vigilant, for today anything too brightly coloured or tight would set tongues wagging. Peeking from a pocket, the edge of a scarf could now and then be glimpsed: its owner had quickly removed it after Dad had gone inside to pray. But Dad 'wasn't born yesterday' and no doubt remembered his own youth, for beside the groups of chattering girls, shifting impatiently from one foot to the other, could be seen more than one younger sister or brother, acting as unofficial chaperone.

Groups were loosely segregated, but now and then a

daring young rebel would break away from his mates to exchange a word or two with a young lady he knew who might fortuitously be standing with his sister or cousin (sometimes female relatives have their uses) before rejoining his friends to bask in their admiration and run a gauntlet of questions.

'Hi Nada.' 'Hi, Laila.' The girls giggled and admired one another's clothes, accessories and make-up (Mum had again been at work and only light touches of cosmetics could be seen). They looked glorious with permed curls hanging down their backs. Momentarily, Wangee Road had been converted into one enormous village square. On a day like today, a young boy and girl might see one another for the very first time and become romantically attracted; two or three years later an 'approved–arranged' marriage might result.

At 7.30 am, long carpets were brought outside for those men who could not squeeze into the mosque or adjacent areas. Everyone else moved back onto the pavements. Little boys and some of the young men, zoot suits and all, joined their fathers or uncles to pray, all facing Mecca, but many stood by, simply observing. Women's prayers took place inside a large marquee that had been erected at the rear of the mosque, as their space in the mosque had been taken over by the men for the day.

'Hey! Did you see him? He's in the fourth row,' someone whispered to her friend.

'Mariam, he's looking this way!' hissed another.

After the prayers were over, it was impossible to move as crowds spilled down the steps and into the street.

'I can see my dad, I've got to go.' 'My uncle's calling me, we have to leave.' Kissing each other three times on the cheek, the young women wished one another '*Eid Mubarak*'. Now it was time for group photos, to be sent back to Lebanon or Egypt or India or South Africa where

Muslim relatives would be celebrating the same festival. For the rest of the day people would come and go, visit the mosque, stay to pray, sit inside or stand outside talking and listening to one another. And gradually the audience of non-Muslim spectators who lived in Wangee Road would take their deckchairs inside from their balconies, tidy away drink cans, cups and saucers, and empty the peanut bowls. The spectacle was over until next year.

Never had I participated in an Eid gathering as big as the Lakemba celebration. I was stunned by the size of the crowd, the sounds, the buzz in the air. The scene tapped many buried memories. I had an awkward rush of nostalgia as thoughts of my youth rose up. I savoured the ritual of prayer and the emotional charge that always lingered from its strange blend of vulnerability, submission and solidarity. The sight of Muslims praying en masse never fails to thrill me. The simplicity and beauty of the natural choreography of communal praying are poignant beyond words. But friends have told me that some Australians admit to feelings of intimidation or unease at the sights which I find so moving. What is familiar and comfortable to one group may seem alien and threatening to another. On my one and only foray into a Catholic church, I'd had feelings of unease verging on distaste as the statues and pictures offended my iconoclastic sensibilities.

How can we feel so threatened by seeing others talking to their God? After all, Christians, Jews and Muslims all believe in the one God. Allah is simply the Arabic word for God — the One God, the Only God.

Many years ago, an acquaintance once told me that the first time she saw a Muslim friend pray she experienced a revulsion so strong that at the time she felt physically sick. Yet the same disgust had not overcome her when she had seen Buddhists or Hindus making their *puja* (prayers).

'Friendly religions' I remembered her calling them. But just as the vague feelings of unease I fleetingly experienced the first time I found myself in a Christian church have disappeared, so have her feelings altered.

Whether your family has been here for five generations or whether you have just got off the plane from Lebanon, as a Muslim you repeatedly experience deep regret every time you are reminded that many non-Muslims in Australia feel hostility towards Islam and, indirectly, towards you. Such people have generally never met Muslims on an individual or social basis. The chasm gapes at their feet as their minds and hearts stumble, refusing to take that step forward. The militant images of Islam that we see on television widen the crevasse even further. Muslims who want nothing to do with non-Muslims are also not entirely blameless, even though their position often stems from a lack of confidence and bad experiences.

'Muslims are arrogant. They set themselves apart by the way they dress.' Just ten minutes before, this good-humoured, polite couple in their mid thirties had asked if they could share my table at a coffee shop in the Roselands shopping centre, about ten minutes from Lakemba by bus. We were joking about inconsequential matters; they were very friendly and seemed interested in why I was visiting Sydney. Their expressions changed, their voices developed a blunt edge, and the air of bonhomie vanished when they heard I was writing about Australian Muslims.

Kathy, the more vitriolic of the pair, stabbed at her cake with the fork she was holding in a way that made me wince, and proceeded to tell me all about the arrogance of Muslim women.

'Just who do they think they are? Where do they think they're living?' Her lips curled unpleasantly.

A raw nerve had been inadvertently touched. Although I

felt uncomfortable, curiosity kept me there. They knew who I was and what I was — their aggression had taken me by surprise and it became a matter of standing up and being counted rather than remaining the impartial observer. I need not have worried. They scarcely paused for breath.

Steve muttered out of the side of his mouth about 'Young girls being forced to marry old men.'

These were the people I had never met in my over-protected multicultural circles — the people who answered opinion polls or telephoned tabloid television shows with a 'no' vote on Asian immigration. These were people I only read about, and it seemed important to try to understand this level of prejudice.

I suggested mildly that it didn't really do any harm if Muslim women chose a different, more modest code of dress; surely it hurt no one? But then it dawned on me that the difference not only in dress but in values affronted them both in a way I had difficulty understanding. Kathy and Steve saw it all as a deadly insult: a refusal to assimilate and a challenge to their own set of values.

My mild-mannered explanations carried no weight with them. Eyes that had been friendly now stared at me icily. They showed no sign of hearing anything I said — nothing penetrated. They wanted nothing more to do with me. The rejection became mutual: I wanted nothing more to do with them either.

Entries from my journal illustrate the obstacles and contradictions I came across when I tried to find out about the Tablighi, the group of men who had so influenced Denise's ex-husband.

> Pondering over the entrails of a pigeon would be easier ... People I talk to seem evenly divided over the Jama'at Tabligh. When I mention the name they roll

> their eyes, look over their shoulders, and lower their voices; or else they begin a lecture on the merits of Tabligh and how criticism of the group is superficial and un-Islamic ... Who do I believe? Responses from both sides always seem so strong! No wishy-washy, mealy-mouthed, middle-of-the-road ambiguities to sort out. The Tablighi movement is quite a visible presence here in Lakemba ... Everyone I ask is happy to talk as long as it's all right to remain anonymous ... Everyone congratulates me on discovering an important undercurrent in local affairs — but no one wants to share in the glory! Why this reticence?

Rumour, strife and rivalry — the three harbingers of local insurrections and palace intrigues. A chance remark grows into a tale of envy and ambition; a fleeting observation woven into plot and counterplot; a joke becomes a malediction. Fortunately there are friends, long-suffering friends who act as soothsayers: men and women who help to explain the signs and 'omens' of village life.

Bearded men dressed in white turbans and white garments had attracted my attention as I walked past the mosque each day on my way to Haldon Street. Who were these dignified-looking men, draped in white shawls, who strode purposefully down Wangee Road and up the steps of the mosque? Was this a uniform or a style of national dress?

From Denise's early tales of the Tablighis I had imagined a group of religiously conservative men, perhaps with misogynistic tendencies, who brought straying Muslims back to the fold. Even those awkward moments with my mentor Sameena started to make sense now, and I remembered the times when I had fallen silent, sensing something I couldn't quite identify. However, one thing stood out clearly — everyone had something or other to say about the Tablighis. Critics asked to remain anonymous not out of fear, but more from the habit of presenting a united Muslim front to the outside world. Muslim women generally were much sharper in their criticism of the Tablighis than their menfolk.

Those who thought kindly of the Tablighis tended to be Indian or Pakistani Muslims who were comfortable with the Tablighi tradition, believing it to have special religious merit. Muslims who had converted to Islam after years of study and self-examination, on the other hand, tended to disapprove of the group, although converts whose religious knowledge was still developing gravitated towards it, drawing strength and solace from the feeling of solidarity and 'family' they discovered. In their early Muslim days, many male converts in particular look around them for religious role models.

'Converts must do everything right. The born Muslim can make mistakes,' Denise had instructed me the first time we met.

The Tablighis belong to the tradition of great Muslim travellers, but neither the way of the merchant nor the path of the soldier calls out to them, for they shun the world of materialism and the world of politics. They are 'pilgrims' in a religious caravan and, as the old Pashto proverb says, 'The world is a traveller's *serai*.' Tablighis are prodigious travellers searching for their roots in the past; their eyes turn back to the days of the Prophet and his Companions in that glorious golden age of pure Islam. They hold to a vision of this utopian past and as they wander they urge others to grasp the rope of Allah. Bands of Tablighis visit Australia and journey around, living simply, praying and discussing the Qur'an and Hadith.

The Tablighis are not a sect but rather a movement founded in India in the nineteenth century during British rule. Their founder, Maulana Muhammad Ilyas, discovered that many Muslims were assimilating Hindu religious habits and no longer understood the rituals and basic tenets of Islam. Although it was founded to help lapsed Muslims return to the path, the movement also targets practising Muslims, who often become annoyed at what they see as the Tablighis' overzealousness. Others who have indeed strayed resent being preached at and are often heard to mutter darkly about Tablighi double standards. Many Muslim women I spoke to thought the Tablighis came down too hard on their own womenfolk, who were left alone to soldier on while the men went off on their tours. Many Muslims wish the religious caravan well but do not want it stopping at their doorstep. Others use it as a refresher course in piety and drop in and out from time to time. The Lakemba Tablighis remain a community within a community, holders of an uneasy status who are best understood by Muslims from the Indian subcontinent.

One day, if you are a Muslim — especially one who hasn't been to the mosque for a while — you might hear a knock on your front door. When you open the door, there they are. '*Salaam alaikum*, brother. We haven't seen you at the mosque lately. Is everything all right? Can we enter and recite the Kalima [the Word] together?'

Many men find the Tablighi movement very attractive while others do not. Ismail, an independent-thinking Muslim, told me, 'There is a basic, fairly simplistic package for followers to understand. You don't find many *ulemma* [Muslim scholars] involved, although some may encourage others to participate because the Tablighis emphasise personal piety so much.' Ismail likes to enquire, to discuss and to see rationality in Islam. The group to him was 'well-meaning but naive'.

Daoud was more critical. 'You can go back in your mind and your actions to the golden age of Islam when life was simple. You dress as you believe the Prophet dressed; you eat on the floor as you believe the Prophet and his Companions did; you spend a lot of time in the mosque, praying a lot, and discuss religious ritual extensively ... and then you go around and tell everyone else they are doing the wrong thing! It's not something for the brain.'

Joining the Tablighis was a strong statement for a man to make, said Nasim admiringly. 'The good side remains that the Tablighis try very hard to live what they believe, and if you avoid the indoctrination, you are given a refresher course in piety — a boost to your waning faith.'

The wives of the Tablighis in Australia have carved out a niche for themselves, although I believe this is unusual. In the main, the group has been male dominated. But Zainab said, 'If you hear often enough that your husband and his friends are modelling themselves on the Prophet (peace be upon Him) even down to his way of dress and beard style, well sooner or later you will begin to model yourself on the wives of the Prophet and you will find yourself wearing the *nikab*.'

Others gave glowing testimonials to the support the Tablighis lent to unhappy and unemployed men, and the sincerity and friendliness they showed to fellow Muslims. They were obviously answering some need, but their lack of interest in social reform disappointed the critics. They involved themselves in reform at the family, but not the social, level.

'Are you a Tablighi?' I asked Sameena.

'Yes,' she answered, and fell silent.

I was puzzled. Never once had Sameena applied any pressure or suggested that I needed to 'lift my game' religiously speaking. She had never been anything but helpful, and without her guidance and sponsorship, finding my way around the labyrinths of Lakemba would have been difficult. We had laughed and joked together and exchanged stories. She was no dour fanatic or moderate fundamentalist, as others had described the Tablighis.

'There are all sorts of rumours and talk that we brainwash people,' she said. 'When I hear this I have to bite my tongue, I really do. It's such nonsense. Some people don't want us to go to the mosque here because they think that if we see bad habits and things we disagree with we will speak out against them.'

'Don't you come down hard on Muslims you see as straying?' I pressed her.

'Some Tablighis are a little too enthusiastic,' she conceded with some reluctance. 'They forget the Hadith which says, "Whoever publicises the wrongdoing of a Muslim, Allah will disclose his wrongdoings to the people — so much so that he will be disgraced sitting in his own house". To follow the Prophet (peace be upon Him) in all matters, to learn about his habits and his utterances, is to stay on the safe path. But what about my duty to others? As long as a Muslim affirms the *Kalima,* no matter what else he has forgotten or has become lazy about, there is a good chance he can be brought over. You must seize the rope of Allah with both hands, and haul him across.'

14

Women in white

I had been forced to change my plane reservation twice already, but nothing could keep me away from Denise and Yusuf's wedding. Their marriage date had changed three times in the last twenty-four hours. Theatrics, confusion — we had run the gamut of pre-nuptial panic.

Denise's *nikab* days were now long gone. Perhaps the most startling sign of the change was her decision to wear a traditional western bridal gown with a tulle headpiece revealing her hair and ears. This was to be the romantic wedding Denise had always dreamed of and she would be a vision in white. This style of dress is not unusual at Egyptian weddings, although the bride's headpiece usually complies with *hijab* requirements and takes the form of a turban or cap. Denise was firm, she wanted an English-style headdress and would not budge. However, as she would be married in a mosque, she would somehow have to cover her head more modestly before she entered.

When Denise's gown arrived I was stunned. She had chosen a tight-fitting bodice with see-through netting and a plunging back. Was this the same woman who only five weeks ago had welcomed me covered from head to toe in *nikab*? Someone who expected to be married in a mosque! Was the woman crazy? Denise's friend Neelie and I looked at one another aghast. Denise agreed to compromise with satin inserts back and front, and we breathed a sigh of relief — the first crisis was over.

For some time Neelie and I had been urging Denise to think about her marriage contract and her *mehr*. Neelie seemed about the only mature, sensible friend Denise had to call on. She was a comfortable-looking woman with a humorous, sometimes sharp edge to her tongue. Denise's other friends had withdrawn in clouds of recrimination and dark prophecies. No one telephoned anymore, for Denise was now out in the cold. But Neelie was a rock. 'Don't forget, you are in a powerful position at the moment,' Neelie reminded Denise. 'This opportunity only comes once in a marriage.' A rather sombre, chilling thought it seemed to me.

Denise agreed to work on a draft with Neelie; I was to tighten up any loose clauses. Her marriage contract would stipulate the amount of her *mehr* and how it would be paid. Grounds for divorce were included: if the marriage turned out to be for permanent residency, if Yusuf physically or (I suggested adding) psychologically abused her, if he committed adultery or if he took another wife without 'consulting' her. I strongly urged her to change the word 'consulting' to getting her consent, although Neelie disagreed. She believed that a husband need only inform his wife. The *mehr* was to be paid in two instalments — altogether a sum of $3000. Denise's earlier puritanical tendencies had been set aside, I noted quietly.

Denise had chosen her Muslim name: two days from now she would be known as Ehsan, which means the giving of goodness without thought of reward. This would mark a new beginning for her — a brand-new life. She now disclosed something I had already begun to suspect and which went a long way to explaining the contradictions, the discrepancies and the denials that had pervaded her accounts of her personal history. Denise had once been a prostitute at Kings Cross. These 'naughty days', as she called them, had been before her marriage just over two years ago: 'I met him while I was still on the game.' For anyone wanting to start a new life away from the Cross, with its subcultures of drugs, violence and prostitution, Islam must hold enormous appeal, I realised. Now I could understand Denise's self-imposed *purdah* and her urge to wear *nikab* as elements of a ritual purification — one which must bring enormous psychological relief. Symbolically, Denise's *nikab* represented an important rite of passage, a kind of rebirth.

Now, too, Denise's innocent game-playing, her friendliness towards men ('men are always talking to me — I don't know why') became understandable.

Having once unburdened herself, Denise seemed to relish telling me about the old days. 'Life was tough and life was rough in the Cross.' She pointed to two side front teeth, obviously false. 'I don't pull hair and scratch,' she boasted, 'I punch!'

'I used to strip too, but I was never on drugs. I had this room upstairs and I decorated it with black and red devils and black and red satin sheets.' (At last the mystery of the satin bed sheets was solved!) I found it incredible that she had spent eight years on the game (that would make her about sixteen when she started) without getting into drugs. Yet I could not think why she would lie about this point. Neelie, too, believed that Denise had not been a drug user.

When one of the girlfriends had learnt of her former life, Denise had reluctantly gone to a shaykh for religious advice. She refused to say what had transpired, 'But I didn't feel guilty,' she insisted. Before her engagement she had decided to confess to Yusuf; others might come running to him with stories. 'He said it was all finished with long before I met him, and that my life started afresh when I became a Muslim.'

Their whirlwind romance had taken just four weeks. When I remarked on the speed of events, Neelie said that

Islam didn't encourage long engagements because that would be tantamount to encouraging young people to engage in premarital sex. I held my tongue. Perhaps after all this way was better for Denise.

On the day of the wedding, Yusuf's cousins — young Egyptian-Australian demoiselles — dragged Denise off to the hairdressers. She returned with a 1960s bouffant style and the requisite silver glitter scattered everywhere. Then began the battle over make-up. 'Okay, but only a little, just a very little,' whimpered Denise. Within an hour the cousins had transformed her into a doll, with lashings of blue eye shadow, dark eyeliner, rouge, lipstick — the works.

Neelie and I came to the rescue and suggested the make-up needed a little toning down. One of the cousins went into a huff, but her sisters took our side and we removed the excess.

Ehsan/Denise was now ready to step into her wedding gown, with its long train. She looked beautiful — like a bride doll on a wedding cake. 'I don't recognise myself,' she said, her cheeks flushed. Neither, truthfully, did I.

Neelie abruptly turned to the cousins. 'You're not going inside the mosque like that, are you?' The girls were wearing smart, tight-fitting suits in chiffon, with skirts barely to their knees, and their heads uncovered. 'We've got scarves,' they answered, unfazed by this attack.

At the mosque there was a separate entrance and a separate ablution block for women, whose praying section was upstairs, apart from the men's area downstairs and sequestered from it by a tall, meshed grille. The men must not be distracted from their prayers by the sight of women. By standing on my toes I could just peep over the railing and through the thick mesh and glimpse what was happening downstairs. A woman laughed at me. 'What are you looking over for? You've already got a husband!'

I find this type of exclusion disturbing; the mosque seemed to belong to the men. But the women seemed oblivious of my misgivings and evidently did not share them. They were completely at home, chatting and catching up with all the news and gossip of the week. It would be wrong to project my feelings onto them and assume that they resent this sequestering, or that they might wish to pray below, behind the men — as is the way at some Bosnian and Albanian mosques.

Denise joined us. Her hair had been covered by a flurry of tulle, creating a turban both striking and exotic.

Down below, fifteen or twenty men — not members of the wedding party — were involved in a variety of activities while waiting for the regular Saturday night *qtbar*, or sermon, to begin — some were sitting cross-legged on the thickly carpeted floor, wearing white turbans and long tunics and engaged in religious discussions. These could very well be Tablighis. Some were standing talking to one another and passing the time. A few had their young sons with them, swinging on their fathers' arms or sitting about. The atmosphere was that of a large male club — for after all a mosque is a communal place and this was not a prayer time — very different from the ambience of *jumma*, or Friday prayer, where individual discipline and absolute concentration characterise Muslims praying en masse in perfect unison.

Yusuf and his small entourage entered. Someone moved to the front and the others knelt or sat cross-legged facing him. The ceremony was simple: a few verses from the Qur'an emphasising the obligations of a husband and the sanctity of marriage. Everyone ceased talking and even though most of the men downstairs were not wedding guests, they too listened intently. We women upstairs — all guests — peered through the grille to try and see what was transpiring below.

Neelie muttered to me quietly that Ehsan would come to regret not marrying in her *hijab*. 'I hope it doesn't come back to haunt her but it will, I'm sure.' A hint of *schadenfreude* lingered in her words. 'You know, she could have had her pick from dozens of men, they really like fair-skinned women.' Neelie was fair skinned, of Dutch origin and for the moment had forgotten where she was and obviously to whom she was talking — or else she was remarkably thick-skinned.

Five minutes later Yusuf came up the stairs to collect Denise, who would accompany him to sign the papers. Marriage in Islam is not a sacrament but a contract. Performed in the home, in a hall or a mosque, it is emphatically an open, public affair. I was still unsure of the legal status of this marriage. As far as I knew it was strictly a religious wedding, not one officially recognised in Australian law.

We were devastated to learn that Denise had forgotten to bring her marriage contract. Neelie was angry that once again Denise had been caught unprepared. 'What have you signed? What is the status of the marriage?' she quizzed her impatiently.

Denise was vague; she had other things on her mind and nothing was going to interfere with the role she was presently playing. All we could learn was that Yusuf's cousin's husband had sworn an oath promising to lodge her document with a lawyer the following Monday. Yusuf asked her again what she wanted as her *mehr* — this must all be recorded. Denise stammered and faltered. Finally he suggested $100. It was an extremely low figure, more symbolic than real. Neelie was spitting mad — the contract which Denise had forgotten to bring with her would have clarified and safeguarded her position.

We set off by car to the reception which was held at the

house of Yusuf's cousin in Campsie, and entered the separate area for female guests. The men sat outside around small tables. There was no alcohol in sight, although I later learned that until the late 1980s it was sometimes served at Lebanese and Egyptian weddings for non-Muslim guests. This accommodation to Australian tastes seemed to have diminished over the years as the Muslim community grew stronger and more confident.

Egyptian music filled the air, accompanied by much hand clapping. Inside the women's room we waited impatiently for the couple to enter and receive our formal good wishes. Neelie and I were the only guests Ehsan had invited. The other seventy or eighty guests belonged to Yusuf's side. Suddenly the older women launched into shrill ululations. They had arrived — a very dignified, stately bride with her handsome, serious but very nervous husband in his dark blue suit. The older women started the traditional, hip-rolling Egyptian dance. Neelie's face froze in horror — it was almost comical. 'I didn't become a Muslim,' she hissed, 'to indulge in these barbaric customs — this is culture, not religion!' Perhaps she had forgotten that singing and music is recommended on festive occasions like Eid, weddings, births and the return of a traveller. It must of course be music and singing to refresh the ear and comfort the soul — nothing too exciting or passionate. Dancing, of course, was something else. Neelie had also noticed that the 'women only' room had been infiltrated by four or five young men with video cameras. Indignantly she swished off into the kitchen.

Traditional dancing is a generally accepted Egyptian custom to which most people — though well aware that Islam forbids dancing — turn a blind eye at weddings. It takes place only in the women's room, usually started by older women who drag their daughters and granddaughters in to dance with them until they form one noisy, hand-clapping throng.

I wanted to assure Neelie that we were hardly witnessing the Hollywood version of *The Thousand and One Nights*. There were no veiled harem beauties slinking around with rubies in their navels, clanking their anklets and generally behaving like naughty nautch girls. This was the kind of dancing women had done for centuries for their own innocent entertainment, segregated from the eyes of men.

Yusuf and his bride sat in splendid red velvet armchairs like royal consorts awaiting congratulations from their subjects. At the same time Neelie was becoming decidedly 'twitchy'. As we moved forward to congratulate the couple, she made it abundantly clear to Yusuf that she strongly disapproved of these goings-on. Judging by the glazed look on his face, it seemed unlikely that he took in anything she said. I said goodbye to Denise. 'Now you have the ending for your chapter,' she whispered in my ear.

Before I left Lakemba there was one person I had to see. Maha Krayem Abdo had returned from Mecca only the day before and I wanted to hear from her own lips the story of her *haj*. Now that her pilgrimage was over she was entitled to use the title *Hajiah*. She was exhausted and her voice was already hoarse from retelling her experiences in the holy city over and over to family and friends. Maha was the president of the Muslim Women's Association, which had offices in Lakemba. Her usually pale face was even paler today and she had dark rings under her eyes, but nothing could hide the contentment in her eyes nor spoil her excitement as she told, for probably the hundredth time since her return, of the thrill of making her pilgrimage for the first time.

'Making *haj* makes you feel reborn,' she said. 'It is the most intense feeling I have ever experienced and it is totally for the glory of Allah. In Medina you visit all the places the Prophet Muhammad (peace be upon Him) used to go to — the mountains, the mosques. In the mountains, I couldn't help crying. I thought they would speak to me. They were tall, rugged mountains, with so much history to tell. My hair stood on end and I felt part of the mountains.

'In every mosque you visit, you are surrounded by friendliness and you see just how multicultural Islam is. I know that coming from Australia I should have expected this mix, but what a sensation — praying next to an Afghan woman, with an Englishwoman on the other side; everyone going to the one place for the one thing. "*Salaam alaikum*," you say, needing no introduction, and then you hug one another, join hands and go off to prayer together.

'There are many different rituals to complete and you are always on the move. After eight days in Medina we went by bus to Mecca.' This year about five hundred Australian Muslims had made their *haj*. 'Shaykh Taj tried to get his bus to the front when we parked, but everyone else was trying to do the same thing,' she said with a laugh. 'The feeling in Mecca is different again. The mountains overwhelm you once more — Mecca is in a valley surrounded by mountains. Somehow I had expected sand. These mountains are made of granite and they are so eerie. You are surrounded by mountains. They are all dark, and I saw reflections of light coming out. I had a strong feeling that this is where all life began. Maybe it's like being on the moon, the terrain is so stark. From here, you will emerge a newborn person. The mosque is so crowded in Mecca that it is impossible to stay together in a group. Men and women pray together in the mosque, almost shoulder to shoulder. It is so crowded and hot, but you don't want it to finish. The men formed a protective shield for the women — we were all in the middle — so we wouldn't get crushed. This was where you really needed to be healthy and fit. Of course, we also circled the Ka'aba seven times reciting "*Allahu Akbar*, God is Most Great".'

Maha had found the crowds incredible. With up to three million pilgrims at a time, the *haj* takes careful organisation by the Saudi Arabian government. Maha praised the excellent medical facilities and the superb crowd management. 'Men with walkie-talkies were everywhere in case you got lost — and that was always happening, you were easily separated from your group. By looking at your ID tag, they knew where you should be.'

Maha is wearing an Eid gift from her mother. 'When you come back you wear white — you left in white and you return in white.' The dress is embossed satin, with wide puff sleeves, tight at the wrist. It is a radiant white that dazzles your eyes, whiter even than Denise's bridal dress. The finest and softest white muslin forms her *hijab*, beautifully draped around her tired face. She wears soft white kid boots and a single piece of jewellery. Except for the anachronism of the gold watch, Maha would not be out of place in a Renaissance painting.

Two women dressed in white. Ehsan/Denise in her bridal gown, longing to be reborn, searching for something in Islam: 'I know it's there, I just have to find it,' her voice echoed. And an exhausted but radiant Maha, dressed in a long white robe telling me she felt spiritually reborn. 'I carry my *haj* with me. I feel more responsibilities now; I am aware of my mortality.' The signs indicated a long spiritual journey ahead for Denise. The inner peace that Maha had found might be further away for Denise than she realised. It is simply too early to tell.

After six weeks in Lakemba, I was still fascinated by the people's energy, and by the organisations which brought religious and cultural vitality into their lives. Lakemba was still a village to me: capable of acting as one body on certain matters, but also capable of individual capricious, unpredictable behaviour. Circles within circles, leaders and followers, deep undercurrents and tensions — altogether a strange blend of vigour and waywardness. I recalled Sameena's words that first day in her house, when she had tried her best to explain to me what living in Lakemba was all about and how it felt to be part of a believing circle. 'Muslims in Lakemba are like a fortress, a stronghold for Islam ... If you don't want to be a practising Muslim, you don't live in Lakemba.'

IV

The women's caravan

Woman is a ray of God, not a mere mistress, The Creator's Self, as it were, not a mere creature!

Rumi, Sufi poet

15

Gentlewomen of Cairo

The caravanserais of old were unseemly places for women to venture, unless you happened to be a serving girl or the wife of the landlord. Women rarely left their villages or towns. The world of trade and bazaars, of games and competitions, of the excitement and dangers of war, were the property of men. A few women, it is true, enjoyed the freedom and uncertainty of nomadic life. Romany, or gypsy, women wandered together with their clans through kingdoms and across borders which existed only on maps for the tiresome, greedy officials they encountered and had no place in their world of ancient trails and annual gatherings. Other nomadic women, in bright dresses and unveiled faces, moved each season with their families and herds forming their own caravans, camping far from the haunts of settled folk. Over the centuries they paid dearly for their freedom and unconventional ways, ostracised and looked down upon wherever they went by the good farmers and townspeople whose walled settlements they silently passed. But most women were not free to roam, and most had to content themselves with local festivals, or with a visit to a holy shrine or a famous mystic to grant a secret wish or cure an ailment. Monotony ruled their lives.

Aziza Abdul-Halim is a master storyteller in the old tradition. Everyone admires the way she weaves together colourful moments and breathes new life into old tales. Most of her stories come from the Hadith, that compilation of the sayings and actions of the Prophet and his Companions. They are stories with strong moral overtones not unlike the parables found in the Bible.

Three months had passed since my Lakemba stay. I now travelled with ease on Sydney's trains so Aziza and I agreed to meet at a Turkish coffee shop in Auburn over *halal* pizzas and cappuccinos. We started off discussing one of her passions — the Muslim Women's National Network of which she is president. However, before I became too lost in the charm of Aziza's conversation, I thought I should learn more about this teller of tales herself, and so our talk gradually drifted from the changing world of Muslim women today to the days of her childhood in Egypt. Slowly Aziza unlocked the doors of her past.

'My grandmother was a very strong woman and it was from her lips that I heard all about my grandfather, for he died many years before my birth. He was an upright man, always on the side of the underdog. He served as an officer in the late nineteenth century when the British were routing the Mahdi and his followers from the Sudan. My mother was born in the Sudan during one of his later campaigns, for in those days the officers' wives accompanied their husbands and lived in dusty, crowded garrisons; so my grandmother shared in those exciting times as well.

'"Your grandfather," she would tell me as I sat listening to every word, hardly daring to move in case she stopped, "your grandfather wrote his memoirs when he retired. They were serialised in the official government newspaper until they were banned by command of the British." His writing exposed the truth behind the legendary campaign, my grandmother told me. As usual, the British were up to their old tricks.

'As soon as Grandmother said the magic words, "Your grandfather always said ..." I used to sit up attentively, hoping she would begin one of the Sudan stories. "Your grandfather always said that with the British it never mattered whether the soldiers were Egyptian or Indian" — or even Australian,' Aziza added — '"They were sent in first under heavy fire. 'Native' troops suffered terrible casualties. They would accomplish the impossible and win the battles — and then the British would ride in with trumpets blaring and flags flying and be acclaimed the victors! And so another British legend would be born."

'My mother took after her father — always upset over injustice. She went to a Catholic high school in Cairo in the 1930s and when ordered to recite the catechism or go to mass, she would calmly reply, "No, I'm a Muslim. I don't do that." Even the Mother Superior couldn't frighten her!'

In the old photograph of her mother that Aziza handed me, I saw a classical beauty with a small straight nose, masses of brown wavy hair and a dreamy expression on her face. Another photo was of her grandfather. A man of obvious military bearing and background stared proudly back at me. Dressed in full uniform with his regimental insignia, he was wearing a distinctive fez with a feather on the side, designed for the Sudan campaign. His waxed moustache suited his stern face. His family, I learnt, had originally come from Saudi Arabia.

'Prince of the Haj' was a title Aziza's grandfather received just before he died. Egypt, in those days, always provided the outer cover of the Ka'aba, that ancient sacred rock of Mecca. The enormous splendid cover, known as the Kiswa, was made of black velvet and embroidered all over in gold thread with verses from the Qur'an. Each year a newly embroidered Kiswa was ceremoniously transported from Egypt to Mecca by camel caravan where it was presented by an appointed leader — the Prince of the Haj. It was an old custom, dating back more than a hundred years. The day the caravan began its journey was always a national holiday in Eygpt. Today the Saudis weave the Kiswa in their mills, but it is still beautiful and highly sought after by pilgrims who pay large sums of money to take bits of the fabric home with them as a keepsake of their sacred pilgrimage.

'Grandmother ruled the family. Every morning after getting up we dutifully kissed her hand, were kissed on the cheeks in return and then ate our breakfast. If I woke up early and crept downstairs, I would find her sitting out on the terrace overlooking the gardens, grinding coffee beans or some such task and reciting the Qur'an from memory. Our visits were lengthy because we lived in Al-Iskandariyah, or Alexandria, named after Alexander the Great, while grandmother lived in Cairo, or El-Qahira, as it was called. We would journey for about six hours by train, although the trip is down to two and a half now, I think.

'Grandmother's house was a big two-storeyed white building with beautiful parquet floors, french windows and, outside, a small herb garden with hutches for the rabbits. It was in Shubra, an area very close to the Nile.' Aziza talked casually of the Nile River as a familiar and friendly playground.

'On evenings of the full moon we would sail out on the Nile and enjoy a moonlight picnic. Boatmen would play the drums; someone would sing and the rest would clap their hands in time to the rhythm. Lying on the cushions, staring at the moon while the boat rocked from side to side, I often fell asleep and had to be carried home.

'Grandmother dressed like a grande dame in the European style, with fine dresses and parasols. The house was full of artists and someone was always playing the piano. Two huge lounge rooms were full of paintings because one of my uncles kept up with the world of art and had a circle of artistic friends who dropped in occasionally. But although the outward appearance was western, the mood was Egyptian and Muslim. People prayed, kept up Islamic ethics, and always dealt with the opposite sex on a proper level — friendly but not familiar, with no segregation but certainly always correct.

But there was more to the 'grand bourgoise' lifestyle than Aziza intimated. In the 1920s, behind the picnics, the family gatherings and the festivals, the gentlewomen of Cairo — many of them veiled — were protesting in the streets. Egypt has a long list of female activitists who at this time were emerging from their homes and organising themselves into associations like the League of Women, which was established in 1923. Side by side with their men, they protested against foreign occupation, shouted slogans and organised strikes and demonstrations. Through their participation in the nationalist movement, upper middle-class women emerged from their lives of seclusion. In the following decades they won the right to education and finally, in 1956, to political equality. Today Egyptian women are encouraged to work as a national duty.

The history of Egyptian female activists is not well known in the West. These women belonged to the elite and had they been told that they were activists they would have been horrified; they were simply doing what they thought was their duty. Although there were the 'lady bountiful' types with traces of a noblesse oblige ethos, they worked tirelessly as unpaid social workers, nurses, teachers and organisers.

In the late 1950s, thirty years after Egyptian women first took to the streets, as the tides of nationalism gathered force, sixteen-year-old Aziza marched with her girlfriends in an anti-British protest. It was to be her first, but not her last, demonstration.

'The key to understanding my mother,' Aziza's daughter Doà had explained to me once, 'is her revulsion towards anything smacking of injustice.'

What would be Aziza's reaction, I wondered, to a tale of female disobedience which had recently drifted to my ears?

'I have heard,' I said, 'that in some quarters a woman's piety is measured by her absolute obedience to her husband.'

Aziza listened intently to my unhappy story before replying. 'Some extremely traditional Muslims are hard on their wives to the point of emotional abuse,' she said. 'Yet the Prophet Muhammad (peace be upon Him) never ill-treated a woman in his life!' Her voice sounded stern and her eyes were serious.

Aziza is famous for having a Hadith for every occasion. She was bound to have one, I thought, on the subject of female obedience, and of course she did.

'"Do not obey your husband if he transgresses" is an authentic Hadith,' she said.

Unlike many other Hadith experts I have listened to, she made the Prophet's comments and moral examples come alive in the social context of their time. With her, you wandered down the narrow, dusty alleyways of Medina in the time of the Prophet and his Companions.

'Caliph Omar did not like his wife going to the mosque to pray five times a day,' continued Aziza. '"Once is enough," he said. His wife, Ateka, answered her husband saying, "If you want to stop me, do so by religious decree!" And he could not, because he was a just man. The Prophet's Hadith says clearly, "Do not stop women from going to the mosque".'

'And yet,' I said, 'overseas, and sometimes in Australia, obstacles are put in the way of women who want to pray at the mosque.' There were a string of excuses to keep women away: '"Females are too emotional and tender-hearted, in danger of crying and other inappropriate mosque conduct", "If women love God it shouldn't matter where they pray". Knowledgeable women who have studied the original sources know that in the time of the Prophet the whole family would meet five times daily in the mosque — men, children and women, without curtains, walls or partitions separating them, praying in their own rows.

'Those who try to keep women out of the mosque,' said Aziza, 'are playing on a Hadith in which a woman came to the Prophet and said, "I cannot go to the mosque regularly because I have only one garment and it is torn and patched and I feel ashamed to attend like this." The Prophet told her that in this case, prayer in her own home would be more rewarding for her than going to the mosque. But what has happened over the years? Some people have taken this very specific Hadith out of context and extrapolated it to all women on all occasions.

'That is why women must be religiously educated so that they can find out for themselves. We are given a duty to go to the source, to find out the truth, to use their own minds. We are to follow the Prophet's own advice and to reject those Hadith which are weak, which contradict the Qur'an or more logical and authentic Hadith, or which contradict the spirit of Islam — the spirit of justice.' The learned Aziza would leave nothing to the haphazard interpretation of a non-expert!

The more I read and talked to experts, the more fascinated I became with the complex methodology of assessing the historical and religious authenticity of the Hadith. Within one hundred years of the Prophet's death, records of what he said and did were being made. The names of those who transmitted them were meticulously recorded so as to ensure accurate and reliable chains of human reference.

There are thousands and thousands of Hadith. However, as Islam's boundaries spread, forged Hadith flourished in certain periods in Islamic history, bolstering the political careers of corrupt rulers. In my search for 'shady' or suspect Hadith, I found some that seemed unsympathetic to women.

Reading Muslim feminist literature had taught me that after the Prophet's death, women slowly started losing ground as a number of Muhammad's reforms were eroded. Tensions were already discernible in the Prophet's time, something he was forced to contend with politically, as his sweeping reforms had rocked many followers by attacking their power and privileges. Exactly when this decline began is unclear, although some writers say it came about after the time of the four orthodox caliphs, Abu Bakr, Omar, Osman and Ali. It is thought to have intensified during the Umayyad and Abbasid dynasties in the seventh, eighth and ninth centuries when Islam had spread beyond the Middle East as far west as Spain and as far east as Central Asia. Others have argued that the political corruption that gradually eroded later dynasties was the cause of the waning of women's rights. However, most writers agree that as the *ulemma* (religious scholars and authorities) increased their power and authority, women became the losers.

16

A disobedient woman

'Matters came to a head when he tried to force me to wear *hijab*. I became frightened that if I gave in, the demands would continue to grow until there was nothing left of me; that his commands would feed on me like a giant spider. I felt I was fighting for my honour and for my children.'

Zareena eloquently conveyed the anguish of her experience in her French-accented English, lapsing into French whenever a word escaped her. She was from Algeria, the former French colony which had won independence in 1963 after a long and bloody war. Underlying her speech, one could feel the authority and sway of Arabic as it infiltrated the rhythm of her words and phrases and the lyrical imagery she used.

Zareena was a beautiful woman in her late thirties, pale and green eyed with long henna-red hair. She sat in her lounge room, hands clasped tightly, her voice, usually passionate and clear, turning tremulous now and then. Only these small signs gave her away, for usually she showed nothing but implacable resolve. Zareena was obsessed with the idea that if she had given in to her husband on *hijab* he would have become more and more demanding. 'It was my last refuge; I had to make a stand.' She stared ahead, her eyes fixed on me, daring me to disagree.

The family had arrived in Sydney two years previously. Soon it became evident to Zareena that her husband, Omar, was unhappy and finding it difficult to settle. Give him time, she had thought; once he finds a job, everything will be all right. But everything was not all right, and finally Omar insisted that they move to another suburb.

'We're leaving,' he said quietly one night. 'I need to be close to an Arabic-speaking mosque.' The loss of his language had affected Omar badly. Once a laughing man who enjoyed the company of others, since arriving in Australia he had become more and more silent and morose. Without his beloved Arabic, he experienced enormous difficulty in negotiating his way around the new systems and structures he needed to influence. His self-esteem shrivelled up and in Zareena's eyes he seemed half the man he used to be. In English he was like a blind man, groping his way from sentence to sentence. Although they all spoke Arabic at home, his loss of competence in the outside world continued to trouble him — and everyone else in the household became infected by his unhappiness.

Zareena had been startled by his announcement. They had always discussed things together before. Yet over the past few weeks his mood swings had worsened and she had imagined she could hear him crying softly as he lay in bed. He was changing and she didn't know how to help him. All she could do was make sure that the children did not know what was happening to their beloved papa. He was a proud man who always had the answers to all of their problems; she didn't want them to lose this picture of their father.

'Why upset the children's schooling?' she asked. 'They've just settled in.'

'We're moving. I've found a house for us in Canterbury.'

They had been so happy as students in the United States, she thought. Where was the man who had spent $3,000 a month on telephone calls when he had gone to Syria while she stayed in the States? Theirs had been a love marriage;

they had been true companions of the mind. But since their arrival in Australia Zareena had been so busy settling in and making sure the children — Suad, ten and Jamil, eight — were all right that she had not noticed the early signs of Omar's wretchedness. She often thought now, as she lay awake at night unable to sleep, that immigrating was the worst thing they could have done. But Australia had seemed the answer for a modern Muslim couple with university degrees and a young family.

After they moved to Canterbury, life for Zareena and the children changed irrevocably.

'He started slowly, taking a little bit away at a time. First it was something small like going to McDonald's.

'"It is *haram*," he would announce. "The meat is not killed the *halal* way. We can make our own hamburgers at home and we can go on picnics together." It sounded reasonable, so I agreed. But every day he asked for more and more.

'He wanted to enrol the children at a Muslim school and the one he chose insisted that Suad wear *hijab*. I needed time to think about this. Suad had been happy at her old public school and didn't need a sudden change, I thought. And I was troubled about my daughter going to a school which promoted *hijab* and coming home to a mother who wasn't covered. I didn't want Suad thinking of me as a foreigner. What could I say when they asked me, "Mummy why are you uncovered?" They might come to see me as a bad woman.'

But Omar insisted on having his way. In desperation Zareena rang the principal who told her brusquely that he believed the problem lay with Zareena herself. Zareena, who had expected sympathy, now suspected that Omar had already won the principal's support with tales about his 'neurotic wife'.

Suad had cried when she and her brother came home

from school the first day. Zareena telephoned the principal again and asked him not to force the girl to wear *hijab*. He refused to budge.

'You hurt me,' Zareena told her husband later. 'You humiliated me. I could hear you laughing in the background when I spoke to the principal on the phone. I have this right as a mother. She is my daughter! For me putting on the *hijab* is not a trivial thing; it has big implications.'

'Papa, I don't want to wear it. I don't want to go to that school, Papa,' Suad said to her father the next morning. But he was intransigent.

Like most couples, Zareena and Omar had fought in the past, but they had always been good friends and equal partners; fighting was something all married couples did from time to time. But now, everything seemed wrong between them. 'Every day there came another argument. The children were becoming confused. I knew they were caught in the middle, but I couldn't stop the arguments and the bad feelings which festered.

'One day he said, "Why did you buy all this furniture? We should eat on the floor and sleep on the floor, the simple Islamic way, just like the Prophet (peace be upon Him)."

'"Why do we drive a car, then?" I retorted. "Why do we watch television and use the telephone? You are not consistent."'

The next day Omar pronounced his second *talaq* ('I divorce thee'). He had given her the first a month earlier as a warning. Under Islamic law, a third *talaq* could mean the end of their marriage. They were playing a cruel game of marital suicide.

'My big mistake,' Zareena said, 'was when I started to compromise.'

'What do you mean?'

'Maybe I should explain our early years. When I met him [Zareena refused to use her husband's name], I was twenty-four. "You are a human being," I told him, "I am a human being and we respect each other." I wanted to explain to him that we were not competing. Just because I had a Master's degree didn't mean I was better. "We are two individuals sharing our lives."'

I wondered if Omar had ever truly accepted this.

'I made a compromise when I came here,' Zareena went on, 'because I had two children with this man.'

Zareena believed that the characteristics Omar was now revealing had lain dormant in his personality for many years. She gave me yet more examples of his unreasonable, tyrannical behaviour. 'He started telling me that I shouldn't mix with women who did not wear *hijab*. He was now allied with new friends who seemed very devout and spent a lot of time at the mosque. He had no work, so with all this time on his hands he went down to the mosque every day and they began to influence him. All I will say is that they are very traditional and so are their wives.' Zareena suddenly became very careful and for the first time looked away, refusing to meet my eye. What now I wondered?

'So there I was mixing only with the women he wanted me to mix with. Of course I was the only one who didn't cover. He thought it would happen sooner or later, especially as there was one woman in the group who took it upon herself to make it like ... what do you say ... a contest of wills? She was more like the group leader and she used this to show how strong she was. If and when I wear *hijab* one day, it will be by my own will,' she finished off categorically.'

But although Zareena held out on the scarf, she began to give in on the other little things that she thought didn't matter as much. 'No. 1, the people he wanted me to mix with. No. 2, no more short sleeves — even in summer. (Between you and me, this suited me fine because my upper arms aren't so firm any more.)

'He wanted more though. I was always under pressure. I wear long sleeves — and he starts talking about the *hijab*. "You should start reading the Qur'an," he said, and I did. That helped, because now I could base my arguments on the Qur'an and not just rely on my own ideas.'

Zareena had discovered what the many Muslim women who were reading the Qur'an now knew to be true. Muslim feminists overseas were going back to the Qur'an to bring about change, arguing and reinterpreting many of the explanatory texts. In many cases they were taking on the Muslim religious establishment.

'I don't like the perfume you are using,' Omar told his wife one day.

'It is my old Christian Dior. What is wrong with it?'

'Christian Dior is *haram*. You must wear the perfume that Aysha used in the golden age of Islam.'

'Certainly. Is it still available?' replied Zareena with heavy sarcasm.

Zareena had had enough.

'Please let us talk,' she cried, over and over again.

'No. I don't want to talk to you,' was his inevitable answer.

So she went ahead and filed for a legal separation. Of course he didn't believe she would go through with it, and even after moving out he still spent nights, she told me, praying that the *shaitan*, or devil, inside her would vanish.

He met all his financial obligations and didn't seem to want custody of the children. But he refused to talk to her or write to her.

'He still doesn't think the divorce will take place,' Zareena said.

'I know he has psychological problems, and I know it is a power thing with him, that he needs to feel a king in his own house. But I am convinced that these characteristics were always there and in these bad circumstances, they floated to the surface. My obedience became the most important thing to him. He wanted to break me.'

When next I met Zareena eight months later, the conflict had worsened. Suddenly one night, after five months absence, Omar returned to the flat without warning. He paid the rent, he said, he had bought the furniture, he was still sending her money — it was his home! His lawyer's idea, she immediately thought. She became hysterical and called the police.

'I played into his hands again. By the time the police arrived he was calm, had stopped shouting and stood there the very symbol of a perplexed husband who could not understand the hysteria and theatrics of "My poor wife who is frightening the children."' He had struck her but there was no mark and the police seemed to believe him.

She turned to legal aid for help and took out a restraining order against him. By now her son Jamil wanted to live with his father, so she agreed. The boy was becoming confused and father and son had always been devoted to each other; perhaps it was for the best.

Still, Zareena was worried because Jamil now made critical remarks about women who were wearing even a little make-up. She was afraid that one day he might even reject her as his mother. The boy and his father were inseparable and she acknowledged their closeness and affection, but did not want him spending so much time at the mosque at his young age.

'I have one staunch ally, *Al'ham dulillah*! The shaykh does not believe the stories that I am an unfit mother and a *kafir*.'

Now it was my turn to be surprised. I had always assumed that a shaykh would see it as his duty to urge an estranged wife to show obedience and return to her husband.

'I could not believe it myself at first,' she said, laughing. 'But I could not have found a better friend and adviser; he is kind, helpful, compassionate ... he did not automatically side with my husband, as I had expected. He said, "Do not go back to your husband until he comes to his senses and gives you back your dignity." He intervened and made sure my husband returned the washing machine and refrigerator he had taken away in spite. A man must be generous to his wife even if he is divorcing her, he told him.'

'But aren't you the one divorcing your husband?' I asked.

'Yes, but Islamically he is divorcing me, and anyway it makes him feel better when it sounds like he is the one doing the rejecting.'

'What does the shaykh think about women initiating divorce?' I was curious.

'If a man has not slept with his wife for more than three months, she has the right to initiate divorce, he believes,' she said soberly.

The second of the two questions I often use as a kind of litmus test as to the progressiveness of members of the *ulemma* revolved around individual interpretation of the Qur'an. Where did the shaykh stand?

'He is not against individual interpretation itself,' Zareena replied, 'if the broad knowledge is there to interpret the Hadith. Many women are illiterate and some partially educated women try to interpret in their own way. Of that he is critical.'

To an outsider, Zareena's story might appear at first glance to be the typical tale of a tyrannical Muslim husband forcing his wife into submission and using the *hijab* as his symbolic weapon to bludgeon her into obedience. Indeed that remains one level of interpretation, but one that turns Omar into a complete monster and that would be an injustice. In a strange way this story was as much a story of his unhappiness as of his wife's.

I admire Zareena tremendously; my sympathies are instinctively with her. But power, not religion, was the problem here. I often wonder, when I hear of divorces in which conflict between western and Islamic values seems to play a part: Is this happening because the husband is a Muslim, or is it related to his role as a male? Are we talking about a marriage breakdown or a universal problem related to patriarchal issues of power and control? At the heart of this unhappy chronicle lay the psychological misery of a man who was unable, for many reasons, to adjust to life in Australia and who had turned on the person closest to him. His last retreat, his last link with his lost pride and dignity, had become his family. Here he could exercise some control over his life when it seemed to be falling to pieces. He had clung to them and eventually lost them. I did not want to excuse his extreme behaviour, only to try to understand.

'He made one bad mistake,' Zareena told me at the end. She smiled at me — a tight smile showing satisfaction but not much joy. 'He should never have brought me to Australia. Here I have managed to fly out of the cage he tried to build for me.'

Which is very often the way with disobedient women.

17

Daughters of the wind

The days of caravans and caravanserais have for the most part vanished. Storytellers of old have given way to a new body of social commentators: efficient, serious-faced speakers delivering papers on subjects liberally laced with the incantations of modern social justice. At a conference of Australian Muslim women, I saw the spirit of the caravanserai reappear from time to time in the drama behind the scenes, away from the dais. They came from every corner of Australia, travelling in pairs or in groups for modesty and protection, to exchange their personal stories — modern-day adventures — before returning home to their world of men, children and responsibilities.

Like conferences everywhere, this Muslim women's conference had that low buzz of anticipation, a feeling of energy held in check, waiting for an outlet, for something useful and productive to happen. Executive members attended to last-minute details while delegates embraced and greeted each other in warm and demonstrative shows of affection. Hidden agendas were sharpened, allies confirmed and likely antagonists singled out. Amidst the loud calls of '*salaam alaikum*' and laughter, microphones squawked and people busily located their name tags, marking with coats and bags the seats they would occupy over the next two days.

Half-a-dozen female public servants representing

various government departments — Health, Immigration, Education and so on — stood out amongst the hundred or so Muslim women like tourists at a bazaar. Most wore the uneasy look, the small telltale signs of discomfort, of individuals not quite at ease in an unfamiliar culture and in need of a prop or a colleague to rescue them.

Looking around, I noticed two types of uniform. Practically all the Muslims were wearing *hijab*; the two or three Muslim mavericks who had not covered their heads (of whom I was one) looked singularly conspicuous. (Was there truth after all in the old Dervish saying, 'A woman without a veil is like good food without salt' — unattractive?) Surrounded by our more devout sisters, properly clad and serenely confident as they glided about their business, we were living examples to some of what could happen to Muslim women if you were not careful. Non-Muslim women had their own corporate-style uniform, the mandatory jacket with shoulder pads and sleek briefcases.

Muslim women en masse are a marvel to behold in Australia, breaking every stereotype in the book. Yet outsiders retain a persistent view of them all as victims. Is this an apt description of the situation of Muslim women in Australia? The 'victims' think otherwise. 'Western women are always trying to save Muslim women!' came the complaint. 'We want empathy, not sympathy!'

The stories unfolded. Some illustrated simple misunderstandings between Anglo-Australian and Muslim women. Other stories told of dealings that would have been embarrassing had the non-Muslims ever realised that their well-meaning but clumsy efforts were condescending.

Reading between the lines, one notices a strong desire among Muslim women to solve their own problems in their own way. In many other countries they are striving to do just that — empower themselves but remain Islamic. It doesn't happen with a wave of some legislative wand and it most certainly doesn't happen overnight! To onlookers it can be an agonisingly slow process, but many believe it can only be brought about from inside Islam, by Muslim women themselves. Most western feminist groups have problems coming to grips with this.

'If they don't want to be rescued by white women's sympathy, they should get around to doing it themselves!' is a common cry.

And so the misunderstanding continues.

'The newspaper accounts make me feel like a walking tent: a breeding machine with a vacuum under my headscarf. Mind you, this vacuum should properly be filled only with western, feminist ideas.'

'I read this article about ethnic women in Australia. It focused on a Greek woman, a Jewish woman and a Turkish woman. The headline was THE PROBLEMS OF MUSLIM WOMEN.'

I circled the conference, tape-recorder in hand like a collector of rare butterflies. The conference was my own personal bazaar, full of bright colours, strange delights and memorable characters. But was it merely another occasion for preaching to the converted? Inside the conference caravanserai, did everyone agree? I noticed a staunch wall of sisterly solidarity, but were there certain lines and shadows I was missing?

I found myself talking to Jutta Wern, a tall blonde public servant who, though not a Muslim, had studied Arabic and Islamic studies in Cairo, even visiting the famous Al-Azhar university as an honoured guest. Many women present would have gladly traded their gold bangles for such an opportunity! Behind her impassive bureaucratic exterior lay a wealth of Islamic knowledge. Jutta could not be easily fobbed off with hazy theological explanations from the dais. She recognised a contentious issue when she heard one and adroitly deflected questions. 'One shouldn't take things too literally,' I heard her say to three short, smiling Muslim women. 'There is so much in Islam which allows for interpretation! Okay, you have your golden tenets, but there is so much that is mutable.' Just in time, Jutta stopped short of launching into a lecture on Islam and losing her small fan club.

'I lived in Egypt with a very strict family,' she said. 'The mother remained definitely traditional, but not so the daughter. Living with us was also a niece, who swam and did gymnastics. She wore swimming costumes and shorts — clothing that didn't restrict her movements. What was her *niyyat*, her intention? Simply to keep fit and win a race.'

Talk switched to the young Algerian runner Hassiba Boulmerka, at the time the world 1500-metre women's champion, who had recently visited Sydney. Her bare legs, shorts and competitive running had earned her the censure of many ultra-orthodox and militant Muslims in Algeria. The three women said that although they admired her, they would never have had her courage.

Later that day I cornered Jutta, curious to learn how she had come by her knowledge. Years ago, thanks to a Muslim mentor at the Australian National University, she had become interested in Egypt, and in 1977 won a scholarship which led to her visiting, on and off, the renowned religious university of Al-Azhar, widely regarded as a beacon of Islamic theology. Five years later she made a second trip. 'I was so well treated: they literally rolled out the green Islamic carpet for me at Al-Azhar. I wore a scarf and a long robe. There was no pressure, but it seemed the appropriate thing to do — after all, I was going to meet the famous Shaykh Gadd al-Haqq, a greatly revered figure. He told everyone around him, "Treat her as you would treat my daughter."'

On her second trip Jutta noticed many changes, especially differences in dress and demeanour among the students on campus. 'I thought it more of a political stance by young people disillusioned with western systems — both capitalist and communist. All of a sudden young women were voluntarily putting on the *hijab*, much to the shock of their mothers.

"How can they attract men wearing the *hijab*?" the mothers cried.'

You'd be surprised, I thought, thinking of Denise and Lakemba.

One day Jutta was picked up by a Nubian taxi driver. 'Are you married?' he asked her. The man was not being cheeky — questions like this were often put to foreigners simply out of curiosity. Jutta, feeling out of sorts, snapped, 'Yes! And I've got five husbands!' 'Five husbands?' echoed the shocked driver and, touching his tiny Qur'an on the dashboard (all taxi drivers had a Qur'an on their dashboards), he quickly recited a prayer. 'Why not?' said Jutta, starting to enjoy herself. 'You're allowed to have four wives!'

When he saw her smiling, he realised she was only joking and roared with laughter. From then on, whenever he could, he always tried to pick her up outside the college and would tell all his other passengers about the Australian girl with five husbands. Jutta would sit jammed in the back seat with three or four other women, sharing the taxi as was the custom. The *badawi*, or Bedouin women, cloaked in their black *galabiyyas*, sitting crammed together with children or chooks on their laps, shrieked with laughter at the scandalous joke. The taxi dashed along the road, the driver sounding his horn, his religious objects swinging from his rear-vision mirror. 'What a cheeky foreign woman,' he told his laughing passengers, as the taxi swayed from side to side, doors threatening to burst open at any moment.

How did Jutta think the conference was turning out? By way of reply she referred to a remarkable event that had taken place that very afternoon. Someone in the audience had risen to her feet and courageously had her say about women marrying outside the faith — the pinnacle of taboos for a Muslim woman. 'I know I shouldn't be saying this, but if it was me, I couldn't stand by and watch my daughter mentally and emotionally disintegrate in front of me or, worse still, take her own life. If it came to that,' she quietly uttered to a hushed audience, 'I would be forced, reluctantly, to accept her marrying a non-Muslim rather than lose her forever.' She paused while ripples — mostly of shock, a few of understanding — passed through the hall. 'Five years ago I would not have said this; five years ago I would have insisted that she must not do this, but I've seen what happens.' We later learnt that she was a professional counsellor at a Sydney clinic.

This moment of absolute honesty created a stir, as if a time bomb was waiting to go off. Later this woman might well run the gauntlet of unkind remarks from people accusing her of breaking ranks, of a kind of cultural betrayal in front of outsiders. Her critics failed to understand that this glimpse of painful honesty and private torment from a devout Muslim who knew exactly what she was talking about had touched non-Muslims in the audience in a way that dogmatic accounts of the role of women in Islam failed to do. It showed a human side, a small chink in the armour that was a million times more appealing in its humanity than the arguments from puritans clinging to the moral high ground.

Jutta later told me another anecdote about her time in Egypt. 'President Carter caused a major hullabaloo when he visited Egypt while I was there. The poor man kissed

Jehan Sadat, President Sadat's wife, on the cheek the first time they met!'

'He didn't!'

'He did! It caused a major scandal at the time. Newspapers debated it for weeks, religious scholars made comments on the *haram* nature of "his unseemly act".'

Rather like Paul Keating touching the Queen of England on the back, I reflected. The British tabloids in particular had slammed the gesture as gauche and presumptuous, the kind of gesture only a wild colonial prime minister could make — in its own way, a kind of *haram* faux pas.

'The Carter kiss created a big stir in Cairo until an eminent scholar finally calmed the raging elements by asking rhetorically, "What was Carter's intention — his *niyyat*?" His intention had obviously not been sexual, therefore his action was permissible on this occasion.'

Talking about Islam and living with Islam are two different things, and Jutta had lived with Islam at close quarters. 'It is such a gentle way of life, the complete opposite to the way it's presented in the movies and on television,' she said. 'Muslims are very compassionate; their hospitality is unbelievable and they are so soft-hearted — they cannot go past a beggar without giving something. I remember the garbage carts pulled by donkeys and accompanied by dozens of poor children. Without fail the women always put food out for them on plates. I found this instinctive generosity everywhere. And what messages do we get over here?' For a minute she became very upset. '"They chop off people's hands and stone the women." It's so distorted! It's not representative of those countries at all!'

For a non-Muslim to make supportive statements about Islam is a very effective way of answering the religious bigots. Muslims never quite achieve the same credibility in their own defence.

Jutta had lived among Muslims overseas; she respected them, but was also capable of calling a spade a spade and voicing her disappointment. 'I felt disapproved of today,' she said quietly, 'not because of my criticism, but because of my values. I sensed a lot of disapproval of Australian women in the air. You know, I may not wear *hijab*, I may colour and perm my hair and wear short sleeves, but that doesn't make me a bad woman.' And by extension, I thought, wearing the *hijab* might not make you the perfect Muslim woman either. But that day, at the conference, it certainly made the participants feel like 'one of the mob' for a change.

'After interviewing a number of Muslim women, I believe they really do think Australian women are sluts!' Pamela Bone is a leader writer and columnist with the *Age* newspaper. Her fascination with Islam grew gradually, starting in her early days as an ethnic affairs writer.

I winced at her opening remark. Our discussion centred around the tensions I often thought I observed between Anglo-Australian feminists and Muslim women. I was testing my theory that this might be partly caused by Muslim women appearing to speak from the moral high ground of the modest, chaste homemaker confronting the 'painted Jezebel'.

'How can you be so sure that that's how they feel? Is it something you sense?' I asked.

'I know it because they've said it to me ... not in so many words perhaps, but more like, "We don't want our daughters to grow up like Australian women." They think we are loose women and I have had this said to my face!'

I was staggered. I had imagined that the 'moral high ground' reproaches took a slightly more subtle form. Pamela was a well-informed journalist whose reporting on Muslims was usually balanced and reasonable.

'I once interviewed a young Muslim woman from

Yugoslavia,' she said. 'She told me she was a practising Muslim but that she refused to wear the *hijab*. I included her views in the article I was writing on Muslims. The following week I heard from several Muslim women who were upset that I had included her in the story. They insisted she wasn't a representative Muslim woman!'

But fortunately all was not hubris and folly. Pamela was very respectful of the strong family-values messages she had received from her readings of the Qur'an and her meetings with Muslims. 'What Muslim women are saying today is the same as Catholic women were saying thirty years ago.'

'The irony is,' I agreed, 'that Islam's emphasis on morality and family values has so much in common with mainstream Anglo community values, yet it never gets a mention.'

I found no shortage of women at the conference wishing to talk, but most wanted to remain anonymous. Non-Muslim women were happy to talk to me on the spot, and I stored away the names and telephone numbers of Muslim women who wanted more time and privacy. One woman, whom I shall call Deirdre, quietly observed that from an outsider's point of view there were two different levels of dialogue going on: 'official speak' from the dais and private conversations behind the scenes. 'The *hijab* makes everyone seem the same, but don't believe it! Who are the representative Muslim women, and does it really matter?' she argued. 'I sense that there are many different kinds of Muslim women out there who keep their mouths tightly closed.' She thought they appeared wary of each other, watching. 'It's as if they're waiting for someone to make a slip — "Oops! I've gone too far!" They don't want to open up in front of non-Muslims.'

18

A small piece of cloth

'When we see a Muslim woman walk down the street wearing the *hijab,* it makes us feel as if she is betraying everything we believe in. You can try to convince us otherwise, but that is the general belief among our feminist circle. We simply can't identify with Muslim women.'

Symbol of betrayal or symbol of religious commitment and solidarity? Travelling from state to state, I sensed an ambivalence — even outright hostility — towards that small piece of cloth. Each side regards the scarf as a symbol with a different meaning, as the pendulum of misunderstanding swings from side to side: to some, a sign of betrayal or female submission to male oppression, and to others a rallying point on a range of fascinating religious, political, psychological and other personal issues all to do with self-identity. Within Australia, in the vast majority of cases, a remarkable spectrum of motives for wearing the *hijab* is held together by the element of personal choice. This is often the antithesis of what those who oppose wearing the *hijab* want to hear and are prepared to believe. We all show a reluctance to rethink stereotypes we are wedded to. It's like parting with a favourite pair of boots or an old jumper — we know we should throw it away, it really is getting tatty, but we've had it for so long ...

Staring one another in the face, quite angrily at times, are two different ways of looking at power, status and male–female relations. One belongs to a western, often white, middle-class framework and causes problems when applied gratuitously outside the historical and social contexts in which it developed. The other way is diverse, complex and bound up with the continuing efforts of feudal and traditional societies to shrug off colonial pasts — efforts which put them in danger of stumbling into fresh pits of cultural imperialism dug by well-meaning but impatient western women.

Narrow-mindedness is universal and not the preserve of one side only. There are also opinionated Muslim women in danger of stumbling into pits they themselves have dug with their constant and automatic rejection of anything western as un-Islamic and inferior.

Hostility towards the *hijab* comes mostly from non-Muslim women rather than men. The anti-*hijab* wave cuts across boundaries of class, ethnicity and education. You find these feelings hiding in shopping malls, government offices, classrooms and on university campuses. 'Who do they think they are?' 'Where do they think they are?' 'When in Rome …' — a long, wailing Greek chorus of disapproval.

'We have this custom in our part of Lebanon,' said Afraa. 'When you are newly married you stick a piece of dough on top of the door. If the dough stays there, it means good luck!'

Afraa came to Australia from Lebanon eight years ago in an arranged marriage. One day she enrolled in a community development course at her local college. She was excited because for the first time she had a real opportunity to meet and talk to non-Muslim women on a regular basis. Unfortunately, things didn't work out as she expected. Perhaps she was naive not to realise that others would see her as different. Each time she attended it was almost like running a gauntlet, she explained. Lined up on either side were young women who displayed, by her account, a voyeurism tinged with childish overtones. 'What's it like wearing that bag?' 'Let me try it on !'

'They laughed when I told them how I got married. "When you get older," they said, "he'll take a second wife and then a third."

'"It's not like that," I tried to protest, but they didn't seem to believe me.

'"Don't tell us that," they'd say. "We know the men have four wives!"

'"Do you wear your scarf in bed? Do you have any hair on your body at all? Do you use condoms?"'

This was beyond teasing and jesting; much more like a form of harassment. We were not talking about schoolgirls picking on the newcomer with the funny accent and the funny name; these were young women doing a community development course — which, one would imagine, had something to do with social justice and sensitivity. Common decency would seem a part of it too.

In effect, Afraa said to them, 'This is my life. Would you like to know about it?' and they answered, 'Don't tell us, we already know, thanks, and what we know we don't like!' And the door slammed shut.

Afraa lurched from one mishap to the next. In a class discussion on gay couples adopting children, she announced that while she could imagine lesbians adopting and raising children, gay men shouldn't be allowed to do the same. A lesbian classmate walked out and later made an official complaint about Afraa's intolerance. The class lecturer formally requested Afraa to read the class rules on respecting other people's beliefs.

For many non-Muslims, the veiling and seclusion of women symbolise Islam itself.

An Arabic-speaking Christian, cheerful, articulate and

intelligent, Joe Wachim knows everybody and everybody knows Joe in Melbourne. For some years now, Joe has been monitoring the Australian media's treatment of Muslims and people of Arabic-speaking background. He has a river of stories showing the media's propensity for moulding stereotypes and presenting them as authentic portrayals.

As a non-Muslim Arab, Joe and his community found themselves vilified during the 1991 Gulf War along with Muslims both Arab and non-Arab. 'At the height of the war hysteria, a certain commercial television current affairs program contacted me. They needed help in organising an interview with "some Arabs".' His voice dripped with sarcasm. 'The enthusiastic young reporter made some suggestions. He would really prefer "A room full of Arab women," is how he put it to me, "preferably wearing those things on their head, and it would be really terrific if they were all covered in black"! He was really placing an order — for the standard Muslim female doll. The Australian media concentrate on producing images of difference and contrast; the headlines and the television cameras seem to thrive on that. I am convinced that if camera crews were given the opportunity to film a group of ten Arab women, this is what would happen. First they would write off the women not wearing the *hijab*, that is the Christian women and the Muslim women who don't cover. Of the remaining "veiled" women, anyone in black would be seen as ideal, but one whose face and hands were also covered, leaving only her eyes exposed, would be even better!'

Dr Ahmad Shboul, Associate Professor of Arabic and Islamic Culture at the University of Sydney, relished the opportunity to talk about the media's 'distorted images' — the images audiences love to hate. He believes the camera distorts reality brazenly. 'There is little truth in the expression that the camera never lies. What the camera does is fall in love with the exotic image: the fierce eyes, the turban and beard, the veiled woman. With television, rationality simply disappears — you lose the story because the image takes over.' Often, he said, someone the camera will love is chosen ahead of someone who knows what he is talking about. 'What do journalists read about Muslims?' he wondered. 'How are they educated? Are journalists new-wave orientalists without realising it?' He was referring to the tendency of westerners to stereotype the 'mysterious Orient' as a land of oil, sand, camels, mirages, harems and so on, and the power of those stereotypes to reduce any actual experience of the Middle East — in all its complex diversity — to a set of predictable conclusions.

Why do Muslim women wear the *hijab*? And in Australia of all places?

Dr Shboul thought it might be in part a reaction to media distortions. 'When the images in society around you are so different your identity becomes tied up with questions of self-esteem. One way of handling this psychologically is to deny this part of you. Another way is to show solidarity.'

Lakemba had taught me about the religious revival in the 1980s. The vast majority of Muslim women immigrants had worn no head covering until they came to Australia. I had encountered many cases of women only starting to wear it after living in Australia for twenty years or more.

'My mother wore *purdah*, but I was brought up the modern way with western education, and *purdah* was associated with traditional ways and not modern, progressive ways. Then a few years ago I made my *haj* and it seemed so natural to wear traditional garments. I thought, why take them off? I wanted to be close to Allah, to please God and so I continued wearing them. I don't understand why Australian people object to this. Mary, the mother of Jesus, wore the same clothes. What can be wrong with this?'

'I used to be very fashion conscious, but last Ramadan I thought it was about time. I was getting older; it just seemed time to settle down.'

Jamila Ahmad, my friend from Sydney, offers a number of reasons — some religious and some psychological. She also told me she enjoys the bonding with other Muslim women that wearing the *hijab* offers. As a convert to Islam she found this important. 'I have opted out of competition with dressing. I no longer get whistles on the street, just straight-out abuse, but I think I prefer it that way.'

Wearing *hijab* may symbolise variously a reaffirmation of faith, an assertion of Islamic identity, a rejection of western values, and revolutionary, national or political sentiment. In Australia some educated second-generation Muslim women see it as a feminist power statement by which women restrict access by men to their bodies, their looks and their personal space.

Women who do and women who don't:

Lina was adamant. 'I am not being weak, but I think the *hijab* of the mind is more important. Islam for me is an internal thing. Prayer and how I behave to others are also important. I know too many women who wear the *hijab* but their actions and the way they talk about other women make a mockery of the *hijab*. Covering doesn't necessarily make you a better Muslim. This doesn't apply to everyone. I respect those devout women who are models for us all.'

Zora said, 'Sometimes I'm looked down upon for not wearing it by certain Muslims who consider that the *hijab* symbolises all the qualities of a decent, virtuous Muslim woman.' By now, she had learned to turn a deaf ear to the whispers and innuendo.

'Have you heard of the saying,' I asked, '"Each strand of hair you show means you have slept with forty men".' She nodded, yes.

Zora had her own offering. 'My mother used to tell me that every hair that shows, in the life hereafter will become a snake biting at you. It's a very old superstition. Mum says I should wear *hijab* as a sign of decency and respect for God's wishes and the commandments we all have to obey. The *hijab* is a badge of honour and if I don't wear it, then I, too, am without honour. That makes me mad — I really resent it!'

Khulsoom said, 'I don't wear it because I honestly don't think it is required or necessary today. But of course I cover when I go inside a mosque — that is compulsory — and if I were in the presence of a shaykh I would also cover my head out of respect. So now and then I wear the *dupatta*, the scarf Benazir Bhutto wears. I do not wear the Middle East version. Why should I? It is not my tradition.'

'Times have changed,' said Halima from Fiji. 'You can see this in the way that Muslim men dress. How many in Australia or even in their homeland wear clothes like the Prophet (peace be upon Him)? In the Prophet's time men wore turbans. Yes, in those days they covered their heads inside and outside the mosque. Today men only wear a head covering inside the mosque. But if the Prophet were alive today he would be dressed differently. It is not a big deal with my family. I believe the religious injunction is more to do with dressing modestly than with covering your hair. Anyway, that's my interpretation and I'm sticking by it!'

Everyone seemed to have a favourite *hijab* story. Adeeba is the soft-voiced fashion designer daughter of my Melbourne friend Rokaya. She wears *hijab* proudly and elegantly. 'Being stared at is a part of my life and it doesn't bother me now,' she said. She had fun classifying the stares: 'There is the plain curious stare with no animosity attached — some look away when you stare back, and others don't; there are the hostile stares from those with their minds made up, and this comes more from women than from men. But the kids are really funny! A little four-year-old girl came up to me and asked, "Lady, are you a witch?" On another occasion I was out with a girlfriend who really dresses up exotically in bright coloured clothes and turban and this sweet little boy grabbed his mother's arm and yelled out, "Look, Mum, there's the Queen!"'

Not everyone, however, saw the lighter side. A male colleague said, 'One day an elderly Catholic nun came up to me. I will refrain from mentioning her order. She told me, "It is the poor Muslim women who particularly concern me. We run a number of programs aimed at disadvantaged women whom we want to see empowered and taking charge of their lives. We come across these Muslim women — totally oppressed — and it makes me really, really angry." She went on for some time about these victims and the veil and her anger at this.

'I said to her, "Wait a minute, sister! How long is it since you stopped wearing the veil? And do you feel that same level of anger when you see elderly Catholic nuns who still wear the veil?" In a sense it was a nasty question, I admit. But this intelligent, sensitive woman could not bring any of her understanding of the journey of Catholic women and their faith into her perspective on Muslim women and Islam. After all, the veil worn by nuns not so long ago was once a symbol of intense faith. She couldn't sympathise with Muslim women as she no doubt could with the "old, fuddy-duddy nuns" as she probably fondly thought of them.'

'It all comes down to that peculiar Aussie obsession with the importance of outward appearance.' Moira Rayner was Commissioner of Equal Opportunity in Victoria, though soon to leave that office. 'When I first saw women wearing the *hijab* in Melbourne,' she went on, 'I recall a feeling of slight distaste. But until I actually met a woman who wore it, all I saw was someone in unusual clothes and my initial reaction was, this is startling, this is odd. Very soon after, I met intelligent, articulate, strong women who covered as a matter of choice. But until then I was as guilty as anyone else of stereotyping. The one thing I wouldn't like, however, would be a community that *insisted* that women wear the *hijab* — that would be horrible! But in the end it really is none of anyone's damned business what Muslim women wear!

'When you begin to draw the attention of the ordinary Aussie to the injustice of taunting women and children, tearing scarves from heads, spitting at them, throwing rocks at Muslim school buses and other dreadful incidents, they will tend on the whole to behave. I really admire some of the Australian Muslim women I've met. You should see them getting stuck into the men about the equality of women in the Qur'an, arguing the toss with them politely but firmly. It was a real eye-opener for me!'

And so the fuss continues over a plain piece of cloth. Nuns wear habits, Christians wear crosses and Jews, the Star of David. What does it matter if other people, for religious reasons, want to wear distinctive clothes as a religious sign — a reminder of God and a show of solidarity?

Symbols change and often the very symbol of oppression from the past is reinterpreted and becomes adopted as a rallying point — redefined all over by subsequent generations.

Today many young Muslim women in Australia choose to wear 'the veil' or *hijab* — their symbol from the past. Yet not so long ago, their grandmothers and great-aunts marched in the streets demanding the right not to wear the veil for what it symbolised to them — exclusion from education, public life and employment. Seventy years ago Egyptian feminist leader Huda Sha'rawi symbolically threw her veil into the Mediterranean at Alexandria. Her husband divorced her for refusing to wear it. Overseas the struggle still continues. But for migrant women, in Australia at least, wearing the *hijab* is a way of asserting their religious and cultural identities.

19

Hypothetically speaking

Nada Roude and I first met under difficult circumstances. We were both taking part in Geoffrey Robertson's ABC Television discussion program, 'Hypothetical'. It was shortly after the end of the Gulf War. On the night of our debut in front of a large live audience, I mentioned to Nada in the tiny make-up room, that of the three women on the panel — there were thirteen men — we two were Muslims. Our religious styles were dissimilar and I half suspected that the wily Mr Robertson might try to set the cat among the pigeons by bringing up some topical Middle Eastern issues. So I proposed that we declare a moratorium. Nada agreed to a show of overall solidarity which would still allow us to differ on minor points.

There had been no rehearsal, no list of questions or advance notice of any topics. The theme was multiculturalism, that was all we knew. Geoffrey Robertson, QC, paced around the stage like a restless tiger with steel claws hidden, waiting to pounce as the mood seized him. His velvet tones duped nobody, for we all knew by now what to expect given his reputation for cut-throat scenarios.

Nada showed her true colours that night. Others like myself might field questions with attempts at humour and flashes of cynicism, but Nada knew that to many watching, she represented the face of Islam in Australia. As she grappled with one hypothetical dilemma after another, the camera revealed a face unused to masking its true feelings. She refused to play at being flippant, and not a soul watching could have doubted her honesty; there was no guile, no game playing, no seeking the approbation of the audience — just Nada and her conscience.

The final dilemma Mr Robertson presented for us to wrestle with was a nasty one, which manacled a question of life and death to one of loyalty.

'You are on board a Qantas flight which strays over Iraqi airspace and two Iraqi fighter jets force the captain to land. Armed men board the plane, ordering all passengers with American or Australian passports to identify themselves and leave the plane — they will be interned. The other passengers will be permitted to fly on to Greece.

'What would you do?' he asked one of the panel, a former Hungarian citizen. Under pressure, the man admitted that he would conceal his Australian citizenship and use his Hungarian documents instead. Two other panellists joined him.

Our ringmaster turned to Nada. 'So, Nada, they look at you and think, "Ah! A Lebanese sister!" What do you answer, Nada?' She paused and frowned, biting her lips. 'Well, make up your mind, Nada,' he continued relentlessly. 'It's either off the plane or onto Greece! Are you more Lebanese than Australian, or more Australian than Lebanese?'

'I would ...' she hesitated, 'I would have to say, Australian.'

'Are you being patriotic?' he persisted.

'Australia has become my identity. I'm an Australian Muslim. I can't compromise on that.'

On that evening at the World Trade Centre in Melbourne, Nada's reply slammed the door in the face of the many people who around this time were accusing

Muslims and Arabs of being traitors to Australia and un-Australian in their values.

Abu Anees wrote a regular column called 'Fair Dinkum' in the *Australasian Muslim Times*. He had recently written a bold article based on an idea that I found interesting. Instead of talking about the role of women in Islam, he suggested, why not talk about the role of men?

> I would love to see a woman speaker talking to a gathering of men and reminding them of their position in Islam. What [women's] rights are and how [men] have failed to fulfil them.
>
> I would also love to see an imam talking to a gathering of women and describing how men are not fulfilling their obligations towards them. How much of men's behaviour is guided by Arab, Afghan, or Australian culture and how much by the teachings of Islam.

'I'm getting a bit tired, and I think many women are too, of listening to talks about the role of women in Islam,' Anees complained when we met. 'Whenever there is a meeting where Islam and women are raised together, this is the only topic you hear. It seems never ending. When an imam from the mosque is invited to speak to a group of women, it's always about the role or status of women in Islam. Editors and journalists are no different. And even if you find someone more enlightened, they only broaden the topic to the family in Islam, or polygamy in Islam. And so it continues — you can't seem to break the cycle!'

'You almost feel you know the passages by heart. What would you rather people talked about, then?'

'Real life,' he said without hesitation. 'It's time, I think, for women to stop playing roles and for men to stop reassuring women about their status. Women could also contribute to discussions on education, human rights, politics, conflict resolution and anything else at all.'

'Why, then,' I asked, 'do women continue with the same old monologues about their religious status, religious obligations and so on — almost like a set piece?'

'Well,' Anees said, 'it's very simple — because they are patronised by men and the agendas are also set by men. Too many women are conditioned to accept men setting the limits of their discussion! Women need to take the initiative more! I can't find any basis for this so-called traditional behaviour in the Shari'ah or the Hadith.'

Whenever I looked at the books on sale at Islamic bookshops, I never noticed any by Muslim feminists like the Moroccan sociologist Fatima Mernissi, Egyptian Salwa Bakr, Palestinian Liana Badr and Lebanese writers Ghada al-Sammam and Hanan al-Shaykh. So far such writers were unknown to all but one or two of the Muslim women I had spoken to. Perhaps they were regarded as too secular? Too progressive? Too expensive? The majority of the pamphlets and books available were written by religious scholars and teachers, often in apologistic tones and without much of a critical framework, at least to my mind. These were mostly inexpensive publications, directed especially at women without tertiary education who might want to teach themselves more about Islam and prime themselves with ready-made arguments to convince their critics that Islam was not an oppressive religion. They also appealed to busy women who might want to refer quickly to a salient point — women who often represented groups and associations and regularly faced tricky questions. Many of these publications were subsidised by large religious bodies and also, no doubt, by the Saudi Arabian government, whose petrodollars often supported the more formalistic and conservative Islamic schools of thought.

Asking for more critical, interrogatory books would once have earned you a ticking off from men and women alike who believed that most non-Muslims, and even some western-educated or western-conditioned Muslims, drank from a poisoned chalice — a deadly libation poured by biased orientalists. Lately, however, the sheer volume of literature by Muslim women and men taking a critical approach has muted their complaints.

Many of the staunchest allies of women seeking reforms in countries like Egypt, Algeria, Pakistan and Jordan have been liberal, educated Muslim men. They are implacably opposed by conservatives — men and women — who are unwilling to relinquish power and want to go forward by going backwards. Yet as Fatima Mernissi reminds us, both groups seek change. Women activists want access to education and employment and more power both in the public domain and in their own lives. Ultra-orthodox men and women want to turn the clock back to what they see as the golden age of Islam. Mernissi sees the two groups as bound together in an almost perverse tug of war.

While the acknowledgement that Islam was originally a great instrument of social reform for women seemed to be the starting point for progressive Muslims overseas, it often seemed the end of the journey for Australian Muslim women. Why was this so? Perhaps the answer had something to do with the drive to retain a religious identity in a secular state, the feelings of a beleaguered minority seeing itself perpetually under attack. On the other hand, many of the resources which middle-class Muslim feminists overseas were struggling to obtain for themselves, or for their less fortunate sisters — education and legal resources in particular — were more readily accessible in Australia. Surely the advantage of being able to control your own fertility and determine how you would space your children was invaluable? The institutions of social justice in this secular society were helping the development of a strong cadre of Muslim women who were making choices, changing their lives and acting as role models for others. But sadly, it seemed that if they wore the *hijab*, they faced discrimination in employment.

True, we were not living under Shari'ah law, as many would like. But one could argue that in many Islamic countries, the courts administering Shari'ah family law were failing to provide women with the kind of legal protection available to them in Australia, and often not implementing the law as it was originally intended.

Bilal Cleland, a red-headed Muslim convert of Scottish descent and ruddy complexion, traced his Australian ancestry back to the First Fleet. A former Anglican, he strongly supported Muslim women's rights. It was always a relief to visit him, for I knew I could voice my thoughts without fear of censure even if we disagreed, as we sometimes did. 'Many westerners,' Bilal hammered home with his usual energy, 'think Islamic fundamentalism is dangerous. There is fanaticism among some Muslims and that is dangerous, but to go back to the Qur'an to find out what it says about the rights of women and children, for example, is not wrong or dangerous.' (How strange, I thought, that no one ever called the Saudi Arabians fundamentalists. Was the term 'fundamentalist' reserved for the perceived enemies of the West?)

'It is clear,' Bilal continued, 'when you do go back to the Qur'an, that women's rights have been taken away from them by men. This is not Islamic, by which I mean that it has been done without the authority of Islam, but in the name of Islam! Women have to learn to fight back! In a society where women are being denied the opportunity for education, you can be sure that their rights are being taken away.' He paused, and mentally I started to tick off the countries in my mind.

'Look at Muslim women in Australia. First, there are those who are very aware and conscious and active, but there are also groups of women who are deprived of their rights — the non-joiners who sometimes aren't *allowed* to join.' He stopped to glare at me as if I was personally responsible. 'And it's not always the wicked husbands, you know. It's often grandmothers and mothers-in-law, aunts and an entire female network who insist vehemently that "Muslim women don't do this!" and that all Muslim women need is to learn how to read the Qur'an and know a few Hadith. They determine this to be proper religious behaviour for women and their sole obligation.'

But Bilal sees some light at the end of the tunnel. 'Change is in the air and more and more women are being drawn into activities. Ignorant pre-Islamic practices, especially, are being challenged as never before.'

Female genital mutilation. For weeks I had been procrastinating, but finally I wrote down the three words, and as they stared back at me, I wondered how to proceed from here. Initially, I had considered omitting any reference to this dreadful practice. Like other Muslim women, I hesitated to speak openly lest I be misunderstood and once more expose Islam to attack. But with the increase in immigration from the Horn of Africa and the spread of community health centres and midwives, there was growing evidence of women who had been mutilated as children in their homelands. Most of these women were now mothers themselves and there was increasing concern that they were having their daughters 'circumcised'.

By mentioning female genital mutilation in a book on Muslims, would I be fostering the idea that it was an

Islamic practice? Or was I, the arch-critic of the 'defend-Islam-at-all-cost' approach, about to fall into the same trap myself? But distancing oneself from abhorrent practices does not help stop them. Protecting one's religion from persistent and ill-informed attack is laudable, I told myself. But it would be reprehensible to ignore wrongs that are associated with it.

The fact remains that neither the Qur'an nor the Hadith contains any mention of — or justification for — the practice of female 'circumcision'. It seems essential to repeat this, ad nauseam if necessary, as it continues to be wrongly identified with Islam. Today in Australia, more religious leaders are declaring this publicly, urged by Muslim women's groups to announce it loudly in the mosques.

Still, there are in Australia small numbers of Muslim women who have been mutilated as children in societies where this is a traditional practice. Many feminists fear that these women will continue the practice with their own daughters. How do you break the cycle of tradition, the cycle of pressure and expectation placed on women by community and relatives?

Special legislation was the answer, said former Labor MP Franca Arena — and others — in New South Wales where this solution eventually won the day after considerable community debate in 1994. Workers from community-based organisations in Melbourne, where many women from the Horn of Africa have settled, opposed this approach. 'It's already illegal under existing laws against child assault and grievous bodily harm,' they argued. 'Why drive it underground? Why further victimise the victims? Spend the money on education.'

However, in 1995 all states decided to fall in line with New South Wales and opted for special legislation specifically outlawing female genital mutilation. Western Australia is the last state to fall in line, but expects to pass its own law in early 2003. State and federal governments since 1994 have, therefore, moved from implacable opposition to the acceptance of the need for special legislation. Australia has thus joined a number of western countries prepared to take a stand, including Sweden, the United Kingdom, Canada and France. The old arguments that the problem should be contained within the Child Abuse Protective laws have been defeated.

For twenty years Franca Arena listened patiently at international conferences, concerned by the lack of global progress towards ending the practice. She had no time for women who said, 'Leave us alone and let us handle this tradition in our own way.' She found this proposition unacceptable, especially as women were perpetrating this practice on other women.

'If the Chinese had brought the practice of foot binding with them to Australia when they first immigrated here and if we had seen young girls with the bones of their feet broken and their feet bound tightly, what would we have said? We would have been outraged! But because genital mutilation involves a part of the body that is not visible and because people do not know much about it, we leave it alone.'

Not any more.

V

Waiting in the wings

Youth is strength, for the sun does not brighten the afternoon as much as it does in the morning … and during its youth a tree brings forth its fruit, while after that all trees give nothing but wood.

Mustafa al-Rafi'ee, twentieth-century Muslim writer

20

Soban and Anna

'I lived with my parents until I was thirty and got married. For a Turkish guy that's nothing unusual. Who better to look after you than your mother or your sister. Hey, I shouldn't be saying this to you, I know, but in my teens life was pretty good. I had the best of both worlds. "Sis, bring me a glass of water!" or "Sis, prepare something for me to eat!" — no matter how late I came home at night. Looking back now, I feel ashamed, but at the time it was normal practice.

'My wife has changed me a lot, but I still tell her, "Darling, Allah forbid that anything should happen to you, but if you should pass away, I would be back with my mum like a flash or I would have to get married again," because I just can't live on my own! Did I mention that my wife's a devout Catholic?

'As I say life was pretty good. My parents indulged me; after all, I was their son. You say I sound like a tyrant? Oh! Thinking back, I was really awful! I liked to control my two sisters, even the one older than me. If I caught any boy talking to them I would chase him away. I mean it. Once I saw this boy talking to my sister, who was about fifteen or sixteen at the time. I grabbed my baseball bat and ran downstairs. I hit him, and he didn't come around again. My older sister missed out on a lot; she got married young. When my young sister kept crying to Mum that she wanted to go to a disco like everyone else, I said to her, "Look, Sis, I'll take you," and I did. A few years later, when she went to uni, I would hear her say, "Sorry, Mum, I'll be home about ten tonight, we've got something on at uni."'

Soban was thirty-two and had a natural charm born of confidence nurtured by a doting mother. His open, sunny personality simply expected to be liked. This and his good looks — curly brown hair, a neat moustache and a winning smile — made it hard to take offence, even when he made outrageously chauvinistic statements. His unselfconsciousness and absence of vanity were quite disarming.

But in his youth? What an odious little pasha, I thought. How I would have hated being your sister!

'I used to be a Bald Eagle. You've never heard of the Skinheads and the Sharpies — the gangs? Maybe you remember the Chiko Rolls, the AC-DC? Anyway, in the mid seventies the kids from North Melbourne had a gang against us kids from the housing estates in Kensington. I'm kind of light even for a Turk, but the Australians would say, "Gee, you're dark!" I stood out, so I got belted up quite a lot. They'd gang up on you, slap you a few times, kick you around a bit ... that was it until the next time. That was one of the reasons Dad said I had to go to martial arts. My dad comes from the old tradition, the old Ottoman thing — you know, a very proud race and all that — and as far as he was concerned, you just never lose in a fight. So if I ever came home crying, I'd get belted up by him as well. Even if I lost I'd have to say, "I won, Dad (with blood running down my nose, a black eye), I won Dad. You should see the other guy!"

'The Aussies could never distinguish between the Greeks, the Italians, the Yugoslavs and us. We Turks shaved our heads and called ourselves the Bald Eagles. Back in Turkey you have your hair trimmed very short at school, so some of the parents just thought we were good Turkish boys going back to the old ways. They didn't know we had a gang. We did it just to look mean and tough, of course. And we made a name for ourselves. You know how it is. You win a few fights and your reputation grows, and you become a "living legend". Later on we admitted a few Lebanese and Italians. After three or four years we had proven our group strength, so the young ones coming after us didn't have to go through what we experienced. In fact in the mid eighties it became trendy to be ethnic, trendy to be a wog.

'We'd dress up to the nines — sleek hairstyles, gold chains, suits, and strut along Lygon Street. The Australians never did anything like that! With us it's different. Back home, you may not have enough money in your pocket to buy a can of Coke, but you dress up well!

'How clean do you want this kept? Is this an R-rated tape? The Anglo girls went for toughness and ruggedness in the seventies — the Steve McQueen, leather jacket, macho look. In the eighties they went for class and sophistication. Now in the nineties they go for the quiet, sensitive new-age guy. Anyway, the parents had no idea what was going on. They didn't know the Anglo girls were hanging around us Turkish boys. I'd better remind you that this was long before I met my wife!

'When I eventually met Anna, my wife, I kept her on the sidelines for six years. No one knew I even had a girlfriend. I was twenty-six or twenty-seven then, still living at home of course. Don't laugh! You know how it is with us. Whenever Anna wanted to talk to me on the phone — I couldn't break my mother's heart, you see — she'd let the phone ring once and hang up. Then I would return her call. I'd come home some days and Mum would say, "Son, please ring Telecom. Our phone is broken; it just rings once and then it stops." I'd ring Anna back and pretend I was speaking to a guy, and after we'd finished our talk I'd stay on for a minute faking it, talking rough to a mate. May Allah forgive me! Anna was so understanding, though. That's one of the reasons I married her. At first I thought I'd have a fling and leave, but it wasn't as easy as that.

'Looking back, I don't think my mum was taken in after all. Because after six years, as I was driving her to work one morning she turned to me and said, "You know, Son, I think it's time for you to bring Steve home."

'"Mum, what are you saying?" (I always called Anna Steve, you see, on the phone.) "Your father and I have talked it over and we think it is time."

'I was sure she didn't think I was gay, so obviously she knew. Then I panicked! I completely panicked! "Mum," I said, "she's not like you might think. She's not tall and blonde … she's Italian!"

'"Doesn't matter. You're the one who's going to sleep with her, not me. So just bring her home! Please!"

'Well, I brought her home and they got on like a house on fire.'

'Yes, for six years I played Steve.'

Six months had passed since my interview with Soban before I finally met Anna — just the two of us — in a Lygon Street coffee shop. Anna was sophisticated, intelligent and composed as she recalled this period.

'At first I was rather amused by the pretence,' she told me. 'As a female growing up in an Italian household I had done the same thing. But now instead of a girl doing it, it was a boy. Soban always presumed that I would understand, but that …' didn't remove the hurt, I mentally filled in.

'The day he was told to "bring Steve along," I felt as if I'd been summoned. I was not happy. A few months before, I'd been ready to abandon the relationship. But he pleaded with me. So I did it for him and not for me. For weeks I would get depressed just thinking about it. Instead of feeling relieved that everything was out in the open, I felt it was coming at the worst possible time in our six-year relationship.

'Can I recall that day? Absolutely! It was a day that I would prefer to forget. I hadn't slept much the night before and woke up at six. I started going through my wardrobe because Soban had drilled me about what to wear and what not to wear. In the long run I ended up choosing a skirt a lot shorter than Soban would have liked, just to the knee. With this I wore a long-sleeved blouse — on a hot day — with my usual make-up. When Soban picked me up, he was very nervous and I felt sick to my stomach. "You must kiss my parents' hands," he told me. "You will lose my mother's respect if you don't." So I did. It is the only time I have ever done it, and I still regret it because it was not sincere. I felt phony — it reminded me of my life of pretence with my own family which I'd hoped was behind me; I'd left home years before. I sat there being examined with my knees jammed together tugging my skirt down. I found out later that his mother had given his two sisters the job of giving me the once over. They had to check how long my nails were, the length of my skirt — even how big my behind was!

'Soban's mother didn't speak much to me, as her English was very limited. It was mainly the older sister, the traditional one, who carried out the interrogation. Soban had disappeared by now. The really big question was why I didn't live at home.

'The younger sister seemed more sympathetic, but I was wary because I'd had an unfortunate encounter with her once before — she'd been rude to me, treating me like her brother's short-term floozie. The hours dragged by. Finally afternoon tea was served and as I was drinking my tea and eating the cakes, I could feel Soban's mother watching me like a hawk. Soban told me later that she was very taken with my teeth! Were they really mine? I felt like a horse.

'But Soban thought the day had gone fantastically well. He was in seventh heaven. He hadn't been aware of my discomfort — controlled distress, as I like to think of it now. Finally they had met me, he thought. There had been no scenes and I hadn't made any faux pas. Everything was going to turn out fine.

'What happened next? Well, the family imagined that we would get engaged now. But after that initial visit I didn't see them again for two months. Soban's mother would send me messages through one daughter or the other. I really felt I was getting roped in, slowly but surely.

'But even before the family inspection I had felt really unsure about our relationship. Over the past year Soban had changed. He'd become selfish, self-centred. He spoke like an ignorant man and made ridiculous demands. My clothing, my necklines, my sleeves — everything was wrong. At first I thought it was more male jealousy than Islamic consciousness, but then I noted that he became very uneasy if I was around when certain of his friends were visiting. As our love grew stronger, it seemed my Christianity began to frighten him. He felt out of his depth, insecure. He needed support and so he turned to the group.'

'I admit it. Before I met Anna, I was a bit of a playboy. How old was I? About twenty-five then. I drank and went to discos and lived a double life — believe me, I wasn't alone in this. There were the usual dirty "soccer weekends". "Off to Canberra, Mum! There's a soccer tournament on."

'Really, I'm not boasting about these times. You come home and your mum asks you, "How did the tournament go, Son?" And you do a double take for a minute, until you remember. It happens — Turkish boys having their fling before they settle down and marry a good Muslim Turkish girl. You know deep down that you are not going to marry that other person.'

Have your fling but don't marry them. Soban had broken that rule.

'I became more religious when I realised that I was serious about Anna and there would be children. It was a catalyst, you might say. We have a lot of Turkish groups, or *jummats*, in Melbourne you know — some solely religious, some more political. My group was more religious and I started praying regularly. This was five years ago. Before that I guess you'd call me a cultural Turk rather than a religious Turk. I no longer belong to the group.

'At the moment I'm a four-timer — I pray four times a day. Much better than being a two-timer, don't you think? My aim is to become a five-timer. But the morning prayer is murder for me. That's no excuse, I know, and *Insha'Allah* I'll get better and won't stay in bed. So at the moment I'm not an all-rounder, but with God's help I will battle my *nafs*, my selfish, physical side.

'My wife pledged that our children will be brought up as Muslims. There are no big religious tensions between us — we've resolved all that. We might have little arguments, but making up is always fun! As she is a Christian and a follower of the Book, it is permissible for me to marry her. I usually drive her to church, but being inside makes me very uncomfortable, I get upset with all the statues and everything. Yes, I'm worried about *shirik*, or idolatry. But religion is not a problem and we communicate very well with each other.

'Yes, I would say I have made most of the compromises. There was so much we had to resolve. We had always fought right from the beginning, but the period between my meeting his parents and our marriage — it was about a year

— was the crucial time. There was the question of children — Soban was very concerned about their upbringing. He'd become much more religious since I'd first met him. I have put my foot down on certain things. The kids are to be brought up as Muslims religiously, but I don't want any strict or strong cultural intervention. When Soban says this or that needs to be done, my first question is, "Is it cultural or religious?" I certainly did a lot of soul-searching before the marriage. It's suicidal not to consider these things first when we come from such vastly different backgrounds.

"I knew from the beginning that our relationship was a dramatic step for him. But I couldn't help wondering, is this really worth it? Why am I bothering to do this? He always expected me to understand that he had a very strong bond with his mother and that he feared shattering that bond. At times this would make me angry. Was he more concerned about his mother or about our relationship?'

'My relationship with my father was always very distant. He came from a family where they revered their father so much that they called him uncle. Turkish boys have a much better relationship with their mothers than with their fathers.'

It escaped before I could stop it, 'You must make rotten husbands.'

'The next generation will be better,' he said softly. 'My mother is a wonderful woman. She is so soft-hearted. Once my father accidentally hit our dog with a stone — yes a lot of Turkish people have dogs, even some of my very religious brothers, but they never come inside and you wear a different set of clothes when you're walking them, playing with them or feeding them. Well, my poor father only meant to scare the dog, but he injured it slightly. None of us would talk to him; my mother wouldn't sleep with him for a month — she cooked his food but he had to serve himself. I heard him outside talking to the dog — he thought he was alone — when it came back from the vet's, apologising to it and saying he was sorry he'd hurt it.

'What did my mother think about me marrying Anna? Well, she cried a few times, of course, until I said to her, "Mum, I won't leave her! I won't marry her, then. I'll just leave home and live with her." But she didn't want me to sin. She'd tried her best to get me married once in my early twenties when we were visiting Turkey. All these young girls would come knocking on the door asking to see my sisters or saying, "I've dropped this in for Auntie," an endless parade. Afterwards she would ask me, "Well, did you like her, Son?" I'd play dumb and say, "What do you mean, Mum?" After the wedding, a few of her women friends commiserated with her but I thought to myself, "If Anna's mother had known we were getting married, she'd probably say exactly the same."

'But as I say Anna has changed me. Any sons we have will learn how to cook, iron and look after themselves. The first time my mother visited us and saw me get up to make the coffee, she nearly fell over!'

'Did you know his parents now spend most of their time in Turkey? I personally think it's better that way, although his mother is very nice to me now. I'm still a little distant with her, but it's my fault. We're living in their house at the moment in Lalor. It's our standard joke. I say to him, "You're thirty-two years old and you're still living at home!"

'I didn't introduce him to my parents until after we married. I'd had a falling-out with my mother and hadn't been home for years. We decided to go round one day and break the news. We'd steeled ourselves for the encounter — after all Soban was not just your run-of-the mill non-

Catholic. It was bad. Mum looked at me with steel in her eyes. "Did you get married in church?" "No," I answered. "You must get married in church!" "No," I said. We left and didn't go back for another two months. Now she adores him! Everyone does! He is probably my mother's favourite son-in-law. She's still worried about the Muslim side — she does her shopping in Brunswick where there are a lot of Turks and she doesn't always like what she sees. You know what I mean — little girls of four or five wearing scarves. And she has seen the film *Not Without My Daughter*.

'And she is worried he might take me to Turkey and, you know the story, make me a prisoner. Soban is a real tease and tells her, "Don't worry, Anna can keep the money and the passport!"

'I feel Soban is not so hung up about my religion any more. Once we used to have a lot of fights and he would get quite distraught about the Holy Trinity. He doesn't drive me to church so much any more, but he has come and sat in the church and listened to the sermon at Easter. I know it irritates him no end, but he does it for me and my family.

'My friends think he's great, too. They're predominantly Anglo-Australians. Knowing me would be as close as they have ever got to multiculturalism. You could say they're well educated and wealthy. Soban was the most "different" person they had ever met. And after they got used to the no alcohol, no pork business, they saw him as a bit of a novelty. They knew nothing of Islam and would ask him a lot of questions. Everyone likes his warmth. You know what he's like — he can be very entertaining — he's got a wealth of dirty jokes. People generally pause after meeting us for the first time and finding out that one of us is Catholic and the other Muslim. They seem more curious about me. Am I oppressed? How do we live? Do we have problems? And then they want our story and Soban loves that. As you can imagine, Soban relates well to women.

'I won't compromise on one thing, though. Our children must have a sound education — the best possible, even if it means they go to a Christian-based school. I am not keen on them going to Saturday Turkish school; I don't want them brainwashed. So how will they gain their Islamic education? Soban is confident that he will be able to direct it himself.

'One thing I must say is that I've never felt neglected by Soban. We are equal partners, but he is probably more devoted to me than I am to him. The odd couple is working!'

'Sometimes I get worried about my wife not being Muslim and tell her so. "Look, I have to tell you, darling, it's my duty and I love you." You could say that I'm preparing myself for the worst. What do I do if my daughters want to marry non-Muslims? What if my son introduces me to his gay lover? I would have to live with it, wouldn't I? If it was at the cost of not seeing them again, I would say, "Darling, if you are happy and you still keep your religion, then it's all right."'

21

Youth will dare

Musa Ilhan, a young Turkish-born weightlifter from Melbourne, had represented Australia at the Barcelona Olympics. We sat surrounded by his gleaming Australian Championship trophies and medals, but sport was not on his mind. He spoke from the heart. 'You think, "If I live strictly according to Islam, I'm going to be unacceptable to my friends and my mates and miss out on a lot." So you turn on your religion, run away, change your name to Tom and assimilate, and one day, you wake up crying and wondering why. Or you try and please your parents, because you love them and because of the sacrifices they've made for you, but you remain very unhappy. Or you can try to work out a new position.'

Muslim youth walk on tiptoe down a path of temptation. Their lives are a course of continuous negotiation, bargaining, and attempts to reach compromises with their parents. They want to please Mum and Dad, keep their friends 'on side', and be true to themselves. Parents, on the other side, circle the wagons. Terrible mistakes are made and some of them make headline news. People who think they have lost everything are not going to give up their children, the core of their identity, just like that! The family is the crucible of Muslim life, collective responsibility its lifeblood. It does not admit of infinite freedom for individuals to follow their own whims.

Dorothy Hoddinot, Acting Principal of Wiley Park Girls High School near Lakemba in Sydney, is an expert on the subject of parents' efforts to retain control of their children. She is very popular with Muslim parents, and Wiley Park, with its sensible multicultural policies, is a good example of a school that works hard at dealing with its culturally diverse student population.

'The old cry, "If you don't behave we'll send you back home," meaning they'll be shipped off overseas — always reminds me of the old bogey of threatening kids with boarding school or the convent,' said Dorothy. 'Parents are very clever. Some have their kids absolutely convinced that they are being made seriously ill by the children's disobedience or shows of disrespect. "It's really making Mum sick, Miss. I have to be careful. These arguments are bad for her high blood pressure, you know," one will say. Or, "I got home half an hour late, Miss, and Dad was so sick, Mum said he had heart failure. She nearly called the doctor!"'

Some households in the area were receiving their first dose of secondary education in the family, Dorothy said. She foresaw huge differences in attitudes between older and subsequent generations.

Dorothy was also worried by the attitudes of employers towards 'her girls'. 'Muslim girls who cover,' she told me in her crisp clear voice, 'are oppressed, but not by their own community. They have problems getting jobs no matter how well-qualified they are. The real prejudice comes from the community at large.'

Immigration takes its toll. One expects the changes in language, in customs, in attitudes and so on, but some parents find the accumulated pain too much. They grieve; they devise new ways of hanging on to the past; they freeze their memories in a time capsule, inventing a golden age that never really existed. Some of them become stricter with their children than ever before — everything else may fail, but family and religion are not negotiable. Without meaning to, some drive their children away. But others draw their children closer, through mutual bonds of love and respect.

Jalal Kassab arrived in Australia wearing four layers of clothing. It was 1968 and his father, a truck driver from Tripoli in northern Lebanon, after a few false starts, had finally decided to join his wife's family in Melbourne. Jalal and his brothers and sisters looked like little round Christmas puddings. Because all their belongings couldn't possibly fit into the few crammed cases they could take with them, they had to wear all their clothes at once. Both parents found work immediately. Young and healthy, they were just what Australia needed. Malake (meaning queen), Jalal's mother, had never worked outside the house before. Husband and wife worked together at the Renault car factory and Malake found herself sewing seat covers. After two years they shifted to the Ford factory where Malake earned $37 a week net; a young daughter who worked at the Rowntree chocolate factory earned $15. Jalal remembers his mother later supplementing the family income by buying material at the markets and making blouses to sell for $5 apiece to her Greek and Turkish co-workers. The civil war prevented them from returning home, and by then a new wave of Lebanese settlers — refugees — was arriving.

'I never saw my parents during the week — they were both on shift work, starting at 3.30 in the afternoon. In the mornings we were careful never to speak too loudly. One of my sisters left school early just to look after us. Sometimes when Dad wasn't working we would go with him to pick Mum up. I remember the smell of the apple cakes she would bring us from the cafeteria.'

Sometimes I noted a little rolling of the eyes from young Muslims when their immigrant parents reminded them for the umpteenth time of the sacrifices they had made for them. With Jalal there were no such signs, just a lot of love and respect. His parents sat with him as he told me his story, but their limited English prevented them from following our conversation or joining in.

'We did our ritual shopping at the Vic Markets every Saturday morning. There were twelve of us — ten kids and Mum and Dad, so we always bought boxes of fruit, barrels of oil, a sack of bread at the bakery — quantities like that. In the afternoon we would all work together like a smooth assembly line. Dad would slaughter a sheep quietly in the backyard, dig a hole for the blood to run into and then quickly fill it in with dirt so the neighbours wouldn't notice and report us to the health authorities. Sundays we spent all day cooking and went on barbecues and picnics — all twelve of us packed into our FC Holden! People would gawk at us as we pulled up at traffic lights.'

I wondered how a family managed to stay together without disintegrating when children only saw their parents on weekends. Many families were unable to withstand the harsh winds of change forced upon them by a modern industrialised society. Women who had never worked outside the house and who came from rural villages and towns found their lives changed forever and their health often devastated by factory work. It was a heavy price to pay for the chance of a more prosperous life for their children. Some families crumbled under the stress. Others were still suffering the after-effects. The Kassab extended family seemed intact. Why? The answer may have had something to do with their strong bonds of love and respect. I saw small signs of affection and dutiful behaviour, awkward to describe in a society where such conduct seems mawkish and old-fashioned, and might even be regarded as trampling on one's rights as an individual! I noticed how Jalal, for example, kneeling unobtrusively, removed his elderly father's shoes and put slippers on his feet.

We talked about culture conflict and what tensions this placed on young shoulders. Afraa, Jalal's wife (the same young woman who'd upset her fellow community development students) joined us, bringing in plates of luscious fruits — melon, apricots and nuts, and cups of coffee. Jalal went on, 'We were being educated at home, at school and out in the streets — and they all conflicted. Our parents didn't like us speaking English at home and mixing with too many non-Muslim kids. I guess I was lucky because the primary school I went to had a good ethnic mix — no one group dominated — and this influenced me a lot. But at high school I used an anglicised name and I still remember the humiliation of having my underwear made by my mother and of wearing hand-me-downs. Later things improved, but it was only a matter of degree. When you changed for Phys. Ed. the whole world knew you were wearing $3 Kmart specials. At least at high school all wogs were hassled, not just Muslims,' he said, suggesting that this made it more bearable.

'As far as identity went I had a slight moral dilemma over a game we played called Wogs on Aussies. It was a queer mixture of rugby, soccer and Aussie Rules football — really rough and played with a soccer ball. A few ethnic kids who were socially acceptable ('closet wogs', I suppose you could call them) were allowed on the Aussie side. Guess which side I was on? But deep down, I think we all wished we were on the Aussie team — though we blustered about, full of bravado and wog toughness.'

Jalal believes he is a better person for having faced the temptations and resisted them. And they were there right under his nose at high school and later at university. 'Some Muslim kids did belong,' he muttered. 'They played football, not soccer, went to pubs and joined in the Aussie manhood thing — you know, the swearing and the sheilas. Spiking your drinks is probably still common — how they loved to trick you on that — but personally I always stayed away from alcohol and drugs, although again the chance to be one of the boys — to belong to the dominant culture for just once in your life, was tempting.'

Even the most tolerant of Australians finds it difficult to swallow the idea of parents organising marital partners for their children. It is the complete inverse of western notions of romantic love. The stereotype of young Muslim girls forced to marry old men is difficult to overcome. Everyone has a favourite story they've heard about or read about or seen on television. But forced marriages with their tragic aftermath are far from the norm according to my discussions with social and welfare workers, and are regarded with abhorrence by the Australian Muslims I have spoken to. Such marriages should be seen as an aberration wherever they occur. Fortunately, Australian laws protect young girls from parental madness which is sometimes economically motivated. And Muslim teenagers appear well aware of their rights and entitlements under the law.

Ask most Muslims born overseas and you are likely to hear that their parents consulted with them in arranging their marriages. Others will say that they did their own arranging, albeit with parental approval. Societies which limit interaction between the sexes or impose social segregation are more likely to have recourse to arranged marriages.

Hasim, born in South Africa of Indian descent, said to me half jokingly, half despairingly, 'I want to marry a good Muslim girl but I can't, because I never get to meet good

Muslim girls. A good Muslim girl is not going to be out and about. Without my parents' help, I'm lost! My parents love me and I know they'll help me when it's time.' Paradoxically, mothers and sisters often control the access of boys to young women, which may partly explain the strong son–mother and sister–brother ties I observed in many traditional Muslim households.

Today it is difficult to gauge which kind of arranged marriage is the norm in Australia other than to note that the forced marriage is an anomaly of the worst kind, and against the teachings of Islam. A 'normal Australian' marriage where the boy and girl meet and decide for themselves that they want to marry is acceptable since parents are still asked to give permission and become involved with the wedding. The term 'arranged marriage' is flexible.

I asked Jalal to tell me about his marriage to Afraa.

'Everyone in my family had an arranged marriage. Although it's officially supposed to be initiated by the father, or an uncle, on the girl's side, the mothers and aunts really control the proceedings. Young people in Lebanon and in Australia are willing to accept the decisions of their parents, who are seen to be wiser and better judges in these matters, but the children have the final say.

'I was twenty and just tearing out the door on my way to a school exam when I spoke to my wife-to-be on the telephone for the first time. My eyes were red — I'd been up swotting the night before and I had one foot outside the door when the telephone rang. It was my mother's voice — she and Dad were ringing from Syria.

'"Guess what?" she said. "I've found a really nice girl for you!"

'"I'm not interested, Mum!" We'd been through this before.

'"Son, listen to me! She's really nice; from a very good family."

'"Not interested, Mum! Please! I'm on my way to an exam and the last thing I want to think about now is marriage!"

'"Son, she's here next to me. I'm ashamed of you! The least you can do is talk to her!"

'"All right, Mum, put her on." And so in his broken Arabic Jalal greeted this unknown young woman and asked her what she knew about him.

'"Do you know what I look like?"

'"Yes," came the quiet answer.

'"Australia means a difficult life, and remember it is forever," I told her. She said she knew all of this.

'My mother came back on the phone and I reminded her that I didn't even know what this young woman looked like.

'"Don't worry, Son, just go into the bedroom and in the top drawer of my dressing-table you'll find her photograph."

'I put the phone down and got the photograph.' He paused. 'I was bewitched,' he said simply.

'We communicated for nine months before we got engaged and then we married by proxy,' Afraa said. 'And you already know about the dough on top of the door,' she laughed.

Zahra married very young. One reason for her impatience was the greater personal freedom she would have as a married woman of sixteen. At last she could go out without her brother's permission! Marriage could open up a new world and bring her new clothes and jewellery, as well as freedom. So when her mother suggested it was time for her to get married and brought up the names of a few young local boys, Zahra willingly cooperated. Three years later she was divorced. Within her Melbourne community she was regarded as not much better than a fallen woman, she told me.

Under Australian family law, a girl cannot get married until she is eighteen. Exceptions may be made under special circumstances at the discretion of the court. Some Muslim social workers involved in writing submissions for parents wanting approval for early marriages for their daughters confessed it placed them in a dilemma.

'Sixteen is far too young. I know it in my heart and here I am writing the submission for the parents and arguing it for them in court!' Farida was a Melbourne social worker in her thirties who always looked tired and generally perplexed with the human dramas she was called on to adjudicate. She tried her best, she said. Girls were questioned alone and very carefully to make sure they understood the step they were taking and that this was what they truly wanted. 'But they're children really. What can you say? One young girl I remember well, she was sixteen, the man was thirty-three, but she wanted to be married! No question of force at all! Just the typical arranged marriage. I asked her why she wanted to get married so young. She said she wanted a wedding. It wasn't my job to tell her that real life would be very different. No education, no economic independence; perhaps eventually trapped in a marriage she would grow to hate. This seems to be more prevalent with uneducated parents who in turn don't educate their daughters — the traditional, old-fashioned ones.

'"My mother married at fifteen," the young girl told me. "She's been happy with her life and her eleven children." There was nothing left for me to say,' said Farida.

'People tell you idyllic stories about arranged marriages, but there are those that fall apart, just like love marriages do in the West.'

Zahra, now twenty-two and with a five-year-old son, showed all the signs of being a confused, unhappy woman who had severe doubts about her religion, her ancestry and her own personal identity. She abhorred the Lebanese customs and traditions she had grown up with and now saw herself imprisoned by. Deep in her mind there seemed to be a battle raging. I found her outbursts so vehement and bitter that at first I was taken aback, but I became used to them. Perhaps she would never unravel the love–hate tangle that ruled her psyche. She denied the Muslim side of herself because what she saw in the mirror was so different from the images of women she saw around her in society.

Her looks were striking; she was both beautiful and voluptuous, with long black wavy hair and a smooth pale complexion. She used her make-up with the skill of a Hollywood beautician. Her voice was clear and well modulated and she was always dripping with expensive jewellery.

'My older brother was so strict that he wouldn't even allow me to go on Muslim youth camps or to Eid celebrations outside the mosque. He took the place of my father and even today still tries to control me. But it's the community I really hate. Because I'm divorced and they all know it's my fault, everyone expects me to be living at home.'

We were talking at her elegantly furnished flat in the Melbourne suburb of Prahran, surrounded by framed portraits of herself and her handsome son.

'They're always ringing up my mother and commiserating with her — the hypocrites! Because I live alone, they imply I have lovers.' Her voice rises indignantly. 'I've proven to be a bad wife, and I'm no longer a virgin, so they think they're doing me a favour by suggesting someone. "She'll do for a permanent residency marriage," is the feeling.'

Unfortunately for Zahra, her mother lived close to the

mosque and was entangled in community networks in her neighbourhood. Even though Zahra had moved as far away as she could without leaving her mother completely isolated, the ripples of condemnation still reached out to her, she said bitterly.

'Are you ashamed of being a Muslim?' I asked, trying to penetrate this wall of self-hate.

She admitted to hiding her religious identity and her Lebanese side when she was with non-Muslims. 'My name is more French sounding, too,' she said wickedly. 'Not too Arabic to western ears. I don't like Muslims as a group. It's not easy if you are a nonconformist and progressive.'

'But you're always helping individual Muslims, I've noticed — and it's not part of your job — you don't have to do it,' I said.

The clue to Zahra's self-rejection seemed to lie in part in a lack of role models. 'My father,' she told me, clearly enjoying herself, 'was a bigamist under Australian law. In all, he had twelve wives — one of whom was a Syrian nun!'

By now I knew when Zahra was deliberately trying to shock me. Her father must have forgotten the old Moorish saying, 'The man who marries many wives marries trouble'!

'Naturally he didn't have all these wives at once. Now he's an old man in his eighties and he wants my mother to remarry him and look after him all over again. He divorced her when I was ten. I think we were lucky to be the family he had in Australia — my mother was his fourth wife. If he wanted to bring a new wife to Australia he couldn't do so without divorcing my mother, which he eventually did. My mother is truly an angel. She even made the wedding gown for the wife who followed her! I love my mother but I have no respect for my father.'

'Every time they came to the eighth name on the roll, I knew the teachers would get stuck.' In Brisbane I met Yasmeen, a young woman elegantly dressed in western clothes, with a long skirt, long sleeves and a little discreet gold jewellery. With an adroit show of name dropping, I discovered, as I had imagined, that we both knew many of the same people in Melbourne and Sydney. 'At school,' she went on, 'I think I made the deliberate decision to gain some sort of acceptance by becoming active in debating and sports. I was sixteen and a lot of my girlfriends — it was a girls-only high school — were already going out with boys and starting to eye me as if something must be wrong with me. I tried explaining, but the more I tried, the more isolated I became, and the further I seemed to be from the others. My solution was to become popular another way. So I learnt to avoid the confrontations of explaining my religion, or why I was different.

'Then I went to my first Muslim youth camp in Sydney. I met hundreds of young people just like me. Although they came from different ethnic backgrounds, they had the same restrictions as I did: curfews, no dating, praying, dietary problems — they were forever asking whether foods contained pork. I looked around and saw reflections of myself.'

In a society in which the dominant images are of those who are not like them, many young people begin to reject their own culture and customs. Growing up like this can be a very lonely, sobering experience, but Yasmeen, unlike Zahra, had found a way out without lacerating herself.

From this coeducational camp emerged a group of young boys and girls who wanted to stay in contact with one another. It sounded fun. They would all meet as a group and go ice-skating or roller-skating, or to movies and coffee houses. Now Yasmeen didn't have to explain to her friends why she had to get home by 8.30 — they all did too! The boys were protective of the girls and on the way home they would often stop at a mosque and pray together as a group. 'Where you might tend to slide and say to yourself, "Oh well, I'll miss this prayer, I'm a bit tired," when you are with a group the energy from the circle drags you along. I noticed this silent sharing with my Muslim friends. It was a unique feeling for me — one that had always eluded me with non-Muslim friends. I no longer felt like a nerd. I belonged to a group and it was a group that was normal!'

Yasmeen's young husband did not share her feelings. Osman had grown up in Brisbane. Most of his friends were not Muslims and this had never bothered him. Unlike Yasmeen, he had not felt obliged to explain, over and over again, why he could not do this or that. 'My friends were compatible,' he said. 'They were told once and never made anything out of it, or they wouldn't have been my friends!'

The first time I met Asma Wang she was wearing an Akubra hat. Was this meant to be an icon of Australianness or a tongue-in-cheek joke? Until I got to know her better I wasn't sure. Later I realised it was a humorous fashion statement, tied up with her own identity. The young woman I had spoken to on the telephone and arranged to meet in the Qantas Club lounge in Sydney had sounded self-assured enough to pull a stunt like this, and get away with it. Asma knew how to make an entry.

When you're a Chinese Muslim born in Pakistan, and you grow up learning Urdu for the first ten years of your life, identity questions follow you like phantoms. But Asma's family had been Muslim for hundreds of years. There are more than sixty million Muslims in the People's Republic of China today and it is believed that Islam first came to China around 650 AD.

'Australian Muslims are always bowled over when I say

"*Salaam*" to them. When I pass through Malaysia, the Muslims there always ask me when I converted. Next in line come the Anglo feminists. They don't see me as a Muslim woman at all, so they debate with me in a way they wouldn't do with a woman wearing *hijab*. They are frank and open but we always seem to disagree, and I don't see any positives flowing from these debates. And of course mainstream Australia only sees the Chinese in me — not the Muslim!

'Early on it was a problem because you never knew where you fitted in. You juggled your identities on a day-to-day basis. Some you can put to sleep for the moment but never the Chinese side, of which I'm tremendously proud.'

Confident and comfortable as she now was with her multiple identities, Asma told me that once, when very young and travelling with her family from Pakistan to Australia, 'We did a slight detour to visit my mother's relatives in Taiwan. The Taiwanese Muslims knew that I wasn't exactly like them, and when they asked me where I came from I told them I was Pakistani. They just laughed. There I was so visibly Chinese, even speaking Chinese with them, and claiming to be a Pakistani!'

As she grew older, she gradually overcame the yearning to belong. But not before going through that Pakistani phase, and then the desire to be Chinese Chinese instead of Chinese Muslim. 'Sometimes it is very hurtful not fitting in anywhere. I think I've stopped looking for answers. There are none; I just have to bear with it. My family is home for me, and by that I mean wherever my parents are — that's my home.'

Being married had only underlined Asma's outsider status. She had some Chinese friends who disapproved of her marrying a non-Chinese, and Muslim friends who condemned her for marrying a non-Muslim, and feminist friends who disagreed with her marrying at all! 'I can't win!' she said, laughing. 'So I have to live with it.'

22

The forgotten tribe

So far, all the young Muslims I'd met seemed to be success stories. They were inspiring examples of achievement-oriented, socially mobile, ambitious young men and women. It seemed the ones with educational and social problems were eluding my nets.

Teenagers I spied from train windows loitering around railway stations, escapees from the taming influence of Islam. Where were the less tractable, the less obedient? Not everyone could be having such an idyllic ride.

Entering new terrain meant securing the services of a new guide. Ramsee Jebeile, educator and sage, volunteered to take me into uncharted waters. Ramsee was the first red-headed Lebanese I had met. He had come to Australia not from Lebanon but from Uganda, although that had nothing to do with his red hair. Years spent working with young people in Sydney's western suburbs had sharpened his understanding of the effects of educational disadvantage on Arabic-speaking youth, especially those from working-class homes. If they don't do well at school, they face a shrinking labour market for young unskilled people. These kids know that without those magic pieces of paper there remains little hope.

'Come and meet some of the kids,' he said one day, challenging me to do more than just listen. 'We organise classes on weekends, although I admit the tough cases don't come — the ones you'll meet still have a chance.

'We are trying to stop the ranks of unmotivated, poorly educated young people from growing. We ask where the education system is letting them down.' Unless this drift was stopped, students could be caught up in a hopeless treadmill of repeating their parents' working lives all over again. These were not scare tactics he was using. Here was my forgotten tribe. 'They've failed so many times,' he said with a hint of weariness, 'that they develop an ethos of failure. They stop trying. We are trying to intervene and remotivate students, even though their peer group often pulls them back, telling them, "Don't bother! You'll fail".'

Faces gazed at me blankly, impassively. Eyes moved to my tape-recorder; the machine, I noticed uneasily, recording nothing as yet but an awkward silence.

Ramsee and two of his colleagues introduced me to a small class of Year 11 boys and girls, all aged about fifteen or sixteen. These were the ambitious ones, they explained; Arabic-speaking teenagers from working-class homes hoping to go on to university or a TAFE college — the ones who hadn't given up. Obviously they were not part of the guerrilla movement or they would not be here on a Sunday. I noticed their uniform — neat jeans and sweaters, the girls uncovered, but with no make-up, and fairly 'straight' hairstyles for both sexes.

'Before we begin,' Ramsee said, 'please let me stress the very different social contexts which need to be borne in mind when talking about parental control. There is a big difference between an urban environment like Sydney and village environments in Lebanon. It's all tied up with the western emphasis on individualism, as against Lebanese concerns with community and family.' Many parents, he explained, saw an emphasis on the individual as a weakness of western culture.

'Do the parents really believe that what they see on television is typical of Australian society?' I asked.

'Yes,' Ramsee said. 'And these days this means atrocious murders, wild parties, mindless crimes and senseless accidents caused by drink driving.' The adolescent jury started to come to life, nodding seriously in front of me. 'Parents are phobic about what they see on television,' Ramsee continued.

'Last year, when I was in Lebanon, I was impressed by the number of young boys and girls walking out together at sunset — they could even have been courting, but it was in front of the whole village, open, correct, in public — not in the back seat of a car.' Again the young faces of the jury confirmed what he said.

One of the young girls spoke up. Her name was Kamila. 'When I'm in Lebanon,' she said, 'I have a lot more freedom than here in Australia. There are no strangers in the village; people say hello and you say hello back, because even if you don't know them, someone in the village does, so there's no stranger danger or anything like that.'

Samar, sitting next to her, broke in with her own example. 'I could walk alone by myself at 10 pm. In Australia I'm not even allowed to walk to the corner shop by myself after 5 o'clock!'

Curfews were an essential weapon in any self-respecting Muslim parent's arsenal of control. Or were they a form of protection which sometimes expressed itself as control, rather than concern for the safety of young girls? A family's honour was linked closely to the virginity of its unmarried females. Looking at television, pulp magazines and the tabloid press, parents grew horrified at what they thought lurked 'out there', believing that after dark the streets became a jungle.

Did television really show Australian life as it was? I asked them.

'It's definitely true,' protested Fadila of the brown plaits and serious-looking glasses. 'My dad is a taxi driver and he's always coming home and telling us, "There are animals everywhere out there," and that what we see on television is life as it is.'

How could I compete with the authority of her father? Far be it from me to suggest that her father might have a vested interest in accentuating the horror stories, or that he might be seeing only one image of Australian night-life from the front seat of a taxi — drunks, foul-mouthed youths and vomiting young girls.

Did the boys still keep an eye out for their sisters? 'Yes,' they said. 'But we don't dob them in,' added Abdullah phlegmatically. 'They could get pissed off with you and dob you in, so it would only backfire.'

'If I really want to upset my parents, all I have to do is say, "Just wait till I get my own flat!" giggled Samar, nudging Fadila with her elbow. 'I'm only teasing, of course, but it really sets them off!' Everybody laughed. They'd all been there and done that.

But this seemed to be as far as their defiance went or at least as far as they cared to admit publicly that it went. They had an air of innocence, unsophistication — an obvious lack of 'cool'. They told me in genuinely disapproving voices that there were some Muslim kids who wanted to leave home, or didn't respect their parents, who talked back and so on. Everyone knew of someone or other who had left home — 'the bad kids' they called them, in voices tinged with self-righteousness. Comically, in the back of my head, I could hear the voices and value systems of their parents mixed up with their own feelings. There was a quaint, somewhat old-fashioned air of prudishness floating about which now and then became confused with the kids' own desire to be nonchalant and seem 'cool'. I liked it; they were an endearing lot.

'When my mother heard about that American boy who divorced his own parents, wow! "What kind of a country is this — some little pipsqueak daring to divorce his parents," she said. "I'd show that little pipsqueak a thing or two!" Kamila imitated her mother's expression and voice and everyone giggled. They fell about laughing when I said that I supposed they'd dropped the idea of divorcing *their* parents.

'My mother says, "How can I teach my children discipline if I can't smack them when they're small?" and she's right,' added Kamila sympathetically.

By now, after a slow start, we seemed to be getting on famously. I was inundated with stories about Lebanese girls running away from home. Oh, yes! they knew of such cases. These girls only did it because of the strictness, though — no television watching, early bedtimes and pretty tough homes. The idea that perhaps their own lives might be seen as controlled did not cross their minds.

'If the government didn't support the runaways through the Youth Assistance Scheme, they wouldn't do it,' Fadila insisted. Once more I remembered that I was talking to fifteen and sixteen year olds and not parents, because again the words held a strange echo of mum and dad talking — old words coming from fresh, young faces. But my next question brought us all down to earth again.

'How do you solve parental problems?'

'You don't solve them,' answered Samar. 'You live through them or you split.'

For the girls, trouble meant daring to, or even wanting to, go out without their parents, and for the boys the explosions came if they tried going out after eight o'clock at night. Fadila complained that she couldn't go shopping by herself, even in the daytime. When we females spontaneously turned on the boys, attacking them verbally for the extra freedom they enjoyed, they turned sheepish, shrugging their shoulders. 'What can we do? It's the way of the world,' they seemed to be saying. It struck me that the values these teenagers were articulating held echoes of growing up in Australia forty or fifty years ago.

My young friends were quite convinced that they stood very much in the minority and that most other Muslim teenagers enjoyed much more freedom.

Why were they different?

'Because our parents are strong,' a chorus of voices sang out. 'Strong parents; especially strong fathers.' The rebels with real problems, as they put it, the ones who had stolen more personal freedom or had run away, their parents were strict, while their own parents were strong. 'Strict' seemed to mean very religious: strict parents equalled strict Muslims to their way of thinking.

Ibrahim, who'd sat and listened impassively, finally decided to contribute. 'Children of very religious parents,' he said, 'are the ones who run away because they can't handle the pressure.'

'They try to discipline you in the old way,' Abdullah tried to explain.

What did that mean? What kind of discipline came into play to ensure compliance? My mind went back to Asma, Yasmeen, Wafia and Hossam's daughters, Jalal, Hassan, and all the others whose upbringing and parental role-modelling had contradicted the horror stories one read about now and then.

Time was running out and we gossiped informally, pleasantly passing the time of day. Obviously, they welcomed a change to their class routine.

Samar and Abdullah confided that they were getting fed up with parents censoring their television. 'They hate us watching "Home and Away" and "Neighbours".' I knew whose side I was on.

'You haven't met any of the young people who hang out in the streets,' Ramsee pointed out, 'the kids who see themselves as failures, who have either dropped out of the system completely or who still stay around but no longer try or care.' He believed fervently that the Australian school system depended on students getting help from their parents. 'My daughter is always coming to me with questions of one kind or another. First-generation kids cannot get that kind of support from parents whose English is poor.'

In some Arabic-speaking homes, the children did not even learn to read or write Arabic because their parents were illiterate in their mother tongue. By now it has been proven that without proficiency in your home language, acquiring a second language is enormously difficult. I remembered Dorothy Hoddinot telling me that some of her children were the first in their families to receive secondary education.

The following day I travelled by train to Bankstown where I met John, a youth worker who knew the streets, the teen hang-outs, the gang leaders and everyone who mattered in the local youth subculture. John could have been elected mayor of Bankstown had under-eighteens been allowed to vote in local elections. The streets, the railway station, the malls, the video shops were his office.

He explained the territorial imperatives. One side of the railway station 'belonged' to the Vietnamese gang members and the other side to the Lebanese. Often the police came along to move everyone on, now and then disturbing the activities of drug sellers. Over there, he said, pointing to a clump of bushes, knives had been found last week. Everything seemed normal today, however; it was sunny, and the station was full of shouting adolescents jumping off trains and falling over one another's bags as they escaped from school. The only potential source of trouble seemed to be a small group of Vietnamese students loitering on the wrong side of the 'wall' who, in John's words, would soon have to move on ... or else! The railway station served as the daytime headquarters for many kids who lived on the streets. Those who preferred hanging out with their street mates also found this the perfect place to meet for a few hours before trudging home once more to their parents' watchful eyes. There were any number of discreet little doorways and stairways for boys and girls to meet, smoke a cigarette, talk a little, joke a little, flirt a little.

We were taking a risk. John wasn't sure if the boys he was looking for would surface, but they did eventually turn up. John left me in the hands of Muhammad, a good-looking young man of nineteen or twenty, who took my unusual request in his stride and acted as if he was welcoming me into his own home instead of the area around the railway station exit.

Of course he didn't mind me using his name in the book, he said with a laugh. 'How many Muhammads do you think there are in Bankstown?' (Muhammad remains the most popular name for Muslim boys everywhere in the world.) Calling together some of his mates, he spelt out the purpose of my impromptu visit.

'She's writing a book,' he explained. 'She wants to ask some questions. No, it's not for television. It's about Muslims and she's come all the way from Perth to Bankstown to talk to us. C'mon!' he called, doing his best to marshall a group together.

Any of these young men could have been cast as extras on the television series 'Heartbreak High', which, incidentally, drove Muslim parents crazy with its casual on-screen sexuality and permissiveness, and the lack of respect students showed for teachers.

I suggested to Muhammad that perhaps I could invite them all for a few bowls of noodles and some Cokes and chips. Everyone perked up considerably and I found myself being led to a kiosk–cafe on one side of the railway exit. John had disappeared.

The Sunshine Cafe was a tiny place — three small round tables, eight plastic chairs, a counter with steaming takeaway food, and two Vietnamese shopkeepers probably wondering what on earth was going on.

Some kids ate and ran, as they became either bored or bloated, but a core of three or four remained loyal. After about ten minutes we settled down fairly seriously, having had a good laugh when one or two 'Muslims for a day' (who had wanted to share in this sudden windfall) were unmasked. A few Lebanese Christians came in, shouting ostentatiously to their Muslim friends, '*Salaam alaikum* (Peace be with you), brother.' They were hilarious and didn't dupe me for a moment, which added to my credibility with the others. Distinguishing the fakes from the genuine article had not been difficult. While they of course spoke Arabic, they clumsily mixed up their religious exclamations, saying *Al'ham dulillah* (Praise be to Allah) where they should have said *Insha'Allah* (God willing) and vice versa. Nevertheless, these young men were disobeying the precepts of those guardians on both sides of the religious fence who urged them to mix only with kids of their own faith.

Muhammad told me he spent time helping his father and then every afternoon came down to the station to see his mates and his girlfriend. He fetched her in to meet me, a gorgeous young woman, beautifully made-up, with flawless skin and streaks through her dark blonde hair. 'We hang out for an hour or so; it's a good place to be. My parents aren't so strict,' he said. They were divorced and he lived with his dad. 'He lets me go out, but he expects to see me at home sometimes.' Like many others in the area, his father is unemployed. Young Muhammad left school at fifteen and since then has spent a year in a detention centre. 'I done a year there. What can I say?' He shrugged philosophically and, not wishing to assail his dignity, I intruded no further.

His friends Ali and Naseem seemed to get along with their parents reasonably well. Compared to the young people in Ramsee's class, these kids had more freedom, but they took pains to emphasise that their parents expected to know where they were. Most took it for granted that their parents checked up on their whereabouts, but they admitted to 'jigging school' — playing truant — on and off. 'Who cares?' seemed the general attitude

I'd been warned, 'The language will be pretty rough. Prepare your ears for the worst.' But the only time these boys' speech floundered into profanity was when the question of relations with the police came up. Suddenly everyone wanted to talk at once!

FAMILY BRAWL TURNS CARNIVAL INTO A RIOT one headline had read. POLICE 'TOO HASTY'. RIOT COULD HAVE BEEN PREVENTED read another. Earlier that year, at the end of a peaceful family day with a crowd of forty thousand at the annual Arabic Day carnival, an altercation had taken place which seemed to demonstrate police–youth relations of the worst kind. An isolated fight had escalated into a melee, with injuries on all sides. The police had found themselves under attack by youthful sections of the crowd. They had called for reinforcements — an overreaction according to some who were present — and large numbers of police with batons and dogs arrived. There were sixty police vehicles and one hundred officers, including mounted police.

Six months after the event these youths were still seething. Yes, they understood the police had been frightened and had overreacted. 'But they had no right to push people back and unleash the dogs on grandmothers and little kids and girls!' Three or four were talking at once. They had all been there ... They had seen what had happened! I listened to at least three different versions of how the whole skirmish had erupted. 'And the journalists,' snorted Muhammad, 'they blew everything out of proportion.' He claimed that the girl who had apparently triggered the initial altercation was his cousin.

'You should have heard the language,' said Ali. 'The police called us every name under the sun.' Their own language, he conceded had been pretty foul too.

'How would you avoid the same thing happening again?'

'Community policing,' they suggested immediately. 'Have our own marshalls and keep the fuzz away.'

Somehow I thought it might be a few years before another Arab carnival took place, even though it had been run successfully for ten years previously.

Rumours fuelled these kids' world — rumours from the paranoid to the preposterous, influencing moods and framing animosity to people outside the fellowship of group, family and local community. Muhammad asked me if I knew that manufacturers of cigarette papers coated them with pig fat to deliberately insult and defile Muslims.

'What rubbish!' I said. (Shades of the Indian Mutiny and the cartridge rumour of 1857, I thought. Muslim and Hindu sepoys alike had believed the cartridges they were required to tear open with their teeth were smeared with either pig or cow fat, a first step, so it was rumoured, towards their all being forcibly converted to Christianity.)

'Take it easy,' Muhammad responded, 'take it easy.' So I took his advice and we returned to normal.

For the next half-hour we chatted as young people came in and out. One boy, invited to have a Coke, answered with simple dignity that he would pay himself. 'I have money,' he said, and I respected his pride. Another sheepish youth of about eighteen, with short-cropped hair, found himself shoved before me. 'This is a real man,' announced Muhammad, with a flourish. 'He's married, and he's just had a baby!' Fay, a sharp-tongued twenty year old, told me that the girls she knew wearing *hijab* took them off and rolled up their school tunics as soon as they got around the corner. Suddenly a hundred people seemed to be talking to me all at once.

'Peace in the Middle East!' yelled Fay. 'Break the monotony!' she shouted, holding up her fingers in the V for victory sign (at least that's what it looked like). Somehow or other she had confused my tape-recorder with a television camera.

'Did you get what you wanted? Did you get enough information?' Muhammad asked anxiously. During the time I spent with these young people, I became aware of the hospitality they were instinctively extending to me and the care they were taking with their language. The kiosk was their territory, a part of their clubroom, and they were being good-natured and helpful. Muhammad, in particular, had assumed the role of mediator, a good Middle Eastern trader wanting to ensure that an honest transaction took place — that I got value for money. He played the bazaari, or merchant, and I the customer. We had haggled a little, and I had refused to let more than two packets of cigarettes be run up on the tab. But no one had taken advantage of me and in return I tried not to exploit the situation. I felt comfortable with the final bill of $33. In their own individual ways, these young people exemplified the traditional values of looking after a guest and extending the rules of hospitality to the stranger.

But there were other boys from the forgotten tribe as I'd once called them, boys beyond my reach, though not the law's. These young men had been described to me as the tough cases, the failures, the ones who no longer cared. We never met, although I would read about them years later when stories about a series of pack rapes began to surface. Their crimes and the shock waves they caused stayed in the headlines years after the event and delivered Sydney's Muslim Lebanese community up as scapegoats.

Since the 1991 Gulf War, Australian Muslims had become confident of their future as a religious community. They believed that they were living in a tolerant country —that the 'fair go' meant something after all. Ten years later, in 2001, a series of events would change all this and turn the clock backwards.

VI

Caravanserai revisited 2002

We are part of the family called Australia and because we are part of that family, every part that hurts, hurts us as well.

Noor Dean, Spokesman for East Doncaster Mosque,
target of arson attack in the wake of the Bali blasts, 12 October 2002.

... people want to put a face to their fear. It will be a tragedy if this becomes the Muslim schoolkid who lives next door.

Kevin McDonald, sociologist,
University of Melbourne, 21 October 2002

23

'Of Middle Eastern appearance'

I once met a man in New York who told me that there were two kinds of Muslims in the world: good Muslims and bad Muslims — for him it was as simple as that.

In his mind the 'good Muslims' were those who agreed with his particular world view and the 'bad Muslims', well they were the ones causing all the trouble and had to be dealt with by right-minded people around the world. I tried to picture a vast army of the righteous standing shoulder to shoulder facing an opposing army of virtuous warriors convinced that they too were doing God's will: enemy cultures clashing into each other like comets.

At first I was taken in by the man's air of sophistication, fooled by the 'myth of Manhattan', until I realised that this American's mindset, despite his wit and general savvy, stopped at the Canadian border. Swept up in a cloud of boyish innocence, charming in a man of his years, he spoke with great authority about religion and freedom of speech because, as an atheist, he had made a study of comparative religions.

When he moved on to discussing 'the world of Islam', as he called it, a warning bell sounded in my head. I soon discovered that this otherwise erudite man knew nothing about the modern history, politics and culture of Islamic societies anywhere in the world. He had no idea of their aspirations, their historical grievances, their strong feelings of injustice and the tensions between the drive towards modernisation and the radical movements opposing it — he certainly had no inkling of how his country's Middle East policy was viewed by moderate and extremist Muslims around the world.

We stood on the penthouse roof of his co-op in Greenwich Village and surveyed the Manhattan skyline. It was September 1998. Four years have passed; the skyline has changed and so have we.

My New Yorker still has difficulty in understanding what happened in New York on September 11 and why, but he no longer uses the word 'fundamentalist' so freely; now he uses the word 'terrorist' instead. Since the World Trade Centre tragedy, language has changed, definitions have been reshaped, and mindsets have hardened.

In Australia the lines are drawn in the sand: shock-jock patriots of the airways demand that Muslims publicly declare where their loyalties lie — a symbolic act of public humiliation is part of the ritual of reassuring listeners.

Wrapping yourself in the Australian flag means one thing when Cathy Freeman performs a victory lap at the Olympics, although this icon of Australian sport was also criticised years before when she honoured her Aboriginal flag; it means something else when an Australian Muslim wraps himself in the flag, to be photographed on the steps of a mosque, in order to prove how Australian he truly is, or when a *nikab*-clad woman peers through the slits in her veil, waving the flag at a camera — these acts make me cringe. Meant as symbolic actions, they are sad and humiliating to witness. A younger generation wonders why it should have to appease those whose hatred hardens as the months go by.

Almost ten years ago, as I travelled around Australia on a journey of the mind and the heart, hundreds of Australian Muslims I met predicted that this could happen. I noted their fears then:

> Around Australia, Muslims — butchers, bakers, businessmen, academics, teachers, the young, the old and the unemployed — are convinced that now that Communism is no longer 'the enemy', Islam has become the new global enemy. It's a depressing view to hold of your own position in society. Australian Muslims need reassurance that they are not seen as the enemy; that they are not un-Australian.

As I wrote these words I wondered if the fears were exaggerated or unduly fatalistic. Trying to read between the lines I thought I detected a yearning for martyrdom. Today, I know better.

What has caused this change of mind? The answer is simple but disturbing: I have revisited old friends and travelled along familiar routes belonging to my *Caravanserai* days and found Muslims everywhere, from the devout to the nominal, reeling from events, near and far, which have impacted on their daily lives and their spirituality. I have witnessed a wave of 'Islamophobia' drift across the country and seen this poison infect our policy of mandatory detention for asylum seekers, as the word 'refugee' becomes synonymous with Muslim.

Three terrible events took place in 2001; they were of different magnitude but one followed on the heels of the other and all of them were to affect the lives of Australian Muslims: the Sydney gang rapes in August 2000 which became public knowledge a year later, the September 11 terrorist attacks which rocked the world and the 'Tampa incident' just before the 2001 November federal election. Australian Muslims were under siege and saw themselves lumped together as 'the enemy'.

Months passed and I remained silent. It was hard to foreshadow what the repercussions would be, but it became clearer to me that these three unrelated events would become linked in many people's minds and they would look for a common denominator, a common enemy.

I grew up in the forties and fifties of the last century, almost a lifetime ago, when Muslims were invisible. We were called 'Mohammedans' and nobody knew much about us, or really bothered with us: we were too small to be a threat, there was no Middle East problem, and while the British Empire was running out of steam it still flew the flag; the media hadn't 'adopted' and 'distorted' us — we were pariah-like without being real pariahs.

When I was a child of six or seven my parents would take me to the port of Fremantle on visits which filled my head with adventurous ideas like stowing away and sailing the Seven Seas, or wherever else Sindbad the Sailor might be hiding. Surrounded by new faces and new smells: men in turbans and the strange, comforting aroma of engine oil, rope, spices and ghee, these excursions were the most exciting events in my life. Getting dressed up in our Sunday best is what the Dean family did when certain ships came to port and my father came to learn of it by what I imagined to be some feat of magic, but what was probably no more than looking up the shipping news to see what vessel was on its way. I'm not sure what other families did on weekends, but it was our habit to visit the Muslim Indian or Pakistani crews of ships coming into Fremantle harbour.

These were the days of the White Australia policy, which gave us the unique status, in the late 1940s, of being the only Muslim family in Perth, a distinction I was always uneasy about. My dad would sit sharing a hookah, drawing the smoke into his lungs, and talking in Urdu or Punjabi to the serang and the crew, men who fed us fabulous curries and rich parathas. I was always a favourite and came home with my pockets full of money and chocolates, for the lonely seamen, once they had signed on, saw their own families only every three or four years if they were lucky.

I always believed that I was linked to these strange ships because of my mother's father — the Kashmiri who had stoked many a ship's furnace until one day, in the late nineteenth century, he jumped ship in Melbourne, came ashore and stayed for the rest of his life. Maybe he'd had his fill of the sea for he became a landlubber; a hawker in the Latrobe Valley, making his living with a horse and cart loaded up with bolts of material, safety pins, cotton and tins of curry powder, meandering along the dusty tracks of country Victoria in the late-nineteenth and early-twentieth centuries. He was the first boat person in my life, although I never met him.

I enjoyed those visits where men with liquid brown eyes and gleaming black moustaches would fuss over us; I was at home in their company although their language was strange to me — it was the faces that were so familiar. The only white faces on board were the occasional purser or the ship's captain — always a sunburnt Englishman or Scot — with crisp white shirt and shorts, long socks, a cap and lots of gold braid. Everyone stood up when he entered the crew's quarters, and I understood that he was a person of authority because of his cap, his gold and black epaulets but most of all because his skin was white. Why he came to see us I was never quite sure for we were a modest family of no distinction. But years later I understood that my mother was a great beauty and perhaps that is what drew the captains below deck, or perhaps they thought it kind of us to visit their homesick crews, not understanding that my father used these visits to ease his own feelings of loss and nostalgia for the places of his youth. For although he was Australian born, his childhood and his youth belonged to the small town of Sri Alamgir in what is now

Pakistan. After our ship visits I would return home with a new sense of identity, albeit a confused sense of place. One thing was clear — the British captains belonged in Australia.

The years passed, the White Australia decades drifted by and, one day, when I looked in the mirror of society, I started seeing reflections of myself. The Colombo Plan brought Malaysian and Singaporean students into our homes, and in the seventies people of South Asian ancestry began immigrating to Australia. You no longer needed to be affiliated to the Catholic Church like many of the Anglo-Burmese, or be Christian, and for the most part pale, like the Burghers of Sri Lanka — both groups suddenly out of favour when their browner countrymen farewelled the British.

My sense of place grew stronger and so did my confidence. But there were certain lessons that stayed with me always, certain ways of looking at the world that I never forgot, or put to one side. By the time I was nine I was honing a razor-sharp tongue to deal with bigots and bigotry.

Perhaps these were the occasions which prompted my mother to tell me the Scone Story, a story she repeated so often that I came to know it off by heart. 'When God was creating the world and it came time to fashion mankind he made three kinds of people, just like there are three kinds of scones …' Years later I came to understand the inherent racism in my mother's story, woven to protect her own children and to hell with anyone else's!

'The first batch of scones God cooked up,' Mum said, were burnt, which didn't taste so good (she avoided using the word 'black'), then came the undercooked pale scones which were also pretty yucky, and then (slow roll of drums) came the perfect scones, browned on top — just the way God liked them.' At this stage of her story I would lean against her crying out, 'Me! Me! Me!' Looking back, how can I blame her for the strategies she used to bolster our self-esteem, especially when we came to her in tears? Mothers everywhere tell their children stories to protect them from the cruelty of others; it has always been so and perhaps my mother's mother passed these stories onto her when she was little and in pain.

I have my mother to thank for turning me into a fighter; I have my father and John Steinbeck to thank for their stories of injustice: whether Indians were being gunned down at Amritsar by the British, or the Okies oppressed by rich farmers and anti-unionist cartels, the message was the same for me. I knew who were the oppressed and who was doing the oppressing.

And then later in the fifties, when I learnt how governments won elections by punishing some groups and favouring others, and why it took more than a decade for my uncle to obtain a tourist visa so that he could come to visit his older brother, my father, I understood another of Mum's stories and what she meant when she said with folded arms and a tight look of grievance on her face, 'If Jesus Christ wanted to come into this country, they wouldn't let him in.'

By now I knew that Jesus had brown skin, even though my schoolmates and picture books testified that he was white skinned and blue eyed. He was from the Middle East wasn't he? Even though we were not followers of Christ it comforted me to know that Jesus was really one of 'us' and not really one of 'them' as everyone pretended. This was mixed with strange feelings of how lucky I was to be born in a country which even Jesus was barred from entering — unless he jumped ship like grandfather, or had the right piece of paper in his hand — but my understanding of racism at the time was experiential; there was no historical context and I knew nothing about indigenous Australians, nothing of how the Chinese were mistreated and the Kanakas abused and deported — my world was myself.

All around Australia today there are mothers and fathers who are explaining to their children that they really are Australians; that in spite of what they are hearing and reading they are not the enemy, they are not evil. These times will pass they are told. Parents and teachers must put in plain words what is so hard for young minds to understand: the climate of hate they hear on the radio and the repulsion they see reflected in strangers' eyes on the trains, the streets, even as they walk to school. If you're living in Sydney or Melbourne at present, and are of Lebanese or Arab background, whether you are Christian or Muslim it makes little difference, it's doubly hard. Sane explanations have to be found for insane reactions.

Nada Roude, my old friend from our 'Hypothetical' show night of fame, was shocked when her fourteen-year-old daughter asked her, 'Mum, what am I? Am I Australian, because they don't let me feel that I'm one of them.'

Nada had no doubts about her own identity as an overseas-born Australian Muslim; she had made that clear when the velvet-voiced Robertson had interrogated her before the cameras. 'Are you more Lebanese or more Australian,' he had asked her, pacing up and down with his tiger-like energy. But to hear her Australian-born daughter confess that she didn't feel accepted made her understand what young people faced outside the home.

In the months following September 11, children at the Noor al Houda Islamic College in Sydney's west stopped walking home from school by themselves. Silma Ihram, their school principal and the woman I once likened to a 'woman warrior', tough and articulate when we first met in 1993, told her students' parents that it was no longer safe for their children to be alone in the community.

Silma drove home the lessons of history by constantly reminding her students that Catholics were once marginalised in Australian society and that Germans and Japanese were interned during both world wars. 'There is no guarantee that this will not happen to us — unless we win over the general community and convince them that we are good citizens.'

Muslims living in other cities and towns might have difficulty in accepting Silma's sombre warning. However, the chain of events which unfolded in the Harbour city caught everyone unawares. If the hate mail I have read, and the level of vitriol on talkback radio is any indicator of popular opinion, then Silma's fears, at the time, were legitimate.

As I revisit my old friends and haunts after eight years, the tensions, worries and underlying anger are everywhere. What people took for granted over the years has vanished. Muslims do not feel safe any more.

Silma expects her students to be model Australian citizens — she believes this is how they will survive. 'I make a personal point not to respond to provocation and to be polite and respectful with others at all times,' said Silma, who seems to have mellowed in the intervening years.

'I try to give the dry-cleaner, shop owner, waiter, secretary and everyone I meet a positive image by my behaviour and friendly comments, and I try to make the students understand that they must present the image that they want the public to feel about them. Through dress, manners and appearance,' she says, 'they can present a positive or a negative image and create a positive or negative response. This is up to them, for I believe that we get what we earn in terms of respect and understanding. The more we present a personal image that is aggressive, impatient, impolite and lacking in integrity — or downright arrogant — the more rejection we will face.'

Not everyone agrees with Silma's approach — they call

it burdening the victim — and I think I side with that point of view; it is a heavy load for young shoulders to carry. Yet, I also understood why she feels this sense of urgency. Only the day before I'd sat through an unpleasant experience where a handful of young Muslim women had personified the aggression and arrogance that Silma warned her students against. I'd finally left the meeting in disgust, no longer willing to tolerate what seemed to be a form of 'cultural bullying' being played out by this group of Muslim women against a smaller group of non-Muslim women, who were not strangers to each other. The young Muslim women displayed a level of bombast I found highly offensive in an impromptu discussion comparing Islam with Christianity. What I witnessed was loud, irrational and plain rude. I was left wondering if it was an expression of their current vulnerability as Lebanese Muslims, or a special display put on for me. In the end I decided it was perhaps both, tempered by the opportunity to turn the tables for once.

Teachers at another Muslim school, Rissalah College in Lakemba, tried explaining to their confused young charges that the world was not at war, that Muslims were not bad people and they must be strong and understand that many people would blame Islam and Muslims everywhere for the terrorist attacks in New York. They were called on to feel compassion for those who died and for the families left behind to grieve. Teachers reminded them that no one has the power to take another person's life.

Elsewhere across the country, Islamic schools held special assemblies to explain to their students what had taken place and the effects it might have on Australian Muslims generally. Special commemorative services were also held for the victims in New York. In spite of everything done to prepare them for what they might face from non-Muslims and hear about themselves on television and radio, it was the blackest year in most of their young lives.

Six months later, at a state government school on the other side of Australia, a non-Muslim friend listens in horror as her son's classmates reveal how much they want to 'Blow up an Afghan' yelling, 'Death to bin Laden!' When she complains to the class teacher about this overt demonstration of hate from eleven year olds, his answer is a cool, 'Well, why not?'

The Sydney gang rapes, the New York terrorist attacks and the 'children overboard affair' outraged mainstream Australia and shocked Australian Muslims more than anyone outside their communities and homes ever realised. In the eyes of many non-Muslim Australians these three episodes merged together like a relentless tidal wave, moving against Australian society.

Women were in the front-line because of their traditional garments, especially the *hijab,* which made them easily identifiable. There was no mistaking the hostility when they went beyond the safety of their front gates: on trains, at work, in shops, people who had smiled good morning at them in the past would no longer meet their eyes; en masse people turned away as if Australian Muslims were personally responsible for all the terrible events which had happened over the last year. There had always been a certain social distance between non-Muslims and orthodox Muslims — a distance which both sides often seemed to prefer, but now Muslims faced an abyss and overnight they had become non-people. The reaction was far worse than it had been ten years before during the Gulf War.

If they were lucky the reactions remained at the level of silent suspicion; if they were unlucky they were sworn at, spat on, jostled and abused; hate mail and pornographic material was stuffed in their letterboxes and they were physically attacked — pulling off scarves was a favourite ploy. Mosques in Adelaide and Brisbane were firebombed and graffiti daubed on mosque walls in other towns.

Old friends, who'd permitted me to use their real names before in my writing, now asked to remain anonymous — they hoped I'd understand. One of the bravest Muslim feminists I knew described to me how she curled up inside and died with shame after the events of that year; she no longer wanted to leave the house and for the first time in her life this champion of the *hijab*, actually thought of removing her scarf in a paradoxical attempt at disguise. She baulked at the last minute 'Because it would be like walking around naked,' she said.

But Nada was still Nada. Her face was thinner but nothing else seemed to have changed; if her hair had an odd grey strand or two, they were well hidden beneath her *hijab* which disguises age as well as a woman's beauty. I asked Nada how Australian she felt these days. Had her faith in her identity as an Australian Muslim been shaken?

It hadn't, she answered. 'My commitment to Australia, my dedication and the joy of being able to fuse my Islamic identity with being an Australian surrounded by cultural diversity has strengthened if anything over the years and nothing can alter that.' But for the first time she was forced to ask herself if others accepted her as an Australian.

The Muslim community throughout Australia was shocked beyond belief in 2001. What would come next? Every time a media story broke about a bank robbery, a building set on fire, a case of welfare rorting or insurance fraud, everyone took a deep breath, 'Please God, not a Muslim!'

'What we have endured over the last year,' Nada said, 'would make your hair stand on end. The harassment and the attacks were bad enough but on top of everything the community was constantly being asked — as if we were subhuman with no regard for human suffering — "Do you condemn these attacks?" or "Why do you hate Americans?"'

Explain yourselves, the media demanded. Nada dashed from one media interview to the next; it was like standing before an inquisition, but she felt compelled to try to make people understand that the religion she so loved was not the violent creed they thought it to be, that it had much in common with the other great faiths of the world, that 'Allah' was not a foreign god, but just the Arabic word for 'God' — everybody's God, but this was not what interviewers wanted to discuss. Within a few weeks she had participated in about twenty interviews trying to explain that Muslims were not all the same, that politics played a role in the New York tragedy; from one breakfast show to the next she travelled and she was not alone. In every capital city in the world, wherever Muslims were an immigrant minority, men and women did their best to 'explain Islam' to their frightened fellow citizens.

'People were repelled and disgusted by us and the feeling was that we did not belong, that there was no place for us in this country,' Nada said.

Talkback radio in particular was obsessed with questions of loyalty and whipped up the old 'them and us' feelings. Muslim community leaders were careful about what they said, but some, like Shaykh Taj-Din al-Hilali, inadvertently fuelled fires instead of putting them out. This was seized on by many of the Shaykh's critics, people who make a business of sifting through every word the Mufti says, looking for something with which to hang him. Other spokespeople who tried to look behind the event and explain some of the political complexities were likely to find themselves labelled traitors by talkback radio listeners and the tabloids.

I remembered the wise words of my *halal* butcher in Lakemba, Anis Kahil, a man of little formal education but great wisdom.

> You need a heart big enough to love two countries if you are an immigrant; it shouldn't be a case of choosing one over the other. It's like having two children; your heart must be big enough to love them both.

Nada and many other leaders worked around the clock, often in tears, trying to make people understand. Muslims, in spite of what the wider Australian community thought, were not locked in to one solid block of opinion, there were always a range of views. As they worked to put out the communal fires, they grew to resent how they were automatically expected to prove their Australianness and how, more than any other community, they were held accountable for the actions of individuals and renegades. This state of affairs filled them with a deep, abiding sadness: the sadness of one who is constantly rejected but keeps on trying, hoping that one day they will be accepted.

Nada overcame her despair and continued speaking out but other Muslims retreated and became silent because they did not believe they would receive a 'fair go'. Was there a different set of laws for Muslims? Matters grew worse when a number of Muslim homes were raided by ASIO after September 11.

Looking back over the last ten years, from the Gulf War period to today, I could not help but think that the organised Muslim communities in Australia, the religious societies and ethnic organisations, and the leaders — for all their activities and ecumenical speak fests — had failed to build bridges between Muslims and non-Muslims, and now the ignorance and lack of understanding was threatening to bury them. They concentrated on explaining the teachings of Islam at the expense of human-interest stories, family tales which could show what they had in common with other Australians, not what set them apart. The theological explanations the devout transmitted might earn them religious merit but often frightened non-Muslim Australians into believing they were out to convert the world. The communities had concentrated on building mosques and schools — the icons they yearned for — and had forgotten that if they lived as an island unto themselves, they were setting themselves apart. Mosque communities like Lakemba were seen as changing the face of Australia.

The level of harassment, as Nada put it bluntly, 'Scared the hell out of everybody.' So much animosity had been hidden all this time, 'So that what we'd thought a safe place,' she said, 'was not safe at all.' They would have to start all over again.

'Our existence as a community has been focused on defending our position — always, always! But in spite of everything I've said I believe in the intrinsic fairness of Australians; they are incredible people, truly original, and underneath it all they are fair, but they don't interact with Muslims and their only information comes from listening to the radio and watching television, and what is conveyed to them via the media, they take as gospel.

'The media entertains people by giving them topics that are weird and strange. We are not human — we are weird. We've got to change that perception.' In their own ways Nada and Silma were articulating similar messages with the same level of urgency.

Nada has put any residual bitterness behind her; she is too busy. The Lebanese Muslim Women's Association and the International Muslim Women's Network are commited to building bridges — no matter how long it takes; they are searching for allies, especially among other people of faith in the Christian communities. They attend workshops to learn media skills — Nada would one day like to take on Sydney's leading shock-jock hosts. Silently I wish her luck; I think she understands my feelings on the subject, how I personally consider it a tactic akin to walking through a minefield — a waste of energy and resources with all the dangers of backfiring and supplying the tabloids with yet more sensationalist copy.

But there were other women outside the organised sisterhood, an older generation whose bitterness could only find outlet in symbolic utterances. They would never travel to *kafir* countries, not ever again they vowed, not even for a holiday, only Muslim countries would receive their tourist dollars from now on. These women had arrived as first-generation immigrants; their lives were spent in the house surrounded by extended families and friends, women who shunned non-Muslim circles and whose large families were the centre of their lives. I hoped their bitterness would fade. One of the dangers of telling people that they're no good, that they are indeed a threat to society and that their religion is violent and worthless, is that eventually they may begin to embrace the hatred swirling around them and send it right back, even passing it on to their children in some cases.

The 'children overboard affair' again presented Islam as an alien culture in which parents were so barbaric, so subhuman that they would endanger their children by throwing them into the sea to stop the Australian navy from doing its 'duty'. The *Tampa* Crisis, as it was called, took place when the Royal Australian Navy was used to prevent a Norwegian ship, the MV *Tampa,* from landing 438 asylum seekers on the Australian territory of Christmas Island.

If a poll of Australian Muslim opinion had been conducted the week the *Tampa* headlines broke you would have been hard pressed to find anyone taken in by the government's election gambit. 'I certainly don't want people like that coming to Australia,' the Prime Minister said. Everyone understood the subtext: 'people like that' meant people like Muslims from Afghanistan and the Middle East, or Pakistan or India — religion was now a surrogate for race. Not only were asylum seekers demonised, Australian Muslims took this massive insult as being directed at them as well — I know that I did. Even though my family history in Australia reaches back more than a hundred and twenty years, Prime Minister Howard and ministers Ruddock and Reith were insulting me, and the memory of my parents, when they demonised the *Tampa* refugees and won an election.

Still, after some hard searching I managed to find one Muslim from Malaysia who told me that yes, he'd believed what he'd read and seen on television, reluctantly, he added, but the Prime Minister had said it was so and he knew that a prime minister wouldn't lie — the man had not been in our country for very long.

Muslims, regardless of their ethnicity or birthplace; non-practising Muslims who lived in affluent green and leafy suburbs (many of them professional people well integrated into mainstream Australia) and the truly devout who chose to live as part of mosque communities — were for once united: they all believed that justice was not being done nor being seen to be done. For that matter, why was no apology ever made to the asylum seekers falsely accused of throwing their children into the sea? Why weren't Christians coming out of Sunday church services stopped and asked to explain why their men of God were abusing children?

Nada still refuses to lose hope. 'I've worked hard at

making this country my own, I've worked and contributed from the moment I came. I want to tell all those who hate us, don't you dare question my commitment, loyalty and love to this nation, because I wouldn't be here if I didn't feel so strongly!

'A fascination with us has become a source of entertainment for the whole world,' are Nada's last words to me. I hope it won't take another eight years and another catastrophe before we meet again.

Stereotypes now define people as less than human and what a litany there is to choose from: veiled women, fierce bearded men, barbaric parents, rapists and suicide bombers — these are the images taken to represent Islam. But where is the human face that I know? Where are my parents, my brother and my sister. Where are my friends?

Dr Ahmed Shboul, at Sydney University, is still the same overworked academic I met in 1994; his office must surely rank among one of the most 'overflowing' anywhere in the world, with papers and books toppling from chairs and visiting students dropping in and out, for he is a man not known for turning his students away. His room is more like a chamber, much larger than the rabbit hutches most academics teaching in the non-sandstone universities endure, and it has a medieval charm: I half expect robed monks to wander by or at the very least a scholar or two from the Great Court of Harun al Rashid.

On the surface nothing seems to have changed — in reality everything has. It is not all bad news, for student numbers are up since September 11 and his courses on the history of the Arab world and Arab and Islamic thought are popular. His courses look at oil and politics and culture and Islam. Most of his students are non-Arab and non-Muslim — everyone is interested these days. But understanding the Middle East, he warns, is not just about reading the Qur'an and understanding Hadith.

I am curious about how he sees his role as a teacher and expert on the Middle East in these troubled times. Does he feel like a man walking a tightrope? How does he react to the numerous 'instant experts' on the Middle East?

Ahmed Shboul sees himself as, 'Striving to contribute to a better understanding, based on a critical analysis of Islam as a religion and as a civilisation, with emphasis on the diversity and the often-neglected secular dimensions of the Islamic world.' He wants his students to see different points of view, to be critical and have what he calls, 'A healthy scepticism — not only towards politicians and religious leaders, but also about the media, the think-tanks and the intellectuals.'

Ahmed's impatience with 'instant experts' surfaces when I mention American scholar and international relations expert Samuel Huntington, just to provoke him. He has no time for Huntington's 'clash of civilisation's' theory, which pits Islam against the West; this he believes is ideologically driven and thrives on the notion that Islam and the West are two opposites destined to remain in conflict.

'Civilisations are not watertight entities,' he tells me in full lecture mode, 'or monoliths. They are all complex and interconnected; each of them has its own diversities and what is most important, they learn from each other through a historical process of change.'

He has spent an academic lifetime teaching his readers and students that at present Muslims and Arabs are not unique; their history and their present situation is capable of being understood like any other human society.

The morning after September 11, Professor Shboul entered his class and immediately sensed the tension and confusion amongst the mainly young students. Only the Muslims were silent. 'The event charged us all with foreboding,' he recalled. 'It was not easy to come to terms with what had happened. From my perspective it was even more difficult to think of what was going to happen as a result.'

To help his stunned students come to terms with the 'why?' and 'what does this mean?' and 'what could this lead to?' type of questions, Professor Shboul threw the lecture open to a free discussion, the details of which he can no longer recall, for, as he reminded me, his curiosity was not that of a journalist: he saw himself first and foremost as a teacher. I suspected that like many others, he was coping with the shock waves of September 11 at a deeply personal level.

He turns to a favourite topic: the media as a distorting mirror, which is exactly where we left off talking eight years ago. Many media experts, he believes, pretend to seek an understanding of what lay behind the attacks on the United States. They are hunting for a causal link between the Muslims who attacked America and what they believe is inherent in Islam — this is the only explanation they seek. 'We need to have an understanding of Islam,' they say, as if this is a talisman which will protect them from harm.

'What is it in Islam that lends itself to violence?' they ask. Dr Shboul sees a problematic pattern to this kind of questioning. 'What does the Qur'an say about jihad? About the role of women? Why does Islam breed martyrs? Please explain it to me!' These frequent questions, Ahmed Shboul explains, are not relevant to the events of September 11.

The word 'oil' runs through my mind; where are the questions about oil supplies, oil bosses and oil interests, and the sale of armaments? History, culture and politics — and of course 'national interests' — would supply answers that theology cannot, if anybody bothered to ask.

Susan Sontag, author and public intellectual, bothered to

ask in an article in *The New Yorker*, 24 September 2001, and caused a furore in the United States which has still not died down:

> Let's by all means grieve together. But let's not be stupid together. A few shreds of historical awareness might help us understand what has just happened.

Ahmed Shboul does his best to explain how agendas are political and that men like Osama bin Laden are ideologically driven, and use religion as a tool to fight another ideologically driven force, the United States of America. In his lectures he makes it clear, in case anyone may be wondering, that he is not on the side of the bin Ladens of the world, nor does he support the Taliban ideology.

Nor does he side with television journalists who want people to play up to the cameras. 'They roll up and interview kids in the western suburbs and get them to act in a certain way, to mouth off and act macho and anti - American: it is like a script.' On one occasion he was asked to help a television journalist locate a Muslim 'type' who would show anger about a set topic.

'He was quite explicit that he wasn't asking me to be interviewed, but wanted me to help him find a man or boy who would show their rage. "Do you want a Muslim fanatic?" I asked him. "Sorry, I can't help you." I think he found someone in the end, not a fanatic, but he kept egging him on and trying to lead him into saying something until the guy got angry, responded and the cameras rolled!'

We hold no crystal ball in our hands, but Ahmed and I both understand that television cameramen wandering around the streets of Lakemba might well be able to find such angry responses.

Six months later that is exactly what happens and three cameramen from SBS television are attacked as they stand outside Lakemba Mosque on a Friday after main prayers are over and the crowds are leaving; they take their footage and apparently ask questions — it is the day after one of the rapists has received a fifty-five year sentence. The cameramen are badly beaten by a group of up to ten men who, according to a witness, stopped their cars when they saw the SBS crew; some Muslims come to the cameramen's aid and try to stand between them and their attackers while others stand and watch. One angry bystander vents his feelings. 'You don't see them camped outside Catholic churches when a priest is accused of abusing children.' Nobody knows who their attackers are, or so they say. It is a cowardly attack, a shameful episode.

I traded happier stories with Ahmed like storytellers once used to do. 'Not long ago,' I said to him, 'Circus Oz donated free tickets to a group of twenty or so refugees — men, women and children — to see their first circus ever. It was a wonderful, generous idea with the added bonus of providing story ideas and photo opportunities so that refugees could be seen as people. A newspaper photographer kept insisting on a photo of a Muslim woman refugee in a veil looking at the scantily clad circus artists and registering SHOCK! The Afghan woman laughed and refused: she found the circus artists' costumes charming, she said through an interpreter.'

I last saw Joe Wakim in 1994; he has since moved to Sydney, away from his beloved Australian Arabic Council based in Melbourne, which he helped found ten years ago. He serves the community with his pen these days and his words are angry, but it is a steady anger which motivates him as he picks his way through the evidence. As usual we drift into a lively discussion about media culture.

Joe Wakim was in for a rude surprise when he moved from Melbourne to Sydney. Arabic-speaking taxi drivers wanted to know as soon as they picked him up, 'Are you Muslim or Christian?' In all his years in Melbourne he had never been asked that question before. Joe is a Christian Australian Lebanese with close friends in both the Muslim and Jewish communities.

I had observed that over the last decade anti-Semitism in Australia was extending itself to attack the tribe of Ishmael along with the tribe of Isaac: there was more than a passing resemblance between the hook-nosed Arab of today and the hook-nosed Jew of yore. I wondered if now that hating Jews is beyond the pale in polite circles, and has been driven underground, is it more permissible — even fashionable — to hate the Arab?

'The Australian public has been raised on a diet of anti-Arab stereotypes and has a predisposition to believe any stories which fit neatly into our stereotype about people like that,' he said. 'Hollywood films systematically demonise Arabs and Muslims as terrorists to be feared, the new enemies of civilisation.'

Forget the Gestapo, the Cong or the Red
Look out for the hook-nosed Arab instead.

The words flashed into my head without warning and I surprised myself at how quickly I'd made up this ugly couplet. They were the bitter harvest of my own cynicism. Action heroes now battled swarthy, sweaty, bearded villains who spoke Arabic and hijacked and bombed almost at will, now and then stopping to roll out their prayer mats; they were monsters whose own mothers would have a hard time loving them and, as I knew, Lebanese mothers are very forgiving.

The series of gang rapes in Sydney in late 2000 blackened the name and wounded the honour of the Lebanese in New South Wales, especially the Muslim Lebanese of south-west Sydney. Fifteen young men broke with decency and turned their backs on Australian law and society's sense of what is civilised. They also dishonoured the cultural and religious codes that many of their parents and elders lived by. They chose or, under peer-group pressure, succumbed to a kind of vileness alien to followers of any religious or humanist code. Their acts were brutal and their collective gang mentality showed a macho contempt of dreadful proportions for their victims.

They showed no mercy and in return received no mercy, as reflected in the heavy sentences handed down — fifty-five years in one case. The media told us in great detail how the public reacted: strangers and office staff punching the air, even uncorking bottles of champagne. Turn the clock back to the days of public hangings and the same crowd might well have jockeyed for a vantage point overlooking the gallows. The resulting media hysteria and huge public outcry delivered the entire Lebanese Muslim community up as scapegoats. Egged on by irresponsible sections of the media and pragmatic politicians responding to 'the mood of the mob', there was now further proof of how evil Muslims were the whole world over.

Where had these boys emerged from? I knew where they were headed: straight into prison. If they managed to survive prison violence, they would be middle-aged men before they ever came out, forgotten by everyone — except their parents and their victims. It was hard finding the right people to talk to, everyone was defending a position; the wounds were fresh and I suspected that the people who worked inside the youth culture were not being interviewed by journalists.

Where were these young men when I'd made my rounds

of Lakemba and Bankstown eight years before? Nine year olds at primary school, or maybe attending high school. Were they the kids playing in the park as I walked from Denise's house to the train each day?

Talking to local high school teachers helps me fill in some of the gaps and a picture emerges, hazy in some respects but nevertheless telling. Young Lebanese criminals are often boys from the lowest rungs of the 'forgotten tribe'. They have low self-esteem; their thrills come through violence. Many of them fail at school and have records as juvenile offenders; they seem destined to repeat the cycle of their parents' low-skilled jobs. Often they are children of large immigrant families where parents may be illiterate in their own language and have limited spoken English. Their parents generally have no understanding of Australian school culture and little involvement with the education system. Sons and daughters lie to their parents, who are shocked when they finally hear that their children have been suspended or expelled from school. Drug dealing and protection rackets amongst Lebanese youth is a growing problem, Muslim and Christian alike — everyone seems to know this except their elders; some parents don't want to know, others are completely ignorant about youth culture, and boys in particular know very well how to exploit their parents' ignorance. Boys drift into the drug culture and easy money. Not much contemplation goes on in their young lives and sadly they lack the skills to reflect: they come from an oral culture, rich in imagery and hyperbole and are ensnared in a literal concrete world.

The mood of many young men trapped on the outside between two cultures is easy to read. At home they are too Australian to be Lebanese but outside, in the eyes of the Australian population, they're too Lebanese to be Australian. Nevertheless, they are very adroit at exploiting both cultures with the opportunism of youth.

How do boys fall into these gangs? Joe Wakim worked with street kids in his days as a social worker, before he put on a suit and tie and transformed himself into a businessman. You can change your profession but you can't change your memories, and he still remembers what it was like being Lebanese in the 1970s.

'As a teenager, I had the same hierarchy of needs as my peers: to be accepted, to be inconspicuous, yet successful at school,' he said. 'But being Lebanese was a burden, not a bonus, and I was tired of all the "Where are you from?" questions.' At the time the Lebanese were a minority among new Australians.

'I hoped that by denying my Lebanese heritage I would become Australian, once and for all. But then I grew up; I was at Melbourne University in the 1980s when it dawned on me that denying my "Leb side" did not make me Australian. There is an Arab proverb which says, "They who deny their heritage have no heritage." I had come full circle.

'The boys we are reading about in the papers are boys who resort to their own tribe for safety. They move in homogeneous circles of fellow Muslims and they stay within their local demography dominated by their own majority — hence their territoriality based on a need to belong somewhere and make their mark.'

In Joe's analysis, their only sense of power comes when they are surrounded by each other. 'These boys lack dreams,' he said, 'their actions are far more crude and based on selfish opportunism and immediate gratification.'

Joe points the finger at certain cult television shows like the SBS show 'Pizza'. He calls them 'Wogorama revisited', except that they send up the more recently arrived immigrant groups, not the Greeks and Italians who had thirty or forty years in Australia as a safety barrier before their comedians emerged from a generation that could send up ethnicity with all the confidence of people who know they belong.

'Some of the "Pizza" characters are Lebanese chick-chasing meatheads with an IQ of three. It's not Australian-Leb culture they're sending up,' argues Joe — it's Leb-American, with the hip-hop, backstreet black gangster image from the Bronx and boys calling each other "bro" instead of "mate".'

Comedy cults convey certain messages and you can trace a continuum between the chick-chasing culture which the boys glorify and capitalise on as 'cool' and the other end of that same continuum: ganging up on girls as sexual predators, which is also seen as cool. 'Until,' he adds, 'the boys are imprisoned and then gang raped in gaol themselves — how cool is that for their macho image? But they never think that far ahead in their search for immediate pleasure.'

I myself have struggled for some time to grasp why these particular young men singled out these particular young women to rape, and why they used racial insults to mock their victims. I was not looking for excuses; I was looking for explanations. I was not interested in defending them — how could anyone outside their own families claim any feeling of kinship with them? My need was to understand, not to justify. Were they the racially motivated attacks the media claimed? Everything that I was reading in the papers pointed in that direction: a victim's account on 'Sixty Minutes', even the rapists' own police statements — it seemed to all fall into place, but something was wrong, something was being overlooked in these reports. Playing the sensationalist race card seemed to shape and satisfy the public's expectations in 2001; they were ready to think the worst of any Arab or Muslim, and it was something that certain sections of the media carried out with missionary zeal. I suspected the real answers were just as dark, but far more complex.

Men who rape often use vile epithets to terrorise women as a tool to further intimidate, humiliate and brand their prey. Their taunts enhance their act of defilement and perhaps, in some perverted sense, increase their own feelings of power and satisfy their need to feel superior. Men who rape cross all religious, ethnic and class boundaries.

I believe that the dominant culture in the lives of these young men in question, at the time of their attacks, was one of strong loyalty to each other — all the more in that half of the boys were related — and of allegiance to a set of deviant values they shared: attitudes and poses that they'd adopted from imitating their role models. Their folk heroes are characters that we would normally identify as the 'bad guys' — swearing, misogynist, violent and irreverent. They believed they were as invincible as the television heroes they idolised. Yet while they aped the style of the American youth gangs they saw on screen, their groupings were more loosely structured and opportunistic; they were not organised like bikies or other 'guilds', with a common structure and formal code of conduct.

When the assaults first made the headlines in the Melbourne *Sun-Herald* in August 2001, some sections of the media presented the attacks as 'hate attacks' — racially motivated gang rapes against white girls. 2UE talkback host Alan Jones helped light the bonfire in late July 2001 by painting a picture of a city at the mercy of Islamic gangs, as 'Media Watch' on the ABC pointed out a year later. Along with others, Jones' beat up of Muslims intensified after September 11; pinning the sexual crimes of a group of men onto an entire racial minority became the order of the day.

> Are the Muslim rapes of Australian women in the Bankstown area the first signs of an Islamic hatred towards the community that welcomed them here years ago? Have we now, because of multiculturalism, created an Islamic community that's more aligned with Islam than Australia?

These were the questions Alan Jones put to his morning listeners on 13 September 2001. Underneath it all I could hear his real message: They come here and they rape our women! Jones was the populist leader of the pack, but his was not a lone voice. The moral panic Jones and others spread was unfounded, but it certainly resonated with their listeners and readers.

I think that we are too quick to use the term 'racist' as a general label these days. There are different degrees of 'racist' behaviour and along with 'fascist' it is a term we apply too readily, which often lets the real racists and fascists off the hook. The racial taunts the rapists used, like 'white pig' were disgusting but may not have been necessarily racist per se.

As I sit struggling with my thoughts, the tradition of 'sledging' black and brown cricketers comes to mind. I push the idea away in haste, the comparison sounds obscene. I cannot trivialise the crime of rape; a victim lives with what was done to her for the rest of her life. It's far removed from strolling off the cricket ground and letting bygones be bygones after a drink or two. Yet it seems to me that there are times when the use of racial epithets is an accompaniment to an act, rather than an end in itself. Is it possible, I wondered, to separate actions from the use of racial epithets?

I hesitate to go down this road; weeks pass until finally I know I have to deal with it. Let me be clear about this, I am happy that the Australian Rules Football League has outlawed the racial sledging that was regularly used against Aboriginal footballers, making it a punishable offence — it was long overdue. But I see a distinction between this low behaviour and the deeply held racist beliefs of many Hansonite voters and the criminal acts of Jack Van Tongeren, who together with some of his gang members of the Australian National Movement firebombed Chinese restaurants in Western Australia in the eighties.

Let there be no misunderstanding. The fourteen Australian men of Lebanese Muslim background who raped four young women committed despicable crimes for which there are no nuances to excuse their assault. During my return visits to Sydney I found no one inside the Muslim community interested in defending them. I never spoke to their families. After the sentences were handed down in August 2002, the Melbourne *Age* quoted Muslim leaders who believed that those who committed 'a crime beyond imaginable human behaviour should be put away for life'. They meant what they said; this was no show put on for the media.

I believe the rapes committed by these Lebanese Australians in late 2000 were primarily a re-enactment of their macho fantasies, rather than an immediate expression of racism. In their eyes it made them real men like their cult heroes. These were the kind of young hoods brazen enough to invade a local high school and confront any teacher standing in their way as they search for a sister seen talking to a young man in order to give her the belting of a lifetime for 'dishonouring' their family name.

And herein lies the complexity of it all. What they enjoy acting out from television, porno videos and the misogynist lyrics of their favourite rap music, may be supported by attitudes some of them probably learnt from their parents, sometimes their mothers. These values are not Islamic, nor are they Lebanese or culturally based, although there are certain influences and customs to do with the respective roles of men and women and the authority which men hold over women which can be traced to religious beliefs and cultural practices.

A minority of these young Australian Lebanese men grow up within households where young women are seen as pure and worthy of protection if they behave according to the strictest moral code — and seen as sluts as soon as they fail to do so. In their macho, drug-taking culture, 'chicks' are objects for their consumption and typical western female behaviour is considered whorish. These boys have often been told by adults around them that there are good girls and there are bad girls. Feminists in the West have long noticed similar patterns in Christian cultures: the Madonna and the whore syndrome. These beliefs have not come from Lebanon, but where they are strongly held it frequently comes in reaction to living as a minority in a permissive society with relaxed sexual mores. Many young Australian-Lebanese males are married off in their teens to stop them from falling into 'mischief', a quaint expression used for sex outside marriage.

Young Muslim women of various nationalities, including the Lebanese, are protected by male relatives curtailing their freedom of movement and controlling how they socialise in public places. They are 'good girls' who do not go out alone, especially at night; their friends are known to their parents and many wear the hijab which hides them from the lustful gazes of other men. In an ironic sense, Muslim women need protection against the very misogyny and vileness personified by the young rapists now in gaol.

Not everyone will agree with me, but I believe that the so-called Lebanese/Sydney rapes were opportunistic attacks committed by a group of young men dedicated to acting out their group culture, which included a contempt for the Anglo-Australian girls they met on trains or at bus stations at night — girls who were unprotected and outside the codes which these male types accepted as protecting decent girls. A frightening aspect of their pathology is how they acted with impunity, with no fear or thought for the consequences. They would not have dared dishonour girls from their own communities — they knew the reprisals that would have quietly been carried out, swiftly and brutally.

Nicholas Cowdery, QC, New South Wales Director of Public Prosecutions, in an interview on the '7.30 Report' in mid July 2002, also had difficulty accepting that the attacks were some sort of ethnic act committed by one ethnic group against another. They fell into the category of delinquent male behaviour, he argued. 'The criminality of the crime of rape ... was the primary motivating factor,' he said. He regarded the racial epithets as an embellishment by those who committed the crime.

'But there were seven women and all Anglo-Celtic,' persisted his interviewer, Maxine McKew.

Cowdery pointed to an element of self-preservation on the part of perpetrators who looked outside their own ethnic group: if they attacked someone from their own background they might not even get to court.

Was it possible that the climate of opinion might be shifting? Now that Cowdery and a handful of others like James Murray, Religious Affairs columnist with The Australian and P.P. McGuiness of the Sydney Morning Herald argued against pinning a cultural context to the crimes perhaps the emotion would die down. I soon discovered however that the race card is hard to trump once it's firmly lodged in the public's mind. Over the last decade religion has become a surrogate for race when applied to Islam.

Local Muslim leaders had discovered this for themselves a

year earlier when the rapes first became public. When Shaykh Taj and others tried to explain that rape and violent crime were not a part of Lebanese culture or of Islam, reminding anyone who would listen that the attackers were Australian-born and intimating that the rapists reflected Australia's lax mores rather than Lebanon's, they only made matters worse.

They were not practising Muslims, 'Not true Muslims — just criminals, who couldn't even speak Arabic,' said Shaykh Taj Hilali. His response was more desperate than wise and media commentators declared that the Shaykh was in denial. But the Lakemba folk expected their mufti to rise to their defence; when he makes his media pronouncements the thousands who flock to the Lakemba Mosque are his real audience, not non-Muslim Australians.

There is a current of opinion widely held in Lakemba and Bankstown but not often stated publicly because it is seen to be blaming Australian culture. Muslim parents feel that their teenage children have too many rights and are caught between traditional Arabic culture and secular permissive Australia. 'They have no respect for their parents, elders and teachers because the law and the schools tell them to run to the authorities if their parents show them some discipline,' their elders complain.

But the public and the politicians lay the blame at the door of Lebanese parents and the 'un-Australian' culture they brought with them. Lebanese spokespeople, on the other hand, defended their religion by saying that rape was 'un Islamic'. Singled out, the Australian-Arabic community was told to 'fix the problem' because they were not bringing up their children properly. Talkback radio, letters to the editor, the man and woman on the street all expressed their opinions that the parents and, most of all, their Islamic-Lebanese culture were to blame. According to the *Sun-Herald* editorial, 26 August 2001, 'The burden should fall most heavily on those community and religious leaders with whom they [the rapists] most identify.' What the moral soothsayers ignored was that these boys, according to community insiders and youth workers, did not personally identify with either Islam or their culture, in spite of their 'I'm a Leb' poses. They were misfits who identified with each other and their outsider status which they gloried in.

But imams and other Muslim clergy were expected to solve the problems of 'their' young men in a way that Catholic or Protestant clergy were never asked to do in the twentieth century. The Premier's Office also delivered the message that the community needed to, 'Take control of your boys.' The community in turn asked, 'Why do we have to bear the guilt of the rape attacks?' In the heat of the moment the underground world of youth culture and gang cultures was largely ignored.

In August 2001 the New South Wales Bureau of Crime Statistics and Research put out a release entitled 'The Facts on Sexual Assault in Bankstown'. Included in the release were statistics which put the lie to popularly held convictions:

- Sexual violence in Bankstown, as shown by New South Wales Police data, was not increasing;
- The seventy women allegedly lured and pack raped as reported in the headlines of the Melbourne *Sun Herald* of 29 July 2001 were in reality seventy incidents of sexual assault recorded by the police in Bankstown in 1999 and approximately fifty of these offences were attributed to a single individual with a decidedly Anglo surname since imprisoned for sexual offences;
- The rate of recorded sexual assault in Bankstown was lower than both the Sydney average and the New South Wales State average;

- Despite the large Middle Eastern population in the Bankstown area, arrestees at Bankstown Police Station more often identified as 'Australian or New Zealanders' when asked their ethnic background than Middle Eastern.

To many observers like myself it came as no surprise that the talkbacks and tabloids played the race card, but journalists like Janet Albrechtsen, a columnist with the respected newspaper, *The Australian*, were not slow to join in as early as 3 September 2001 when she asserted that, 'Ethnic community leaders continue to deny an ethnic link when it is obvious there is one — a small but insidious group of Lebanese boys are raping Caucasian girls,' and referred to racially motivated gang rape in France and Denmark.

In the words of Robert Manne, *Sydney Morning Herald* columnist and Professor of Politics at Latrobe University, 'She [Albrechtsen] began to write in a manner which suggested that rapes by Muslims of young women had reached epidemic proportions in the West.'

A year later, Albrechtsen returned to this theme. The trials were over, the sentences had just been handed down. They were severe and in keeping with community expectations; no Muslim voices were heard publicly disputing the sentences, except for the boys' families. Yet the pattern of targeting Muslim Lebanese in the headlines and columns continued in 2002.

According to Manne, journalists who insisted that Muslim men were running amok gang raping white girls, provided almost perfect textbook cases of the 'new racism': a term sociologists use for those who argue that irreconcilable differences between human groupings are based on clashes of culture and religion and not on incompatible genes, as the old racism argued. 'Factually careless, socially reckless and morally cavalier,' was how Manne described Janet Albrechtsen's July 2002 column.

'Pack rape of white girls is an initiation rite of passage for a small section of young male Muslim youths,' said Jean-Jacques Rassial, a psychotherapist at Villetaneuse University, according to Albrechtsen in *The Australian*, 17 July 2002.

But as 'Media Watch' pointed out two months later, Albrechtsen had added the words 'white' and 'Muslim' to the French academic's argument. Tracked down by 'Media Watch', the professor was most upset and strongly dissociated himself from the remarks attributed to him. 'They are,' he wrote, 'the opposite of my views.'

Central to Albrechtsen's argument was the idea that gang rapists floundered between two sets of values: the Islamic values of their parents and the liberal and democratic values of western societies. She also quoted a Danish criminologist: he was supposed to have said that Denmark presented a similar picture to France with its influx of Muslim immigrants. But the man didn't say that at all, according to 'Media Watch'. '... The main explanation of gang rape probably is social, and not cultural or religious,' the unhappy Dane tried to explain.

Albrechtsen in the same July article also turned her attention nearer to home. She misquoted Muslim spokesman Keysar Trad, accusing him of excusing the rapists' behaviour when he was doing nothing of the sort. In a speech made a year earlier he had been talking about the general problem of youth crime in his community. 'We should avoid labels,' he said, 'that apportion blame and isolate a community. There is a problem in the south-west, let all the residents of the south-west take ownership of the problem and let us all work on a solution.'

As 'Media Watch' adroitly pointed out, both Trad and the Danish expert, Flemming Balvig, were saying the same thing from opposite sides of the world — 'Right down deep the problem is not about race or religion'.

But the open season on Lebanese Muslims continued for some time, until it was finally put to rest in September 2002 by the 'Media Watch' report, but not before Miranda Devine from the *Sydney Morning Herald* added her voice on 18 August 2002, calling the rapes 'A homegrown form of "ethnic cleansing" by a group of men said to be of Middle East extraction.' She informed readers that the Premier Bob Carr had told a media student from the Arab community newspaper *El Telegraph* that, '... race was brought into this by things the criminals said. It has not been exaggerated in the media. Not one bit.'

As a woman I shared Albrechtsen's and Devine's feelings of rage and disgust towards the rapists, but I could not enter their world and treat these crimes as race crimes. This did not stop me from wanting to wipe the smirk off the leader's face when he showed no remorse and carried his stupid bravado with him into court. The accused were not well served by their friends and relatives who mouthed obscenities at the young women who bravely sought justice. I wished they could have been punished under the law. These outbursts, however, were revealing in another sense: they showed us the circles these young felons travelled in — it was an ugly picture.

While the ongoing debate raged in the media for nearly a year, the Muslim communities stood on the sidelines; many struggled with their own feelings and distanced themselves from the stigma of being associated with gang rapists. Turkish SBS broadcaster Ayse Kemikoglu was appalled at how the Lebanese community in Sydney was singled out.

There seemed to be no distinction made between Christian and Muslim Lebanese alike. The Christian Lebanese started to move away — and who could blame them — although their religious leaders continued to make public expressions of solidarity alongside Muslim clergy, especially after vandal attacks on Lebanese Christian churches and mosques increased after September 11.

'If you are have olive skin, dark hair, dark eyes, and if you are not tall, then you are second class in Australia, and if you are Muslim, then you are third class,' said Ayse. She stems from a Muslim group in Australia which is part of our Gallipoli legend and therefore well liked. 'Johnny Turk' has a respectable role as our once-gallant enemy.

Very little of the anti-Lebanese feeling in Sydney spilled over to Australian Turks unless their youth were taken to be 'of Middle Eastern appearance', which sometimes happened given the inexactness of this visual description favoured by the New South Wales police with the support of the Premier Bob Carr who said, in an interview, that the question was simple, 'Will a description of a suspect's ethnicity enhance the prospects of arrest? If the answer is yes, police must issue this description.' The Premier went on to elaborate in a comment printed in the *Daily Telegraph*, 22 August 2001, 'Suspects are routinely referred to as tall or short, old or young, dark-haired or blond and so on. Why? Because these characteristics help identify the guilty parties.'

One suspects these descriptors also helped vigilantes in the community in their witch-hunt. Being described as short, tall, dark haired or blonde is vastly different to being portrayed as 'of Middle Eastern appearance' — the latter is pejorative in today's climate, as well as being imprecise. Take the word of someone who has, in her lifetime, been mistaken for Iranian, Palestinian, Spanish, Italian, Greek, Turkish and Indian — and in Paris often assumed by French gendarmes to be Moroccan or Algerian.

Human rights activists opposed to the linking of ethnicity with crime — a longstanding debate in New South Wales — quickly pointed out that the only time the ethnicity of criminals had been made public during the last twelve months was if the suspect was Lebanese, Muslim or Arab. This was bringing home hate to children in the schoolyard and there were reports of children telling their parents how ashamed they were to be Lebanese. Muslim girls were asked by their fellow students 'Are your brothers rapists?' The following month it changed to taunts of 'How's Osama bin Laden going?'

The Lebanese rape issue put the entire community on trial, especially Lebanese youth. An ugly way of thinking about Muslims had developed in New South Wales. Community relations between the state government and the Muslim Lebanese communities further deteriorated in August 2001 during preselection for an important by-election in the strong Labor seat of Auburn, where many Lebanese and Turkish Australians reside. Tensions increased when a candidate of Lebanese Muslim background, supported by Shaykh Taj, was overlooked in favour of someone from a Lebanese Christian background. The following month an anti-racist ticket of independents was organised and there was a sharp swing against the government: many Lebanese Muslims and their fellow Muslims made their protest at the ballot box.

It was around this time that a man called Keysar Trad, from the Lebanese Muslim Association of Sydney, moved to the side of Shaykh Taj Hilali as his media spokesman. It was a strategic move achieved with great delicacy of touch, for the Shaykh is his own man and likes to do his own talking with an interpreter by his side. But it's fairly common knowledge to Muslim activists around the country that some of the comments attributed to the Shaykh have landed him in trouble over the years. His oratory in Arabic is 'simply marvellous' — unparalleled in Sydney and probably around Australia, this is one of his greatest assets — even his enemies admit that, 'He speaks with the most ebullient sound bytes and has a remarkable control of language — his followers adore him,' but the dramatic utterances and colourful hyperbole so suited to his mother tongue and Arab audiences, when translated into English, go down like a bombshell in mainstream Australia and have led to accusations of being anti-Semitic and homophobic, which is not the kind of PR image a mufti likes to garner in these hard times.

To the general public Shaykh Taj-Din al-Hilali has more in common with the stern image of the ayatollahs of Iran and is far removed from the gentle, laughing image of Tibetan lamas or other Buddhist monks visiting Australia regularly. But Muslims in Sydney's south-west see a different man; they look at him through the eyes of the believer. He remains their leading scholar and spokesman who defends Islam and his congregation as his duty and his heart demand of him, and as his followers expect.

Nevertheless, he's made powerful enemies over the years, especially when he arrived fresh off the plane from Egypt, a stranger to the ways of Australian society and Australian university campuses. Some of his verbal indiscretions have become folkloric, and he learnt the hard way that what a religious leader could preach in the great mosques and ancient universities of Cairo would not be tolerated in Australia. Gradually he came to understand that being a Muslim in an Islamic country is markedly different from living as a Muslim in Australia. Of the more than a billion Muslims in the world, two-thirds live in forty-five Muslim-majority countries; the remaining third live as minorities in 149 countries.

Shaykh Taj's strong alliances support him in the fortress-village of Lakemba. Outside the fortress he is more vulnerable; Sydney, after all, is not a one-shaykh town and the environment is competitive. Muslims with more secular leanings say amongst themselves that he does not look favourably on attempts to modernise Islam and that secularisation is not a topic you raise with the Mufti. Outside Sydney there are frequent mutterings from Muslims with more egalitarian leanings who like to talk for themselves and who are unhappy when the Mufti is described as the leader of the Islamic faith in Australia.

Keysar Trad seized the moment and moved swiftly into the prickly space between Shaykh Taj Hilali and Sydney's media. Eight years ago when I did my original research, Keysar Trad was not part of the Lakemba establishment. Within a short time, however, he has become known as the media spokesman for the Lebanese Muslim Association and working in the background quietly, unobtrusively, but with great determination, he tries to steer the Shaykh away from some of his more controversial utterances.

In these sensitive times being the purveyor of local knowledge is not enough and specific media skills are required. As a retired auditor and tax accountant, Keysar Trad had what was needed: the time, a facility at letter writing and enormous faith in himself as well as a belief in his mission, which he saw as transmitting the truth and shattering the misconceptions about Islam. Some Muslims find his style controversial, but few deny his courage. Some of his critics think he falls into the trap of entertaining the media: there is no need to respond to everything; he should be more discerning, they complain. But Keysar Trad believes he's a troubleshooter, not a man who shoots himself in the foot, and although he may make the occasional error of judgement, his *niyet* or intentions, are sound — he wants to reach out to mainstream Australia and show them that Muslims are human beings. And the evidence so far shows that he is gaining ground, albeit at an agonisingly slow pace. Too many Muslims are over cautious when the media interviews them; in the end their words convey nothing and the journalist moves on to less boring game. Keysar is not of this mould, he has thrown caution to the wind and for Sydney's media this is a novelty. In a recent *Sydney Morning Herald* article he was described as 'Islam's man of a million comments'.

At first he is wary of me; we have never met before and it takes more than an hour before the ice starts to thaw; he's not an easy man to tackle. Keysar looks like the ex-rugby player he is: burly, thick necked and physically tough, with a stern unsmiling expression on his bearded face. His Aussie accent is distinct, although somewhere in the background there's the faintest trace of an Arabic accent if you listen hard.

Trad cannot stop himself from answering letters: he is a compulsive letter writer and even replies to the loads of hate mail — filthy beyond belief — that the association receives, although addresses are usually false and they are returned to him. I sit in his small unpretentious office across from the Lakemba Mosque in Wangee Road. Reading through his letter files, I notice that each letter is individually composed — there is no such thing as a format letter; even for short expressions of support from individual Christians and church groups new phrases are coined, everything is original, fresh and sincere, and painstakingly carried out.

In the old days, I tell myself, Keysar Trad might well have been a professional letter writer, a scribe sitting cross-legged in the bazaar hard at work composing letters for those who could not read or write but who needed to communicate with a loved one, or an official, and could offer a few coins for this service. Or better still I can imagine him as a court scribe in the employ of a caliph whose victories in battle need memorialising or whose tax edicts must be recorded for all to read and obey — somehow this suits the Trad I come to know. Yes, a man of letters, and the right hand of the caliph.

At prayer time he leaves me and makes his *salat* returning shortly with Shaykh Taj by his side. We exchange *salaams* and a few words. It is a serious moment and an honour that the Mufti has come across the road to greet me, but during this short informal encounter I cannot stop myself from recalling journalist Vivian Schenker's story of her first meeting with the Shaykh, which she'd only told me the day before — only on condition that I promised to emphasise that her cultural faux pas happened sixteen years ago in her early days with SBS when she was still an inexperienced young journalist.

On meeting the Mufti, Viv spontaneously reached out to shake his hand. To this day she is still unsure why she made this sudden movement because it was not her habit to take the lead in shaking hands, but stretch out her hand she did. The Shaykh pulled his arm back out of harm's way. 'What an unusual custom,' Viv thought as she seized his elbow and gave it a hearty shake.

In 2000 when the rape attacks first happened the police kept matters quiet; the Sydney Olympics were taking place and nobody wanted adverse publicity. Keysar and others never denied that these attacks had occurred, they only insisted that they were unrelated to being Lebanese or Muslim.

'We worked closely with the Bankstown Police at the time,' Keysar said, 'to make sure these youths were arrested. A year later when the media ran with the stories we tried telling them, "Yes it happened a year ago, but it is not happening any more."'

But the hysteria mounted and it was like trying to hold back an avalanche with a shovel. Keysar's approach has always been to admit that, 'There is a problem, a youth problem among a very small element in our community, and we're working on it.' For this he was rounded on by some members of his own community. 'How dare you say this in front of the camera!' How dare he admit that there was a problem? But Keysar stayed firm.

'One thing works against us,' says Keysar, 'and it keeps us apart from other Australians. Muslims are not able to participate in the pub culture which is an important part of Australian life. I could mix with friends at school and uni, play sport with them, but I couldn't drink with them. So much happens around alcohol,' he explains. Keysar knows about the temptations of the Australian lifestyle; he arrived at the age of twelve with French as his second language and no English.

'At lunchtime, or after work, people want to go to the pub. If you don't drink you're a marked man. It works against you when you're going for promotion, not direct discrimination, but indirectly, because the manager remembers the faces of the blokes who are his drinking mates — he doesn't remember you.'

At first I take issue with him, arguing that in the twenty-first century many men order water or juice at pubs, but he insists that even now the drinking culture still predominates. When he used to play rugby, after the match the coach would buy the usual carton of beer for the team and then have to remember Keysar's fruit juice, 'But someone else would knock it off half the time,' he said. And then there was the matter of the change-room culture.

'These people,' he said, 'just undress in front of each other, no modesty at all; we are not raised like this and you end up feeling such an outsider.'

Keysar made the front-page of the *Sydney Morning Herald* when he replied to a remark by the Taliban ambassador in 2001. When asked if the jihad extended to Australia, the Taliban representative had answered yes.

The story broke as Keysar was on his way back from a session with the Department of Defence, a regular session he conducts with Australian soldiers who are going overseas. Asked by a television journalist for a response to the Taliban comment, Keysar replied, 'We are Australians and an attack on Australia is an attack on us. We don't take our instructions from overseas. If anybody attacks Australia we are patriotic Australians.'

But I was more interested in what Keysar Trad had to say to our men and women in uniform than I was in the Taliban story.

'I tell them how to interact with Muslims, the proper Islamic protocol, and try to prepare them for the level of poverty they will be seeing. As fellow Australians I want them to stay safe and not make the mistake of shooting indiscriminately when they see a group of people out late at night who are only going to the mosque. An Aussie soldier might think it's a riot.'

Or, I think to myself, they might mistake a wedding party and the customary exuberant rifle fire as an attack; I am remembering a recent tragic incident in Afghanistan where United States troops fired on civilians celebrating a wedding.

'I don't want our boys to end up as cannon fodder in a war not of our making,' Keysar tells me.

Just to be sure there is no misunderstanding I ask him, 'When you say "our boys" who do you mean exactly?'

'Aussie boys, of course,' he says, looking at me a little surprised.

Keysar's brief honeymoon with Alan Jones, one of the talkback kings of Sydney radio, was also criticised by some of his fellow Muslims. Reading through the transcripts of one interview and the numerous letters Keysar sent off to Jones, it was clear that he set out to woo the Ringmaster of talkback although, at the end of the day, it was a short courtship. Talkback radio is based on confrontation and

Jones, in his program on 24 July 2001, showed a propensity for pulling every hoary chestnut one might ever hear about Islam out of the fire, including the reported banning of Christmas carols and decorations in Bankstown Square because it offended Muslims!

The Bankstown Square management set the story straight when I asked them. 'Christmas is alive and well and always will be in Bankstown Square.' They valued their Christian and Muslim customers; everybody enjoyed the decorations at Christmas and the episode had been a 'vicious rumour'.

Jones continued his interrogation of Keysar Trad who responded with patience, good humour and occasionally an air of bewilderment, especially when Jones barged in wanting to know why no Australian Muslim leaders had spoken out and condemned the New York terrorist attacks. Trad was quick to point out that his association had sent Jones two media releases and there'd been prayer vigils for the victims. The Lebanese Muslim Association, Trad said had received more than five hundred letters from Muslims condemning the attacks. But Jones was not to be denied and turned to a sure-fire winner: the subject of Muslim women — women forced to cover themselves, Muslims condoning 'the genital mutilation of women to curb their allegedly rampant sexuality', and women not allowed to go to a hospital unless accompanied by a male relative! A most extraordinary statement in a most extraordinary interview which now and then resembled a gladiatorial contest between Trad, the gentle-sounding giant, and Jones the man with the microphone, the money and the power.

The radio transcript makes for fairly hilarious reading at one level until you realise that Alan Jones is only repeating what 'the common man' out on the street believes, or is led to believe — and then it becomes frightening.

When the media comes a calling in Sydney, Melbourne and elsewhere in these troubled times, only a handful are brave, foolhardy or confident enough to risk the fallout and sometimes the media must look for new faces.

Imagine a conversation between an atheist female lawyer from Afghanistan, a non-practising Muslim feminist high school teacher, a Palestinian activist and passionate Arab nationalist, a former Iraqi diplomat, an old-style Lebanese shaykh who was once a Bondi greengrocer and, for good measure, an angelic-faced Anglo-Australian Muslim born to convert parents who flies on the wings of faith and serenity. Oh to be a fly on the wall, a witness to the quarrelling, the name-calling and malevolence that might well break out: conflict, drama, 'murder and mayhem' — theatre at its best. A handful of passionate secularists from Muslim backgrounds thrown into a den of practising Muslims.

But all this diversity of opinion never surfaces, to the surprise of Vivian Schenker who acts as the forum moderator that evening. The three-hour discussion later forms the basis for a magazine article. A culturally sensitive television and radio journalist now working for the ABC, Vivian Schenker knows how to establish trust and has the track record to prove it; her credentials usually ensure that people are relaxed enough for a more intimate discussion. Viv had met all of her players before, except for one, and enjoyed good relations with them.

Good Weekend Magazine's idea of putting Islam under the microscope in a wide-ranging forum of opposing views failed, in an intriguing way, although the end result, 'Through Islamic Eyes', published 1 December 2001, makes for a unique piece of journalism not often available to Australian readers. There are moments when it totters on the edge of a comedy of errors: Schenker probing in one direction by setting up a series of questions on 'Islam' while her cast takes off in another direction because clearly they all believe that September 11 is not about religion; it's about politics.

Surprisingly the young, secular members of the forum ward off any criticism of Islam by the simple expedient of declaring these problems 'non-Islamic'. On the other hand, the older shaykh and the former diplomat — both practising Muslims — are far more willing to admit that certain imperfections have crept into the religion. But there is no discord: Muslims of different generations, nationalities and varying degrees of religious attachment present a united front to their interviewer, and I wonder if that didn't surprise Vivian Schenker in the end.

The frustration on both sides leaps off the pages — one doesn't have to read between the lines. When the discussion turns to the subject of fundamentalism, and the moderator suggests that perhaps fundamentalism has shifted from being a marginal part of Islam to becoming its face, she is challenged and reminded of just how powerful a political force, fundamentalist Christianity is in America. Her participants outline a litany of double standards: if Iran is a theocracy what about Israel? Why has every secular and progressive government in the Arab world been crushed by western powers, they argue, and why are the ultra-conservative regimes, which might easily be called 'fundamentalist' — places like Saudi Arabia and the Gulf States — why are they propped up and seen as allies?

'I found it worthwhile,' said Vivian Schenker as we sat together over a coffee in the ABC's noisy cafe in the heart of Sydney three months later, 'because it was so unpredictable, because it wasn't what I'd expected. I thought I knew what I'd get and I came out of it incredibly frustrated but with a different insight.

'I didn't understand the level of anger. I thought people would be upset and hurt but I didn't expect them to be so angry. I thought they'd be more conciliatory, and I suppose that's more my weakness than a criticism of them.'

The forum took place in early December, seven weeks after September 11, probably too early for a frank and full discussion. Journalists were still examining Islam to find the key to bin Laden and September 11; Australian Muslims, who understood the big picture, were angry and defensive and tired of explaining Islam — they wanted to talk about the hegemony of the United States in the Middle East and preferred to leave Islam out of it. The unity of the participants was surprising but real, at least when discussing the politics of the current situation.

On looking back Vivian Schenker felt sad that her participants hadn't felt 'safe enough' as she put it, 'To open up about some of their own doubts and insecurities. My best efforts obviously weren't good enough or else it was the climate, or maybe a combination of both.'

For in the end Viv wasn't sure if she believed some of the answers she was given. I understood what she meant. There were long pockets of stonewalling and blocking out of discussion, more so from the younger progressive representatives on the forum; defensive reflexes were in play and an odd censorship when it came to discussing Muslim women. Paradoxically, this all-round defence of the treatment of women in many Muslim countries came from the younger progressives who resented the spotlight put on third world countries by western feminists. Yet the older generation shaykh had no qualms about admitting that discrimination occurred. Islam was a beautiful thing to him, but some Muslims tarnished its meaning and philosophy.

The one person who lowered his defences and most expressed the social reality of being a Muslim, with Vivian, was Shaykh Khalil Chami, the elderly and highly respected leader with a full head of snowy hair and a beard to match.

He has a way of disarming his opponents and wins over the minds and hearts of most of his non-Muslim audiences wherever he goes with his homilies and anecdotes. Later I made a point of visiting him in his Islamic bookshop and cultural centre in Lakemba, which sells a range of fairly simplistic religious books which do not challenge the intellect and are popular amongst the Lakemba devout.

He is a man with a hundred stories. Here is one about the day he first took his son to school and the teachers asked him what his son's name was.

'Muhammad,' he answered.

'What will we call him?' they asked him. 'Muhammad,' he repeated.

'They suggested Michael or Max. My English was bad but I told them either he is Muhammad or we leave!' All of his children kept their Muslim names at a time when many Lebanese were assimilating in the sixties by adopting Anglo names.

'One day my daughter came to me and said, "Daddy, can I sing you a song?" and off she went, "Mary had a baby, oh my lord, and the baby came to save the whole world." The words were something like that and at first I was upset that my daughter seemed to know more about Jesus than Muhammad and then I realised that it was my fault. Muslim children needed their activities too and so I started a band for young people — it took nearly two years.'

Shaykh Chami has survived years as a religious leader, a fact which is quite remarkable given that none of his three daughters wears *hijab*. Muslims enter his shop to argue with him about this transgression. He says to them, 'What can I do? I was born free and I have taught my children to be free. Should I kick my daughters out of the house?' He has six children and has been in Australia for thirty-nine years.

Outward signs of religious conformity do not overly concern him. 'They are Muslims ninety per cent of the way,' he tells me, 'but not in this *hijab* way which is picked on because it is so visible.' Many of the girls who wear *hijab* do so to please their parents, he says, and are not practising Muslims. Like any proud father he tells me about his daughter who plays cricket in the second top team in Australia. 'In my eyes, my daughter and son are equal.'

Shaykh Chami does not use fashionable Anglo-sociological jargon and he comes across as 'old fashioned' to some of the more radical Muslims, but he is willing to engage with society and smart enough not to fall into the trap when non-Muslims ask him, as they often do, 'What would you do if your daughter married a non-Muslim?'

'I always tell them that I would do my utmost to make him a Muslim. They want another answer: they want me to say I would kill my daughter, but how could I do that?'

A recent benchmark study confirms widespread antagonism towards Muslim Australians, with 52.8 per cent of people saying that they would be concerned if a close relative married a Muslim. Only 27.4 per cent of respondents said that they would be concerned about an Asian-Australian connection, compared with 28.9 per cent who would not want an Aboriginal in-law. The authors of the joint July 2002 university study from Macquarie University and the University of New South Wales said that the results reflected an expanding Islamophobia linked with recent geopolitical events, media representation of Muslims and an accumulated heritage of western antipathy to Islam.

Presently in Australian society Muslims have won the unpopularity contest hands down: they are the least liked of all people. The authors tell us it may be a transitory thing and remind us that society used to be anti-Italian, anti-Greek and so on ... but somehow I think the dynamics are different this time round.

Two months later, on 12 October, Australians are in shock and the nation mourns its lost citizens. The Indonesian-based terrorist attacks in Bali widen the chasm between Muslims and non-Muslims. Australia's Indonesian Muslims are now drawn into the morass of distrust and fear. Community relations between Muslims and non-Muslims continue to deteriorate.

After the *Good Weekend Magazine* article came out, Khaldoun Hajaj found himself in hot water. Khaldoun is a young man in his late twenties who is not at all popular in certain religious circles, although his parents' standing gives him some protection.

Khaldoun was the person I described as the Palestinian, nationalist Arab in Vivian Schenker's forum discussion of December 2001. It is only fitting then that writer and philosopher Edward Said is his hero.

'The focal point of Said's life is exile,' said Khaldoun, 'and I strongly identify with that. I am an Australian citizen but I was born in a refugee camp in Lebanon under Israeli bombardment at the time. My mother was born in a refugee camp and my father was born in Palestine. We come from the Galilee part of Palestine and if you want to know more, look up the Bible.'

He is an engaging young man with a round clean-shaven face, a heavy body and short wavy black hair. He is very much in demand as a public speaker; he uses fluent English but his speech rhythms are Arabic. His energy and vocabulary overpowers his listener; he devours books and has an impressive memory.

I wonder what he will be like in ten years. At the moment he has that passionate certainty we all had at his age. The day I met Khaldoun, within the hour he had described himself as 'the bellicose secular Muslim' in one breath, 'truculent' in the next, and finally settled on 'a bit of a dandy' but changed his mind when I said I thought he was more of a dilettante — I could tell he liked that description.

But charm the twenty-nine year old has in abundance. His life turned around with the Gulf War when he was eighteen; until then he said, he was like any other kid, not caring much about anything.

I asked Khaldoun to tell me about the reaction to the *Good Weekend* article.

'Many people were disgusted that I said openly that I don't engage with the daily practise of Islam, you know what I mean, I don't pray. People blamed my father, who is quite pious, and there were lots of phone calls from people telling him that I was committing a sin. And a shaykh wanted to come and visit me, to put me on the right path I suppose; of course I said no. I really admired Hawra, the Afghan lawyer, for her courage in coming out and calling herself an atheist.

'Here was I thinking we'd done something good for the Muslim community, but no — not one Muslim said, "Well done".'

Khaldoun also found himself roundly criticised for admitting that he had more in common with a Greek or a Lebanese Catholic than with a Pakistani or Nigerian Muslim, but he insisted on emphasising 'cultural continuities' across religious boundaries. 'We speak the same language, eat the same food, we look the same and we share the same history.' Many Lakemba hotheads ground their teeth as they read his 'heresies'. People were outraged and confronted him. 'You must identify with Muslims first and then with the others. You must say that the religion is the supreme identifier,' he was instructed. 'They think Muslims are all the same — we are not all the same,' he said.

I knew it was a mistake non-Muslims made as well. 'There are secular Muslims like you in Melbourne,' I tell him, 'who call themselves Muslims of the heart.' Khaldoun is taken with the expression and shortly afterwards starts using it to describe himself.

We move on to talk of zones of comfort, a topic which intrigues us both; we compete with each other in exchanging stories, but I have nothing which matches his Intifada demonstration story. It illustrates how easily people can be removed from their zones of comfort and it says a lot about the way people keep a distance from each other socially.

'When the Intifada first broke out we had many demonstrations in Sydney,' he said. 'They were organised by progressive left-wing groups and heavily attended by Muslims from Lakemba. At their height there were three to four thousand people. You had the burning of the American flag, shouting and screaming of "*Allahu Akbar*" — the usual mayhem. Men with beards and *jilabs* and women in *hijab*. For the first time it seemed that the radical communists and Marxists were outnumbered, and they felt very uneasy. They were uncomfortable that there was now a religious base to the demos instead of their sole secular face. So you see,' he said, 'even the radicals had established their own circle of comfort which the Muslims inadvertently undermined. In the end they stopped inviting the Muslims and the demonstrations shrank to a handful of people.

'But one young man, Ali, who is nineteen and a kind of born-again Muslim — he and I do not get on at all,' Khaldoun wanted me to know, 'in fact we don't talk whatsoever. Well, he continued to come and chant his "*Allahu Akbar*".

'Ali threw down the gauntlet. There he was standing alone, dressed in his Islamic-style clothing, the beard and the turban. You know, he was really gutsy. Two of my progressive friends said, "Can't you shut your relative up?" They were only half serious, but you know for the first time I started feeling the hypocrisy of the progressives and then I really understood how hard it is for people to move outside their own zones of comfort.'

An old friend once summed up her attitude about Buddhism and Hinduism by calling them 'friendly religions'. Her meaning was clear, and although the lure of Hindu ashrams and maharishis has waned since the seventies, Buddhism has continued to appeal to western minds. The Dalai Lama in exile is a smiling, roving ambassador for Tibetan Buddhism wherever he goes, and if the religion has a 'public relations' problem, it lies with the Chinese authorities who continue to deny Tibet its independence. Many people in the West adore the Dalai Lama. Tibetan scholars and teachers have a reputation for their friendliness, geniality and accessibility; they have saved their religion by exporting it to the West where it has taken root. The warm vibrant colours of Buddhist red and gold, its Four Noble Truths and the sheer pageantry of Buddhist ritual attracts thousands of people who seek meaning in their lives. Australians have embraced Buddhism in large numbers as the recent visit of the Dalai Lama proved.

Unlike Islam, the image of Buddhism does not confront or confuse and it is seen as a panacea for a world locked into consumerism and conflict. The face of a Buddhist monk and the face of a shaykh or mullah evoke widely contrasting responses.

The first time I entered a Buddhist temple I was overpowered by the colour, confusion and proliferation of images wherever I looked. It did not reach out to me as a place of rest or contemplation, although I know that meditation is central to Buddhism and around me there were clearly Buddhists 'taming their minds' and 'cultivating a wealth of virtue'.

I am not a woman who attends mosques but, at that moment, the asceticism and stark lines of their architecture drew me closer to the world of 'the true believers'. The beauty that I see in the architecture of mosques around the world extends to their interior where minimalism prevails: the absence of statues, icons, portraits of any kind and the row upon row of people at silent prayer performing a dutiful choreography has a hold on me in spite of my avowed secularism. We all have our zones of comfort.

During my return visit to the familiar faces and places of Lakemba in March 2002, I was invited to a fundraiser for Afghan refugees held in a community hall somewhere in Sydney's south-west. About six hundred people attended: a noisy multicultural mix of Afghans, Lebanese, Indians and Anglo-Australians, with children running around, mobile phones ringing at every crowded table and music and speeches belting out during the night. There was laughter and merriment, a delight in rich food and an absence of alcohol. During the night I noticed Muslims and non-Muslims from mainstream Australia watching each other out of the corners of their eyes, looking for cultural clues as if they were not used to mixing socially. The plight of Afghan refugees trapped inside their war-torn country had brought them together — this does not often happen and I felt I was witnessing something new.

Two nights later I attended my first formal gathering of Buddhists at the Wentworth Hotel in Sydney. An overseas scholar of renown was coming to give a teaching and I wanted to see what kind of people were drawn to Buddhism and to breath the air of a Buddhist gathering en masse.

The event was also a fundraising activity for refugees, but this time the refugees were Tibetans living in India and I was happy to pay my twenty-five dollars and take a seat at the back of the splendid Wentworth Ballroom where I had an excellent view of everyone as they filed by. Within forty minutes there were a thousand people sitting and waiting patiently for the great master.

The audience intrigued me. I seemed to be caught in the middle of a crowd of what I took to be 'the beautiful people of Sydney': stylish, white and mainly in their mid thirties — a trendy set, one might say, who looked well read, well fed, and well bred. There was an absence of extravagant hand gestures, loud voices and 'strange' accents; the bodies were slim, the minds disciplined. Women of a certain age and élan predominated wearing scarves, shawls and cloth bags in the colours which Buddhists favour, and for a second I was reminded of a football crowd carrying their tribal emblems and wearing their team colours. The audience also seemed a well-educated lot, which was just as well for Buddhist texts are not for the faint-hearted and the deeper one goes into Buddhism the more one needs to study. Those gathered were mainly singles and young couples, and the venue was remarkably child free and quiet, with mobiles tucked out of sight. People talked softly amongst themselves, sipped bottled water, and a handful of late arrivals, who seemed to have missed out on a lesson or two on the merits of unselfishness, tried to talk the ushers into giving them seats closer to the stage.

At the end of the teaching the master told us of his own experiences as a refugee in India. 'Tibetan refugees suffered greatly,' he said, 'but we were content and made no complaints.'

'That's how Australia likes its refugees,' I thought to myself, 'uncomplaining and grateful.'

24

King Power Walker and the Shame Pearls: NOT A Bedtime Story

They were pearls unlike any we had ever seen before. Egg-shaped, puce-coloured globules, so strange and so grotesque that when first discovered they were held in low regard by most folk and people generally refused to trade in them. But it wasn't long before they were persuaded to change their minds. In the space of a few years this sickly variety, cultivated in the low tidal waters of the west, came to be much sought after by collectors, who roamed the coast filling their pouches with them. And before very long these puce-coloured pearls came to be known as 'Shame Pearls'.

Shame was now a commodity in the great wide land down-under known as Woz and it came to be prized above all else. The national mood had changed of late. The Shame barometer was rising, and people were becoming edgy.

For decades rumours had been circulating that the black-brown tribes from around the Indian Ocean were intent on transforming Woz into a coffee-coloured nation, something so abhorrent and unWozlike that people shuddered at the thought. But nothing much had happened in the lazy land of Woz, until one bright summers day, in the year 2001, when two lame emus and a pink and grey galah, minus a wing, were sighted in the bushland behind Catatonia, the nation's capital. The high priests of politics rubbed their hands together for the omens were certainly auspicious and they were anxious to complete their life's work. Surely the time had come to invent new welcoming rituals and learn more effective ways of keeping strangers at bay or at the very least out of sight? There was a lull in the building industry at the time — perhaps a chain of desert gulags might be the answer.

At first the people of Woz, especially the women, were slow to abandon their traditional ceremonies of hospitality until the Wombat Cavalry moved in and began warning the rich farmers and docile peasants of what lay ahead if they failed to support their king. Flotillas of dragon boats from the north, they said, crammed with dragon people, were heading our way with devilish plans to sabotage the country's sacred and best beloved Games by Former Subject Nations, a sporting event held once every four years. There was even talk of a new international contest threatening to take centre stage, The Grand Old Sulewesi Canoe Contest sponsored by their island neighbours to the north. This was the last straw and so they called on the invincible Navy of Woz to do its best to torpedo the canoes out of the water and transport any survivors to the desert camps or better still, to islands of brown people far from their shores.

Some sniffed the air and, picking up the stench of rotting pearls, began to understand that the stories about the dragon people floating in their frail craft from island to island — a tribe so wicked, they were told, that they would, at the drop of a life jacket, throw their children overboard — were works of fiction. However, by the time the deception was discovered it was too late: the country had become spellbound with more than eighty per cent of the populace buying up large quantities of the puce-coloured pearls of Shame. This was now the twenty-first century and the old days and ways of welcoming strangers had disappeared from their memories, as if they had never happened.

In its recent past Woz had been a more or less welcoming caravanserai where travellers, fleeing persecution and poverty, could rest, take heart and move into their new world: after a generation or two their accents would sound Wozlike and they would be accepted providing they stayed on their knees until they had learnt the words to the national anthem Advance Wozlanders White. In some cases a few elite muscular individuals were allowed to bypass this painful ceremony if they could pole vault over cliffs, or lift heavy boulders above their heads.

Now you might well ask who engineered this plot. Who was so dedicated, so ambitious that he would mask his intentions and change the heartbeat of his country; a land whose traditions he treasured, or so he was fond of repeating. At around this time in the history of Woz, a man, small of stature with eyebrows shaped like the wings of a bat, ruled the land. The people tolerated him but did not love him, which had always stuck in his craw, for he yearned to be as popular as the country's earlier rulers: their beloved Silverbird or even the tall, tango-dancing, snake-tongued, antique-collecting pig farmer: the ruler you had to have, and the man the people loved to hate. But by now they were all living under the hegemony of King Power Walker, a king who liked his roast and two veg on Sundays, a man never at ease when foreign envoys from the Orient came to his court, especially those with a penchant for garlic which Power Walker regarded as Satan's favourite additive. Their funny names, their food, their 'otherness' all perplexed him, although he did his best to hide his discomfort and overcome his stuttering whenever he had to say the 'M' word until finally, in a fit of pique, he banned it from his court along with the word 'sorry'.

At around this time King Power Walker was growing weary of his followers asking when he would step aside for Prince Youngblood, his successor, who was panting in the parliamentary paddock like a sheepdog ready to round up any old ewe or ram slow to do their king's bidding. But the old king longed for one more term, one more chance to make the people love him. 'Not yet,' he muttered to those bold enough to confront him.

Finally, it was the Minister for Shame and Border Propaganda who came up with the Final Solution. As was the tradition among the king's personal followers — even among those of his rival, His Most Jovial Highness, Duke Measley — the Minister for Shame and Border Propaganda was a eunuch. Twenty-five years he had spent languishing on the edges of the court, always taking a back seat in the Palace of Shouting. Yes, it was Minister Whey (or Old Wheyface the Eunuch, as he was fondly called) who in the end showed King Power Walker how easy it would be to fool the populace and stay wedged in his throne for yet another four years. Thanks to Wheyface, the old king now had the formula for his spell of Diabolical Diversions.

King Power Walker strode into the Palace of Shouting accompanied by his adoring eunuch. The two men surveyed the hall of snoring, snorting courtiers and smiled at one another. Their spell was working. Except for a few of the feral tribe and those belonging to the reading and chattering elites, who had retreated to the underground caves and salt lakes of the inner desert from where they fired their slingshots, all of the king's subjects had drawn into their lungs the fine mellow dust ground from the fat puce pearls flooding the country. Without further ado they had fallen into a trance. Only the voices of Power Walker, Wheyface and one or two favoured ringmasters working for Radio Programs dedicated to the work of the Department of Shame and Propaganda could rouse the sleepers to do their bidding when a zombie jamboree or hotline of hate was thought to be necessary. With their electric cattle prods the Radio Ringmasters would shock their slumbering audiences into great displays of hate and patriotic fervour which rivalled the ranting, war historians told us, of Überallus the Hun.

But now it's SHOW TIME! The circus is about to begin. Step lively now! Come buy a ticket to see the freaks on show!

'Walk right up ladies and gentlemen! See the wild men from tribal Afghanistan banging their heads against the concrete walls! See the wailing women from Iran cry over their lost children. Laugh at the fools from bombed out Baghdad fleeing from Shadaam the Terrible, devourer of small children. Listen to their screams; can you make out the words? "My enemy's enemy is my friend"? See grown men fight over a jar of jam. Watch teenagers slash their wrists and grow mute! Careful, there's hostility there, I tell you — don't get too close, now.

'Roll up! Roll up! Step this way to the Greatest Show on Earth! Pay attention members of the audience; note the exhibits don't feel pain like us! They can't love their babies like we do. These are a species who throw their children overboard, sew their lips together and encourage self-mutilation. No need to be afraid. Look at them from the other side of the razor wire: the subhuman flotsam from a dozen nations. Relax, lady, you're safe; King Power Walker is watching over you. Never forget the nightly prayer of our good Christian king

Save us, oh Lord, from these kind of people spreading disease with the greatest of ease straight from rubbish tip to you.
Baby Jesus, meek and mild, protect us from the infidels.

'No son! Don't feed them. Well, if you must throw a stone or two, go ahead, there's nobody watching, that's the whole point isn't it?

25

Flotsam

'Slaughter those refugees!' a man roared after them. 'It'll save you food. Heil Hitler!'

Erich Maria Remarque, *Flotsam*, 1941

The only place I would tolerate a detention is placed in El Alamein and that in fact, when the army is training, they can use the recalcitrant illegal immigrants as live target practice, the same as galahs ... [sic]

Mayor of Port Lincoln, Peter Davis,
ABC News, 24 June 2002

Old activists refuse to roll over and die, they simply hole up waiting for troubled times and new causes to drive them to the barricades once more. As I set about making contact with Perth's pro-asylum seeker groups, I knew that I was feeling my way, for a writer spends much of her time alone and my activist phase during the anti-Vietnam War years, and the heyday of the ethnic rights movement, were long behind me.

Living on top of the Darling Escarpment I often look down at 'the flats' to the sandy coastal plains, the beach and riverside suburbs, but rarely venture near them preferring the red gravel, wattles and the jarrah trees of the Perth hills. Working alone is addictive, although the ghost of writer-activist Katharine Susannah Prichard lives nearby: I pass by her old wooden cottage in Greenmount every day knowing that we could have been neighbours and might, now and then, have fought on the same side.

My latest journey was to draw me closer to those who supported asylum seekers: a world where e-mail technology, the Internet, sparsely attended vigils and public rallies marked out the terrain. Student activists, socialists, unionists, Quakers, relics from the anti-Vietnam War days, politicians seeking redemption, environmentalists and people who had never belonged to an organisation in their lives before — typical 'non joiners' — made up the numbers, but to my eyes, they seemed largely Anglo-Celtic with Christian underpinnings, which moved me beyond my own zone of comfort. My winters were behind me — it was time to wake up.

Her name cropped up wherever I went: 'You must meet Katie, the teacher,' they said. Students and lawyers were tight-lipped; they favoured letting people speak for themselves and I was new on the scene — untried and unproven — I seemed to emerge from nowhere, a woman who expected to be taken on trust, who held no membership with any refugee or human rights group.

But my new friends up north, Esa Khan Andar, Afzal and Sameena — interned with hundreds of others inside the Port Hedland Detention Centre — spoke openly to me about their former teacher. At the mention of her name their faces lit up as we sat together in the dry-as-dust visitors' compound doing our best to ignore the guards employed by Australasian Correctional Management (ACM) who were listening in on our conversation. Keeping up the pretence that we were friends visiting one another was impossible; although we did our best to suspend our disbelief for the forty-five minutes we were permitted to spend together each day. The glittering blue of the Indian

Ocean and the red dust of the north, the dry spinifex and the bright yellow winter sunshine were the stuff of tourist snapshots, yet they failed to blot out the ugliness of the razor-wired Port Hedland Immigration Reception and Processing Centre.

Four days later I left the mining town of Port Hedland located in the north-west corner of Western Australia, 1635 kilometres north of Perth, determined to track down Katie Brosnan. I was curious about this Irish woman whom desperate people remembered with such affection, and I needed to take stock of what I'd witnessed and — more urgently — discover what was kept hidden out of sight. What lay beyond the visitors' compound inside the heart of the detention centre where 'guests' were not allowed to go and where our friends were kept?

Katie Brosnan lived in a town house in Perth three doors away from an Irish pub; my stereotypes immediately clicked into place. She looked like a woman who wasted little time on the small vanities of make-up and fashion which preoccupy many women of her age, which I judged to be early to mid thirties. Katie's magic lay in her soft voice with its Irish brogue and the rock-solid calmness she radiated. Here was a woman who would listen to you, never cut you short, or adrift and, if she became your friend, Katie Brosnan would suffer with you. Katie was once employed by ACM as a teacher; after seven months she couldn't bear it any longer. She wants to go back to Ireland, that's all she thinks about now.

'I think I can say that I've lost faith in this country. I can't continue to live in a country which supports this system, and since I've left Port Hedland all I want to do is leave Australia.'

At first you are taken in by the softness and lilt of her accent and you overlook the sense of her words until the power of what she is saying rocks you. You look down, unable to meet her eyes, profoundly shamed by what she is saying about your country.

'Before I went up north I enjoyed life in Australia and I know there are good people here. Part of me says I should stay and try to make a difference, but no, I don't have the energy any more — it's beaten me down totally and now I want to leave. I can't tolerate this any more and I don't want to be part of it. I'm no romantic; I know other countries don't want refugees either but they seem to be able to accommodate them in a more humane fashion — they don't lock them up and they certainly don't lock children up. Nobody should be locked up without just cause.'

I rush in with my own explanation as if I must find an excuse for what we're allowing to go on in our names. Surely if these camps were not in remote areas where few can see them, I try to argue, if the media was allowed inside to report on the conditions, surely there'd be a mass outbreak of civil disobedience and people would tear the fences down? Even as I speak I'm no longer sure, my words are beginning to sound hollow; I've read the focus group reports and the polls showing overwhelming public support for what the government is doing, but I know there is also something wrong when authorities ban their own country's media from entering these camps; where guards push journalists away from the gates. What are they hiding from us? Katie is quick to sense my flicker of disbelief.

'I wonder,' she says, 'because on the one hand, while people don't know what is going on inside, it seems to me that people don't want to know what is going on inside.'

Her words strike a chord, reminding me of German civilians living next door to concentration camps as early as 1933, and later on the others who saw men, women and children packed in trains on their way to extermination camps in Poland and Lithuania but claimed they never knew what was happening in the name of the Fatherland — a collective amnesia of ghastly proportions.

Ireland has asylum seekers and Katie expected her Australian experience to be along similar lines. But Ireland and Australia were like two different planets, although the Irish influence in our myths, our history and politics is a strong presence. Yet Australia's policy, unlike Ireland's, is unremitting: mandatory detention for those asylum seekers arriving without a valid visa while their applications for refugee status are processed. Currently Australia is the only country in the world which places children in mandatory detention.

Like most countries which accept asylum seekers, Ireland does not have mandatory detention and society has not fallen to pieces or been transformed into a terrorist paradise. The language used in Katie's homeland reveals a different attitude towards damaged and desperate people — there is no mention of 'queue jumpers' or 'illegals' — people are not demonised by the government which takes them in and processes their claims. Asylum seekers in Ireland are treated as refugees until otherwise proven, and are immediately placed in the community in hotels or bed and breakfast establishments or even converted holiday camps with the government of Ireland footing the bill.

Residents are not billed for the cost of their mandatory detention which is Australia's style of government hospitality. Currently this is being challenged by lawyers working pro bono for clients charged $70–$191 per night — depending on which 'razor wire Hilton' accommodation they enjoy. For the privilege of sleeping behind barbed wire on thin mattresses in crowded rooms, sometimes with guards flashing torches in their faces, and eating food they'd rather not be eating out of plastic boxes, one Temporary Protection Visa (TPV) holder was charged

$26,000. Lawyers see this as a calculated tactic to discourage asylum seekers rather than an act of sadism for such a debt is impossible for people denied the opportunity to work; the liability would prevent people from ever re-applying for asylum to Australia.

In Ireland, although people claiming refugee status are not permitted to work, they receive food they can tolerate, an allowance to get them by and free English lessons. Most of the asylum seekers are from Eastern Europe and Africa, but numbers from the Middle East are increasing.

Katie taught refugees in Ireland, out in the community — not behind barbed wire — and expected it would be the same in Australia. Her background in teaching was solid and she had always liked 'difficult teaching assignments' as she put it: gypsy children, teenagers with drug and family problems living in alternative facilities. Not for her the comfortable teaching life, she said.

'Mainstream education is very solid and very safe,' Katie told me. 'You live your life by the bell, but I was dealing with people who are marginalised and it made me realise that education is not something which fits into little boxes — it doesn't go into forty-minute periods.'

She likes difficult beats, Katie admitted, but nothing had prepared her for what she would discover inside the detention centre at Port Hedland.

Right from the start the signs were not good: her induction course provided by the ACM training officer on her first day at Port Hedland lasted all of twenty minutes. Two of her senior teaching colleagues were away on stress leave and her remaining colleagues could only give her a hurried welcome.

Katie found herself transfixed by this induction session which concentrated on two points only: what to do if you were taken hostage and how keys were your lifeline. If taken hostage she must 'Lie on the floor and say nothing and eat any food offered. Don't, whatever you do,' she was told, 'enter into negotiations. We have staff who are qualified to handle hostage situations and you only have to remain calm at all times.'

And as for keys, well, she must never let them out of her possession and must lock and re-lock doors wherever she went: 'Carry them on your body at all times.'

'What on earth have I let myself in for?' Katie wondered. Until then she had only anticipated an interesting assignment with a chance to learn about different cultures. Suddenly she was being warned that she was in a life-threatening situation with dangerous people.

'If you put huge barbed wire fences around people, you are telling all and sundry that they are a threat — the bigger the fences, the sharper the razor wire, the greater the menace. Obviously you don't lock up people under those conditions unless they are dangerous. It is a very clear signal,' Graham Thom from Amnesty International had said to me in Sydney a few months earlier. 'You are not going to visit those kind of people.

'Now compare that with how refugees from Kosovo were treated in 1999,' he continued. The Kosovars weren't locked behind fences; they mingled with the community and were given temporary status and received enormous support from rural communities, especially in Tasmania.'

But the media, I reminded myself, and the general public had decided long ago that the Kosovan and East Timorese refugees were 'good refugees' while Afghans, Iranians and Iraqis were 'bad refugees'.

Ask Australian Muslims why Bosnian Muslims from Kosovo were received with compassion and, if they trust you, they will answer: 'It's because they were Europeans with white skin and blue eyes. They looked more like other Australians.'

True or not, such comments underline the process by which people turn inwards and become, in their own eyes, the perpetual outsider because they are visibly different. It marks the beginnings of social distance and a tendency to engage only with people who make you feel comfortable, and where you are not continually having to explain yourself; where respect, not hostility, is what you read in people's eyes.

Like everyone else Katie was oblivious to what was happening inside Australian detention camps. Weeks passed before she fully absorbed the fact that she was free to climb into her car and drive home at the end of the day, but her students remained locked up.

But locals living near the detention camp in Hedland knew what ribbon wire and security fences meant and responded to the signs. They believed they were living near hostile people, probably terrorists, and were most unhappy that a child care centre, school, library, bowling club, church and residences were all standing cheek by jowl with a place which looked more like a prison camp than a processing centre. What if 'they' broke out? These were plausible fears which the detainees understood.

After two break-outs and one or two riots at the Port Hedland centre in 2000 and 2001, community opposition increased but the department would not meet their demand to move the centre, and instead constructed a 3.6 metre high, galvanised metal palisade fence at a cost of 3.1 million dollars. It included security cameras, lighting, a 'sterile zone' and an inner fence of high weld mesh topped with barbed wire. The fence was to prevent further break-outs and stop the media from getting close. Local residents feared it would adversely affect real estate prices.

MHR Barry Haase, whose vast Kalgoorlie electorate includes Port Hedland, said in an interview, 'We need something you can't see through because we have a circus being performed on a regular basis in the centre. Anything that can reasonably be done to prevent that circus being a spectator sport should be done.'

The president of the 'resident' group inside the Hedland centre tried in vain to reassure the locals. 'We are just people in terrible circumstances,' said Doctor Okoli who used to be an African journalist but now had a number instead of a name. Recent violent incidents had been instigated by a few people who'd been moved to another centre, he argued, and made a plea to local people to visit them and come to an understanding of their situation. Only a few brave souls accepted his invitation for by now the detainees or 'residents' as ACM liked to call them, had been transformed into a subspecies who had nothing in common with the rest of us. Public opinion, shaped by the prime minister and his senior cabinet ministers and blown up by the tabloid media was now overwhelmingly against asylum seekers. These were the kind of people who would throw their children overboard or sew their own lips together. How could you bring yourself to visit 'people like these' as the prime minister called them? They were not human — they deserved to be locked up. But some Port Hedlanders were starting to ask questions and in November 2001 a Residents' Support Group was set up and a few visitors found their way inside in spite of the obstacles put in their way by ACM.

Katie's first adult class was a daunting experience. With the 'hostage' warnings still ringing in her ears she walked into a makeshift classroom and found herself confronted by 'a lot of hairy men': she'd never seen so many beards in one room before. Twenty or more 'hairy men wearing dresses' as she put it, mistaking their long tunics and baggy trousers for women's attire.

'Oh, my God! Oh crikey, I'm in trouble now,' she

thought. 'I felt totally intimidated,' she confessed to me.

Having always felt comfortable in the company of dark bearded men, I asked Katie to talk about her feelings. What had she expected? What preconceptions was she carrying with her into the camp about 'men of Middle Eastern appearance'?

'Sleazy,' she said, 'I thought they'd be sleazy types and that I'd be seen as easy prey.'

But never once was she made to feel uncomfortable by her male students; they treated her with the utmost respect. 'In their eyes I was first and foremost a teacher, a person to be treated with respect, and being a woman was incidental. All the teachers at the camp were seen as people of standing; it was a very different cultural attitude to what I was used to, and I never once felt as if I was being looked at as an object.'

The only sleaze Katie encountered inside the camp came from some of the male ACM guards, who made what she considered inappropriate remarks about her body when she used the staff swimming pool. 'I didn't expect to hear that from a western man,' she said.

'Really?' I asked her, truly amazed and wondered if she'd spent most of her life in an Irish convent. But Katie had not been in Australia for long; Aussie sexist humour of the 'C'mon luv, get your gear off!' variety was not part of her cultural baggage.

'Not an Irish thing?' I quizzed her.

'No. An Irishman would know he'd get a fist if he said something like that to an Irishwoman.'

When Katie first arrived at Port Hedland the camp held seven hundred inmates in all: four hundred in the main block with another three hundred locked away in isolation, recent arrivals taken off the latest boat. New arrivals are kept in separation blocks for three months, often longer, under quarantine while they undergo health and security checks. Some people arrive with pre-existing medical conditions, others are suspected of being former terrorists, or Iraqi soldiers; there could be criminals or even people smugglers among them. They are kept inside one large block with the freedom to move from room to room but are only allowed outside into a small yard twice a day for half an hour. This privilege occurs at the discretion of the guards who exercise control by granting or denying detainees certain 'gifts' — like spending fifteen minutes in fresh air. And there are times when the guards are in a bad mood and can't be bothered. A young woman locked up with her husband and two young boys, who is still in Hedland after nearly three years, told me of their seven terrible months in the isolation block there — people start to break down and her husband has never been the same since.

Katie dreaded going into the isolation block to teach. It was bad enough in the school proper but in the separation blocks you had to be adaptable and let things happen. There were confused people milling around showing high levels of distress, 'absolute mayhem' she called it. 'Don't leave,' people would cry when the lesson was over, and the children would tug at her clothes, begging her to stay. She was the only outsider they ever saw, the only human being not wearing a uniform.

The teaching facilities in this section were spartan: a small dark room with a grille window, no natural light at all; pupils would write on the windows for there were no boards of any kind. 'Miserable and bleak,' Katie said. 'No desks or tables and tiny tots sitting on big chairs trying to draw.'

The new arrivals were confused and had no idea that they were in an isolated part of the compound, that nearby another four hundred souls were living in the outer blocks. Months passed before they were released into the main compound. One Chinese man spent three years in isolation before he was deported. Australia is on shaky ground when it dares lecture countries in the Asian-Pacific region about human rights.

'The new inmates were completely isolated from the rest of us,' said Katie. 'They had no idea that the twin towers of the World Trade Centre had come down. I found that incredible. The whole world was talking about this catastrophe and they knew nothing: no papers, television or radio; they were allowed to send one fax when they arrived and that was all.'

The months and years drag on and inmates gradually lose touch with reality until many become institutionalised; their confusion worsens until finally they come to think that all of Australia is like a detention centre. Theirs is the culture of despair and they must battle it every day. One day follows the next: they sit and wait for news of how their visa applications are progressing; they hear nothing and their lawyers are far away, sometimes across the continent, their caseworker down in Perth. Men and women work for a dollar an hour, in the kitchen or on cleaning duties in the yards and the toilets, to buy phone cards to communicate with the outside world. Try as they may, thoughts of suicide and self-harm intrude regularly. And the children stand and watch: witnessing the breakdown of the adults meant to shield them from harm.

By the time I visited Port Hedland the centre was down to one hundred and fifty inmates and they were the bravest of them all for they knew deep down that there was little chance that they would ever receive the magic paper stamped 'TPV', Temporary Protection Visa, and yet they kept fighting back, struggling to get up in the morning and face another day of being counted and marshalled and treated as a non-person. When the camp was at its peak, hope was kindled whenever a friend or neighbour received a three-year reprieve, which is all the time the TPV grants these days, but now the climate has changed and it has become a lottery.

A Melbourne lawyer described to me how luck plays a role in determining a detainee's destiny: two men from the same country might apply on the same grounds with identical cases. One succeeds but the other who got 'The shit lawyer, the shit case officer and the shit tribunal member, is out of luck.'

Even the minister's own officers cannot remember the last time he has exercised his discretion and overturned a Refugee Review Tribunal decision. Men, women and children are trapped in limbo; when will it end, and how will it end?

The uncertainty of never knowing how their claim was progressing drove men and women to the brink, especially in cases where families were separated: a husband out in the community with a TPV (which did not allow family reunion) while his wife and children, who arrived later on another boat, remained incarcerated. Rumours filled their day: Would the Afghans and the Iranians be forcibly repatriated? How would the Bangladeshis, Sri Lankans, the Iraqis and the Palestinians fare? Would they be woken up in the middle of the night, told to pack their bags in half an hour, say goodbye to their comrades and then head south with their guards on board a bus to the Perth Detention Centre and from there onto a plane? And what would happen after they returned to the country they'd fled? Would their persecutors welcome them with open arms? In one grim sense, probably yes, and then the cycle of persecution, gaol and torture might well recommence. What we are rarely told is that at least fifty-three per cent of detainees eventually have their claims recognised as bona fide, according to United Nations human rights conventions; others may be in extreme danger and at risk but their kind of persecution is not covered by international conventions and so they sit in limbo waiting for their appeal, deportation, forced repatriation — or breakdown.

'To live without roots takes a stout heart,' wrote German author Erich Maria Remarque, who found asylum in the United States and wrote a novel, published in 1941, called *Flotsam* about the lives of European refugees in pre-Second World War Europe: Jews and non-Jews alike, who shuffled like lost souls across one border to the next, from one detention cell to a few weeks of reprieve and poverty before their carousel of the damned began turning again. He called his refugees 'flotsam': wreckage from a ship found floating. I bought Remarque's book for five shillings when I was a teenager — it was the kind of novel you never forget. 'A man without a passport is a corpse on parole. All he's really expected to do is commit suicide — there's nothing else,' says his character Steiner to the young student Kern, whose only crime seems to be that his father was Jewish and 'politically unreliable'. The blurb on the back of my tattered Panther paperback calls it '... a tremendous novel of the courage, comradeship, love and misery of ordinary people whom the turbulent upheavals of Europe rendered FLOTSAM.'

A chilling irony clings to the word 'flotsam' when linked to boat people seeking sanctuary on Australian shores — human wreckage that we turn our backs on, pretend not to see or refuse to rescue, although we honour the proud maritime tradition of rescuing lone yachtsmen, making for heroic headlines every year or so.

Self-harm and suicide, bred from despair. When does it start?

Does it begin the day they give you a number and take away your name?

Calling people by their numbers is central to the game

played by ACM: it is part of their culture of control. They are in good company with their employers, the federal Department of Immigration, Multicultural and Indigenous Affairs (DIMIA), whose culture is described by most lawyers as 'hostile to asylum seekers', and whose officers and caseworkers, in the words of another, are, 'Incredibly demoralised and overworked with appalling results for applicants across the board.' This has been obvious since the change in government in 1996. Many officers have chosen to retire or be transferred; others remain with their heads down.

Whenever I write to my friends trapped inside the Port Hedland Detention Centre I hesitate before addressing the envelope. It offends me deeply to write their numbers next to their names, but I must or they will not receive my letter.

TAB 34 was Esa Khan's brand. An inmate's ID is based on the first three letters of their boat's name: the crowded boat aboard which they reach Australian territory. Another of my friends is called YAK 94, yet another COO 26.

Katie and her fellow teachers refused to call their students by their numbers. Guards would enter her room, without knocking, looking for TAB 71. 'I'm sorry,' she would murmur softly, 'I don't know who you mean. What is his name?'

'When captive people are given a number,' said Katie, 'they lose their identities.'

On one occasion Katie tried to break the dreadful monotony of daily life in the camp by organising a birthday cake and card for one of the inmate volunteers who sometimes translated for her. Special permission had to be sought from her immediate manager to bring a cake 'inside'. He was not pleased.

'No, it's not a good idea,' he said, 'because it shows that you want to become close to these people.'

'Good God,' thought Katie, 'it's only a birthday cake and

a plastic knife to cut it with.' But she wisely kept her mouth closed, and in the end permission was granted only because she'd already bought the iced sponge cake — 'But it must never happen again,' she was told.

While Katie was trying to organise her 'little surprise party' as she called it, the detainee was sent out of the room on some pretext while the male students signed the card. When she looked at the card what she discovered was a list of numbers.

'But they're numbers! What is this?'

'This is who we are,' they told her. 'We don't have names any more.'

Katie dug in her heels. 'No, she said, 'we're not giving it to him like this. Please start again — forget your numbers — you are people.' It was the moment when Katie finally understood that the detainees had become numbers even to themselves.

'What's your name?' she would ask someone and they would give her their number in response. 'Please,' she would beg, 'you have a name!'

'That was a long time ago,' they would reply.

Even the children answered by number. A children's Christmas party was organised one year; it was the brainchild of the local DIMIA manager who often had good ideas, most of which were never implemented by ACM. A Christmas party with a concert was the plan, with sketches and songs performed by adults, but the message was never passed down to the teachers who would have welcomed the opportunity to organise activities to relieve classroom boredom. But it was still thought to be a good public relations idea and everyone joined in: children were to receive a gift from local community groups who would be invited inside to see with their own eyes that Port Hedland Immigration Detention Centre wasn't such a bad place after all. 'Good heavens, man! They even give the children Chrissie prezzies!'

But it all went horribly wrong on the night when the guard who was giving out the presents called the children up by number, one at a time, over the microphone. The ACM manager, realising how this looked to their visitors, instructed his officer to call them up by their names instead. 'Well, I don't know their names,' the officer told his boss, 'I only know them by number.' And so the whole evening was abandoned, which meant that half the children had received their presents while the other half had to wait until the next day, wondering what they were being punished for this time.

In order to survive Katie at first played the ACM game; it was the only way she could cope. An officer would say, 'Those dirty rotten Middle East terrorists, who do they think they are?' and she would nod, without saying yes — at all costs she avoided getting into any discussions with the guards who parroted mainstream opinion filtered through the rhetorical partnership of the Australian government and talkback radio. For five months she kept it up; she even became rather good at it. She kept her own views well hidden: namely that the detainees were kind, decent people who'd risked their lives on leaky boats and would never have done so if they hadn't been absolutely desperate in the first place.

But there came a time when she started to unravel: she found herself becoming more emotional and unable to remain detached. Gradually it became clear to her that something very wrong was happening in Australia. In another time and place many of the detainees would have been her friends — she couldn't bear to stand by and watch this tragedy unfold any more: to watch while her friends waited behind the wire fences.

She started to look at the guards in disgust. 'How can

they come in here every day and do this job?' The sight of the uniform was making her feel sick. And then she began looking at herself with loathing. 'How can I come in, day after day and do this job because, in essence, I am supporting this system.'

Even now Katie tells me it is painful for her to admit that she was paid by ACM. 'It grieves me to say that I took their money.'

Every morning she dreaded going to the camp. 'How can I face the ACM staff today ... how can I put up with their crap and how can I make the children smile?' By now she was alone for the other teachers had left when numbers began going down and only she was left, apart from Sister Mary, a volunteer teacher whom she rarely saw.

The irony was complete when Katie realised that she was now looking to the detainees for support. 'I knew for my own wellbeing that I must pull the pin,' she said.

The hardest thing for Katie was to break the news that she was leaving of her own free will, for at first everyone thought she'd been sacked for being too friendly, which had happened before to another teacher and an ACM officer who'd given sweets to the children.

The Department spins the tale that ACM staff are free to develop a rapport with detainees: perhaps they are being kept in the dark by their contractors, or perhaps this line of propaganda is DIMIA policy, but nevertheless, the anecdotal evidence is overwhelming that staff are not encouraged to 'feel' for the inmates. ACM's culture of control and coercion feeds on the detainees' misery. Captives and captors are not friends in spite of the Department's fairytales.

Early in 2002 the detainees hung a banner written in English and Arabic: 'We don't hate ACM officers, only the ACM management!'

Not all ACM officers are made of stone and a few officers

might argue that they are also victims of the government's policy on asylum seekers. They work twelve-hour shifts and central management has cut back on staff numbers. It is difficult for them to show any sympathy — everyone watches everyone else. The majority develop their own coping strategies. How else could they keep on doing their jobs if they weren't convinced that the detainees were 'illegals' or potential terrorists? The staff have their favourites among the detainees and have been known to react indignantly when someone labelled 'a good refugee' is turned down by the Review Tribunal.

One of the detainees I visited was a young Bangladeshi man. The burly guard who escorted me into the visitors' area was apparently fond of my friend. He clapped the slightly built man, who came up to his shoulder, on the back, knocking him off balance, and said in a stentorian voice, 'Oh here's my little mate!' He meant well but his 'little mate' flinched and I knew Shamsur felt humiliated that I'd witnessed the well-meaning but infantile way he was being treated — familiarity but no respect. Apparently a smile epidemic breaks out when visitors enter the centre, and the staff are on their best behaviour, but detainees whisper to their visitors that everything is not what it seems. Detainees are adept at talking out of the side of their mouths to indicate who are the most reviled guards and who are tolerable.

On the other side, certain guards have reason to fear a few of the detainees who suddenly snap and lash out at them, especially if a guard is in the way when they receive news that their application for a visa has been turned down. As one detainee told me, 'Okay, I take the orders, but must they control every single thing that I do? "Stand up. Sit down. Give me that piece of paper you're writing on!" And I don't like the way some of them speak to my children. "F... off!" they say if they're in a bad mood. Is that any way to speak to children?'

It was the children who brought Katie undone in the end, the plight of the children that caused her to unravel, for it was becoming clear that some children were worth protecting and others not.

I discovered this for myself while trawling through the archives of Port Hedland's local newspaper. A reader's letter published in the *North West Telegraph*, Wednesday, 30 March 2001, led with a remarkable headline.

> CENTRE COMPROMISES CHILDREN'S WELFARE
>
> Over the last nine years young people living in Port Hedland have had to deal with watching detainees jumping off buildings, barbed wire fences being put up, the plight of people holding placards as protests at our Government's treatment of detainees.
>
> Recently they have had to deal with a mass breakout, escapees on the loose, police in riot gear, tear gas ... Does this sound to you like Australia? ... What I ask is, don't our children have a right to grow up in a safe and peaceful environment?

Someone forgot to tell the writer that detainees love their children too. The mum who wrote this letter might have spared a thought for the children behind barbed wire in need of comfort, love and protection who stood helplessly by watching the adults they were most attached to break down — at times so badly that their roles were reversed and children looked after their mothers and fathers. A child's social order is like a comforting blanket — their social attachments, their sense of security was being destroyed piece by piece, and some of them blamed themselves for what had happened. 'My father wanted a better life for us. It's my fault we came here.'

What does it take to move the mothers of Australia, I wondered? If they looked at a young girl's drawing of a weeping bird in a cage, would they understand why she told a psychiatrist, 'This is not how I feel, it is how I am?' Would they be touched to hear a young boy say he has never seen a real flower? And what of the babies born in detention to mothers showing high rates of psychiatric morbidity?

The children behind the wire were on the front-line when it came to witnessing people jumping off roofs, setting themselves alight, even hanging themselves. Children at Woomera Detention Centre scream when they see trucks approaching because they remember the trucks carrying water cannons used to quell riots started by desperate people who believed there was nothing left for them — they have no voice, nobody is listening — that is why some resort to sewing their lips together. It is a macabre act, a gross act of self-mutilation, but the underlying symbolism and the psychic pain it represents is not staged.

Prime Minister Howard, who often assumes the mantle of defender of family values, tells us, 'Children in the proper positive care of their parents don't sew their lips together do they?' John Howard is right, but he demonstrates no understanding of what lies at the bottom of these acts of self-mutilation and how parents who are damaged and disempowered cannot guard their children any more. He tells us, 'It is being done to morally intimidate the Australian people and the Government will not abandon its mandatory detention policy.' (ABC Online, 25 January 2002.)

Former prime minister Bob Hawke was moved to tears over the massacre in Tienanmen Square in Beijing and gave carte blanche to Chinese students studying in Australia to be given refugee status, much to the chagrin of Immigration Department officers at the time. What does it take to move John Howard's heart?

The story behind the drowning of 353 asylum seekers bound for Australia on board SIEV-X (Suspected Illegal Entry Vessel) on 19 October 2002 is only slowly being divulged, but what is known so far is a sorry tale of inaction, possible indifference and cover-up. A Senate enquiry will be needed to ensure that the true story of what took place in Indonesian and Australian waters is not lost forever along with the poor victims on board that leaky overcrowded vessel.

Human rights are not worth much these days if you are an asylum seeker arriving by boat rather than by jet with a tourist or student visa tucked in your carry-on bag snuggled next to your duty free bottles and latest electronic toy. But Australians are becoming adept at embracing international criticism as if it was some kind of gold sporting medal. The United Nations expresses its disgust at our mandatory detention system calling it a gross abuse of human rights; UN delegations are taken on conducted tours of spruced up centres (when they are not denied entry) and are appalled by what they see, and our response displays all the truculence of a schoolboy. 'No outsider [read bloody foreigner] is going to tell us what to do, thank you very much!'

The wounded children behind wire on Australian soil have lost their basic human rights, mental health professionals around Australia are telling their peers. An article published in *Australasian Psychiatry* in June 2002 makes stark reading.

'Children are deprived of basic human rights such as adequate education, and opportunities for safe play and development,' the article says. It describes the violence and the effects of unrelieved contact with angry, hopeless, frequently suicidal adults. Even before they reach the schoolyard children were reportedly called 'towel heads' or 'little queue jumpers' by ACM staff, and one mother who asked for clothes to fit herself and her children was reportedly told to make them out of the curtains.

A talented artist inside the Hedland camp has taken to painting murals featuring Mickey Mouse characters, dolphins and a picture of Christ outside the prayer annex. A remarkable cast of characters, I think to myself. In one area of the compound, whenever the coast is clear, a secret alcohol still appears, and then disappears, in a game of hide and seek with the guards. To brighten up this area the artist painted a garden setting with trees — they were soon covered with drawings of people hanging from the trees and crude obscenities. One of the detainees told the artist, 'This is not Disneyland, show it as it is!'

Dr Louise Newman, a child and adolescent psychiatrist with expertise in the area of infancy and early childhood, is currently the Director of the New South Wales Institute of Psychiatry. Louise Newman has worked with grossly abused children in mainstream society and shocks her small Perth audience in the Uniting Church's Wesley Centre when she compares the situation of children in detention centres with what she has seen of children from Romanian orphanages. The parallel is deeply disturbing, and her audience falls silent. 'We will all pay for this,' she says.

She talks of the prevalence of antidepressant drugs handed out inside the camps when sometimes all that is needed is someone to talk to, to offer hope instead of drugs. Offers by the Combined Medical Colleges to undertake screening and work with DIMIA in the provision of mental health services to the detainee population, have so far met with an 'inconclusive response'. At present their entry is restricted and they can only enter if DIMIA, or a detainees' lawyer, invites them to compile a written report on the wellbeing of a particular client.

But as I sit listening to Louise Newman present her grim message I realise that I am at last witnessing something remarkable in our society and that there is hope after all. I cannot remember a time in our recent history when two such powerful establishment professions, the law and medicine, have taken a public stand against government policy. Yet this is happening across the country and there is now unanimous support across the medical colleges for the end of mandatory detention — this is an alliance of the combined medical colleges of Australia, forty thousand health professionals in all. Doctors are speaking out and giving evidence. 'Although we pride ourselves on our mental health policies and child protection laws, that is just rhetoric,' says Louise Newman on their behalf. 'We are witnessing the traumatisation of children,' she warns.

The audience listening that night is deeply shocked by her words — it is so much easier to turn a deaf ear or sink into despondency — but this audience is also full of angry, ashamed people doing more than listening — individuals acting out their beliefs and at the end of the night they will report back to their organisations which all support asylum seekers in practical ways. An outstanding example in Western Australia is CARAD, the Coalition for Asylum Seekers, Refugees and Detainees. Convenor and former Labor State minister, Dr Judyth Watson was startled into action one morning when she read in the local paper that a group of detainees from up north, with newly minted TPVs in their pockets, had been driven down by bus and dumped at a local hostel with no money, no Medicare, no clothes and no local knowledge — even a bale of wool is better looked after in Australia. At the hostel Watson met up with a group of volunteer TESL teachers: teachers qualified to teach English as a second language, who'd also read the news and rushed down to the hostel to do what they could. CARAD has grown into a strong advocacy and support organisation, as have numerous rural networks across Australia. From a hundred small beginnings these support and advocacy bases in Australia have grown into a movement.

The vignettes Newman offers us are heart-rending but someone has to tell these stories and someone has to listen: children at play re-enact endless riots; their drawings show the wire, giant-sized guards and small-sized inmates; a six-month baby born in detention to a traumatised lost mother makes no eye contact, little sound or complaint and never smiles — again Newman repeats that ghastly analogy when she compares the baby to a Romanian orphan — 'A baby with no joy.'

Small wonder that Dr Louise Newman and her colleagues caution their fellow physicians against working within the ACM system; she uses the word 'colluding'. 'I personally would not work within the ACM system,' she tells us. She pulls no punches when she reminds us there were doctors who worked for the Nazis.

I know that there are more stories we must listen to or else they will disappear. They are stories which take on the intensity of physical pain: the children up to the age of twelve who are incontinent day and night; the man who tells his visitors, 'Even if we get our freedom, we will be mad people,' and the parents of a two-year-old and a five-month baby who beg a visiting health professional for help. 'Please take our children, find a place for them away from here. They will change to savages, not humans. He [the toddler] doesn't trust us any more. He can't play, he won't eat, he can't sleep well.'

There are too many people trapped in our desert gulags who may never recover from their wounds. I have met them and so have my friends. They are being cut into a hundred small pieces and thrown to the wind so that they may never come together again. They are left hanging in space, lost in the worst kind of existential loneliness imaginable — a dark alienation.

A steady stream of professionals, former ACM employees, are walking away from the camps. Psychiatrists, doctors, nurses, and teachers like Katie can stand to watch no more and they are deeply frightened of what they have witnessed and the spread of the contamination. They return to the outside world but they are changed people and they talk to whoever will listen; they write submissions to enquiries like the National Inquiry into the Mandatory Detention of Children. The Inquiry's Chairman is Doctor Sev Ozdowski, a former Polish refugee who came to Australia in the seventies after spending years in Germany as an asylum seeker living out in the community on a daily ration of a tin of ravioli and a tin of sauerkraut, which he bought for fifty pfennigs each, a man who once went on a hunger strike in Martin's Place, Sydney, to force the Polish authorities to give his parents an exit visa.

The Perth hearings of the National Inquiry into the Mandatory Detention of Children are held in a five-star hotel. This incongruity only strikes me much later when I visit Port Hedland and hear that the guards have given their camp a three-star rating compared to Curtin or Woomera. The witnesses giving evidence to Ozdowski and his colleagues need no prompting. Only the state bureaucrats use bureaucratese to hide the lack of progress in sorting out Commonwealth and State demarcation lines in service provision. Their voices are barely audible. Are they angry or are they ashamed?

I am especially interested in the evidence about unaccompanied minors which seems to have a sadistic twist to my untutored ears as Mary Anne Kenny, a Murdoch University academic and lawyer, speaks her mind to the Human Rights Tribunal. The guardianship of unaccompanied minors seems to contain a conflict of interest for the Immigration Minister who is not only the official guardian of unaccompanied minors under Commonwealth law but also the man who determines their fate — including giving them the 'gift' of spending their childhood behind razor wire.

Dr Judyth Watson, one of the public voices of CARAD, gives clear examples of children's social order breaking down; two young psychiatrists tell of their observations in Woomera where they managed to last for four weeks before they had to walk away. The evidence is compelling, the litany of horrors being inflicted on children is terrifying: anorexia caused by depression, cuts and scratches because there is no grass to play on, inadequate diets, bed-wetting, ten-year-old children receiving antidepressants. The doctors conclude by stating that they had never worked in a setting as bad as Woomera; they had never felt as intimidated, repressed or powerless before in their lives because they couldn't offer assistance to people in need — and these were the doctors, not the detainees left inside to rot.

Katie's departure from Port Hedland was hastened because there was a change in ACM management culture and not for the better, the rumour mills said. The previous manager had set up a resident's committee so that complaints could be aired, and he appeared to respect detainees as long as they toed the line. 'He was approachable,' detainees and staff said, but the new manager stayed in his office and was unpopular right from the start. Tensions mounted and, on the surface, they were all to do with food.

Food is the focus of a detainee's day because there is so little else happening that meals become the highlight. Katie at first found it hard to understand why the quality of the food upset people so. Under their old ACM manager, the different nationalities could choose people to prepare dishes they were familiar with under the supervision of the ACM chef, as he was called. There would be a vegetarian dish, a South Asian dish and a Middle Eastern dish — we are not talking of three-star restaurant standard here, just food with taste, as the detainees told me: salt and oil in the rice, a few spices, everything had to be low cost for ACM is a private organisation driven by the profit motive. As the numbers have decreased, ACM is making less profit — they are paid per head — and some have cut down on food quality and staff. ACM is a subsidiary of an American corporation known as Wackenhut who make a handsome profit out of running prisons in the United States.

Tensions sprang up between ACM and the detainees when the new manager decided that the kitchen regime was not cost-effective and that henceforth there would be one vegetable dish and one meat dish. Everyone was upset — overnight they'd gone from eating their 'own' food to one choice for everyone, regardless of culture and in spite of the fact that Immigration Detention Standards state that detainees should receive food which is 'culturally appropriate'.

My Hedland friends talked incessantly about the terrible food they were receiving; during my visit they began protesting. As a last resort they refused to help the cook prepare meals and refused to eat what they called 'rubbish food'. A mother told me that on some days her children only ate cornflakes for breakfast and a salad and cheese sandwich for dinner. Food was a symbol for everything that was wrong with their lives and could even trigger a riot.

'Lucky' is the ACM's pet dog at Port Hedland, a stray found by one of the guards. 'Lucky to be alive,' say the guards. 'Lucky for other reasons,' say the detainees. 'Better food, free to roam around and treated decently with affection and respect.'

The Reverend Beverly Fabb, or Rev Bev, as she is called with affection, is a minister with the Uniting Church and has served as an independent outsider on the residents' committee at the Hedland centre for some years. The Reverend Fabb has a remarkable memory and would have made a hard-hitting 'take no prisoners', kind of politician if she hadn't chosen the church. She has seen managers come and go and been on the residents' committee in its heyday and at its lowest ebb. After a change of senior management, and a hardening of management culture, the detainees found themselves blamed for everything that went wrong and friction increased. In Australian prisons, inmates have work and education; in detention centres the inmates work one week in four (if they are lucky) and have no proper educational facilities or courses other than some fairly rudimentary English lessons.

Every request becomes a drama and takes forever, and to me, often seems a queer mixture of malice and incompetence. Eighteen months pass before mirrors arrive so that men can shave properly; a request for a sewing room for women lies listlessly in someone's pending tray and never eventuates. A photocopier breaks down and is repaired by an Algerian detainee who in his past life used to repair photocopiers in his former homeland for a living, but ACM caution him and he is warned off. How could a detainee fix it if they couldn't? After all he wasn't Australian trained, and what would happen if it blew up?

When the resident committee relationship with ACM was at an all-time low many resigned, but two detainees stayed on and when Bev asked why they continued to come and be abused every month, they answered, 'We keep coming because you come and are a witness to what happens.' Now there are weekly meetings and nine detainees attend. Most detainees have a strong sense of what is just and what is unjust; persecution and injustice is why most of them have fled their homelands to begin with.

There was a rumour making the rounds in Lakemba circles which I promised myself to investigate when I finally went to Hedland a few months later. The Christians were out and about, so it was said, proselytising and converting good Muslims into bad Christians and turning the camps into hotbeds of religious and inter-ethnic tensions. Like most rumours of this kind it was partly true, but mostly false. I decided to test the holy waters, especially after being present one Sunday morning in the visitors' compound as a group of Christian detainees from different nationalities, including Iranian, stepped out into the free world with their guards, heading off to a church service.

Katie Brosnan saw no inter-ethnic tensions or religious rivalry during her seven months at Port Hedland. Interfaith slanging matches and occasional dirty looks, yes, but nothing dramatic or violent — indeed she felt there was 'great harmony', as she described it. 'People will help one another if they can, even if this transcends national boundaries,' Katie said.

'There were a lot of "ethnic" jokes going on: the kind of comments we Irish make about the English,' Katie said.

Iranians and Iraqis would sling off at one another — not surprising I thought, considering they'd fought against each other through most of the 1980s. 'Cow worshipper' epithets were muttered at Hindus by some Muslims if something unusual happened to upset them or if they saw something on television about Hindus persecuting Muslims in India. Amnesty observers have noted the tensions which sometimes spill over between Muslims and Hindu Sri Lankans or Iranian Christians and their Shiite fellow countrymen at Villawood and Curtin detention centres. The worse the conditions, the more likely it is that incidents of violence will occur. Woomera Detention Centre is described by former inmates as hell on earth: people are going mad behind the barbed wire fences; it's therefore not surprising that at times inmates turn against each other. Some camps are worse than others: Hedland guards hated going to Curtin Detention Centre which is forty miles out of Broome and very isolated. A volunteer who asked permission to take in the 'Book of Welcome' signed by people welcoming detainees to Australia was refused permission for two years. ACM Curtin management wanted nobody inside to think that any Australians welcomed asylum seekers. Curtin has only recently been closed.

The detainees have their national identities, their different languages and customs but share a common culture based on boredom, despair and a feeling that they are all enduring a hellish existence together. Most work hard to negotiate a bearable existence out of unbearable conditions.

Becoming a Christian helps some people pass the time and puts an end to boredom: for one thing they start getting visitors. There are, however, genuine conversions, it would seem, especially among Iranians. The Woomera camp in South Australia has three visiting chaplains and there is contact from the Persian Evangelical Christian Church which circulates correspondence courses on Christianity to camps around Australia. According to the 'Religion Report' on ABC Radio, two hundred detainees have done the course so far. There is no evidence on hand to suggest that becoming a Christian helps detainees secure a visa. The government is sceptical and wants proof that people had a prior interest in Christianity and are not converting to help their refugee claims.

Sister Mary visits the camp regularly as a volunteer teacher; she knows that most of her students attend English classes simply to break the monotony, but doesn't mind. Conversions to Catholicism have taken place at Port Hedland, but these had not been sought out — she and her colleagues are aware that converted Christians may be deported back to an Islamic country where apostates are reviled generally. At Christmas time a few families were baptised and photographs taken to commemorate the happy day, but the families were adamant that the photos not be shown to anyone else. 'Just for us,' they said, knowing that if they went back to Iran their families would be persecuted. Perhaps this is what Minister Ruddock's department means when they reportedly tell people who've recently converted, and then still found themselves deported, that they can be 'secret Christians' — a term which conjures up pictures of Christian martyrs hiding in the catacombs of ancient Rome and later thrown to the lions.

'Most of the converts are Iranians who have grown up under what they call "Mullah Islam", and who gave up on Islam in their teens,' says the Reverend Bev Fabb. The converts she has spoken to see Iranian Islam as an abuse of power and are disillusioned, yet they cannot live without 'faith'. Some turn to Christianity because they remember at home they once had an Armenian Christian friend or an Assyrian Christian friend who was a nice person. Sister Mary recalls that the Iranian converts are especially taken by the biblical quotation where Jesus says, 'Let he who is without sin, cast the first stone.' Stoning an adulterer remains a punishment under Shari'ah law in some Islamic countries.

The Reverend Bev denies that she has any missionary zeal; her policy is always to try to dissuade those seeking baptism. She has a strong sense of social justice and struggles with the ethical dimensions of endangering people; in the end she knows it will not help them get a visa. Inmates first invited the Reverend Bev to run a service which she now does every Sunday afternoon. Those seeking to convert receive instruction for three months, which provides a moratorium giving them time to 'cool off', as she puts it. In July 2002, the first Afghan inside the Hedland camp was baptised into the Uniting Church.

When Marg Le Sueur is asked why detainees convert to Christianity she moves away from faith explanations to the siren call of modernity. Marg is a woman who has reinvented herself more than once and became a lawyer late in life: a lawyer who sees herself as more of an activist and once worked in rape crisis centres. Beneath the fierce exterior is a big heart; she is adored by the detainees and grudgingly admired by the guards — the woman who won't go away. Lawyers are not often at a loss for words, even when upset, but Marg is a lawyer with a difference. She drifts from one theme to the next with the will of a woman who has seen too much and heard too many heartbreaking stories and stored it all away ... there is little else in her life at the moment — she has made her commitment.

Marg believes that Iranians converting to Christianity reflects the same function as westerners converting to Buddhism. 'If you are on a spiritual search in Australia and disappointed with the mainstream religions you may turn to Buddhism — at the moment it is quite fashionable. For many Iranians, Christianity has the same appeal.

'In Iran there are also disillusioned people for whom Christianity equals the West equals jeans, Coca cola and all the consumer things you long for. I'm not saying these conversions are insincere but image is part of the attraction.'

Other sources suggest different reasons and I hear that Iraqis are slow to convert because their government, unlike Iran's, is not a theocracy. A Sydney man who visits Villawood centre quite often, as a teacher volunteer, informs me that converting is a way for Iranians to thumb their noses at the Iranian government, but I am not convinced. It does not take the Iranians and other inmates very long to understand that being a Muslim in Australia is not an advantage. Stories circulate about an Armenian Christian woman at one of the camps who distributes literature and has converted approximately eighty-five of her Iranian countrymen; the woman experienced no problems with Muslims in the camp.

My own feelings are ambivalent on the matter of conversion. Are vulnerable people being taken advantage of? Are they ripe for the picking? There are many people in advanced stages of depression behind the wire. The Mormons and Jehovah Witnesses enter other camps with an unconcealed evangelical zeal, while some Christian fundamentalist groups in Port Hedland see Muslims as the agents of the devil and are given to muttering obscure incantations which have something to do with being 'covered by the blood of the Lamb' to protect themselves. But in Australia the right to religious freedom is strong, and people cannot be turned away if they decide for themselves to convert. From what I have seen myself at Port Hedland, I would not characterise the activities of the Catholic and the Uniting churches as active proselytising by any means. They have earned the respect of the inmates, Muslim and non-Muslim alike, and provide much needed support.

And while all this Christian activity is taking place, where are the imams, the shaykhs and the mullahs? There is a large Muslim population of Christmas Islanders and Cocos Malays who've lived and worked in Port Hedland for many years, people respected by their employers and the community in general and who have their own mosque in South Hedland — they are what my New York friend would call 'good Muslims' — but when the local imam received a call from the detainees asking for a visit, he became worried. 'Why,' he asked? 'Because we are Muslim brothers,' answered the inmates, who saw the ministers from Christian churches filing in and out regularly. Now there are scheduled visits, it seems, but my friend Esa Khan was in detention for more than three years, he said, without seeing an imam — even at Eid. At Woomera, shaykhs and imams are also in short supply.

Ramdas Sankaran emigrated to Australia from Kerala in South India twenty-three years ago and is the former president of the Ethnic Communities Council of Western Australia. The angry young man has become an angry middle-aged man: white haired, fierce of eye and sharp of nose, his voice still fires off sentences like a Gatling machine-gun and nobody can silence this man. He has maintained his rage and enjoys a certain notoriety for verbal indiscretions which he calls telling the truth.

People were turned against asylum seekers, Ramdas argues, by a carefully planned propaganda program by a government determined to win back the Hansonite heartland at the next election. 'Certain messages were sold to certain constituencies around the country,' he said. 'People in rural Australia were frightened by the idea of germs and quarantine; the feminists were sold the usual anti-Islam message of oppression against women by the Taliban, while everyone ignored the Northern Alliance's record which wasn't much better. The government even won over people who came here as refugees after the last war, or at least the children of these former refugees.'

According to Ramdas some ethnic organisations, like the Federation of Ethnic Communities Council, have a conservative membership base and know how to lobby the minister and indicate support for his policies behind the scenes. The Afghan and Iraqi communities are newly emerging and do not have direct access to the minister and his department; they can't influence anyone.

Even some of the older established Muslim organisations have distanced themselves from the asylum seekers' debate and swallowed the department's line that to allow asylum seekers will mean a loss of family reunion and business migration places for people from their own communities — a line that is quite untrue as these are separate intake categories, each with its own quota. Generally, Muslim groups have kept their heads low and followed a survival strategy since September 11, especially Muslims who are not from the Middle East. Some do not want public contact with brethren who come from the world's trouble spots.

Public opinion is shaped by many factors and the stories carried by the media have a strong hand in shaping people's attitudes, especially if their subjects are locked away in remote desert areas. A story about a vulnerable child, or a family separated for years, swings public feelings towards refugees and then a riot happens at Woomera; student activists tear down the fences and people are on the run providing a grand media opportunity for the television cameras — and public opinion swings the other way while DIMIA hides its smiles and the minister seems vindicated.

A major riot took place at the Port Hedland centre in May 2001 terrifying residents who lived nearby. Tear gas was used to bring the estimated one hundred rioters under control. The riot may have been instigated by one particular family expecting to be deported who, in effect, felt they had nothing to lose and had a record of causing trouble and intimidating other detainees who stood in their way. As usual it was difficult to say what set it off — it could be the smallest thing or it could have been simmering for a long time. The guards know exactly who is bucking the system and who is acquiescent. Punishments seem small but cut deeply: a shopping trip is cancelled, the 'naughty' detainee is overlooked when the time comes to work in the kitchen or on cleaning duty, which means he can't buy phone cards to ring his family or lawyer; chicken appears on the menu for the sixth time in a week.

Twenty-two of the alleged ringleaders of the riot were arrested two weeks later in an early morning raid of more than 170 officers from the federal police, Western Australian police, ACM, Australian Protective Services and the minister's own department, and removed to the South Hedland lockup by police in riot gear.

May was a busy month at the Hedland Centre. A former detention centre guard narrowly avoided a gaol sentence for bashing a detainee. He plead guilty to two charges of assault occasioning bodily harm. The former guard was sentenced to terms of nine months and fifteen months to be served concurrently, however, the sentences were suspended for two years. The man he attacked was a forty-seven year old Iranian man who was smaller than his attacker and handcuffed at the time. The incident was one of the causes of a riot the following day. A witness recalled feeling physically sick hearing the thuds of the blows which fell four to six times.

'There was nothing to help him [the guard] get over the stress of the situation,' said his lawyer. At the time the guard was taking antidepressants and had simply snapped, it was claimed.

Police Prosecutor Sgt. Lewis Williams told the court that 'It is this sort of treatment that the people inside the centre are fleeing their countries to escape from.'

The detainee suffered a cut lip, loosened tooth and a sore eye and cheek. No mention appeared in the article about his level of stress or his psychological state of mind.

The week before Katie left she was in class with her students when she heard a terrible sound like an animal in pain, an unbearably loud sustained wailing that hardly seemed human. As she went to investigate, officers ran past her. 'Lock your door!' they yelled at her. She stayed where she was and a minute later, across the yard, saw nine officers with helmets and shields circling this one small Afghan man, a totally distraught human being crying out for help.

'All he needed,' said Katie, 'was someone to put their hand on his shoulder and say to him, "It will be all right," but no, they put him in a cell for a week. He was so fragile, anyone could tell he was near to breaking, but, to my knowledge, no psychiatrist was called in.'

A few weeks later the same man was involved in another incident. All the poor devil wanted was the chance to show his papers to Shadow Minister for Immigration, Julia Gillard, who was visiting the Hedland and Curtin camps, no doubt believing that justice would prevail if only one person — someone in authority — would listen to him.

The shadow minister's 2002 visit had been planned in advance and she was scheduled to meet with a delegation of detainees and nobody else. The visit was cut short after a disturbance broke out in the single men's compound where this man, Sher Khan, was housed and there was much banging on fences and shouting, whereupon the official party was called on to vacate the area.

Sher Khan, in the afternoon of that terrible day, ended his protest and tried to end his life by jumping from a tree. Sara, a young student activist who visits him every week at the Perth Detention Centre where he's now kept, says he doesn't want to live.

Minister Ruddock argues that episodes like this are all accidents. People fall off roofs and out of trees by accident. And women who become morbidly depressed when they give birth to babies without the support of their extended families, not even their husband to hold their hand, in strange hospitals with no interpreter — in one case a woman didn't understand that she was having a caesarean — 'Well,' the minister says, 'they had these problems before they came to Australia.'

Attempted suicide rates are ten times higher inside detention centres than in the general community, and self-harm and suicidal behaviour is endemic says Dr Newman in a submission by the Royal Australian and New Zealand College of Psychiatrists to the United Nations working party on arbitrary detention, June 2002. Rates of completed suicides are currently before the coroner and it is suspected that they will also be ten times more than the general community, comparable with indigenous people in prisons and our rural youth suicide rates. It remains to be seen whether the minister will continue to trivialise the findings of independent expert opinion, but presently he and his department seem immune to criticism.

Australia's first coronial enquiry into the death of an asylum seeker in detention may change this. Palestinian refugee Muhammad Saleh's story was recently disclosed by Elizabeth Wynhausen writing for *The Australian*, 12 October 2002. In Syria, Saleh was imprisoned, beaten and tortured with electric shocks. He received similar 'treatment' in Australia. At the Port Hedland centre he was put into a dark cell in the isolation block as punishment for thirteen days, for reasons which are a mystery as the case notes for this period have 'disappeared' from his file. Men in these blocks are allowed out of their cells for one hour each day. Witnesses say he emerged mentally broken. He was eventually sent to Hollywood Hospital in Perth for surgery for a tumour that had long been left untreated, Wynhausen says, and also received electric shock therapy for severe depression, later diagnosed as a psychotic state.

Within two months he was dead — 'from rare complications' following surgery, was the coroner's finding in August 2002.

Psychiatrists and other health professionals are called in at the discretion of the ACM. In Katie's time some regarded themselves as ACM employees and even wore the uniform; then wondered why people kept away. Often they are young and without much clinical experience. There are a few professionals who shouldn't be there at all, I believe.

Another former employee, who wanted to remain anonymous, worked alongside a counsellor who seemed in need of therapy herself. This woman was hurting people; she was a professional with a nasty streak who seemed to seek out particularly vulnerable people to come to sessions with her — she seemed to pick out the most wounded.

'I once saw her in action and now I regret that I didn't make a complaint. There was one young boy, a sixteen-year-old, a troubled child but always polite. After the freedom bus came to the camp and people exchanged names and numbers by throwing notes across the fences and writing messages on T-shirts, people inside started getting letters — there was an avalanche of post after January 2002.

'One day I watched this woman as I was out having a smoko. The boy was so excited when he gave her the news that he'd at last got a letter — his first in detention. "Can I read your letter," she asked. After reading it she said to the boy, "Oh this letter is very bad. It's from an old woman and it is no good; it's better if you throw it in the rubbish bin. Shall I do it for you?" And she did. I would watch her hanging around, the type of person who got off on other people's misery.'

Esa Khan was a 'good detainee'; the guards said so, which made him suspect with non-Afghan residents who thought him a tad too friendly with ACM senior management. At our first meeting I recognised the *bazaari* in him: a wily trader used to living off his wits, negotiating his way through the bazaars of Kabul or Kandahar with the finesse of a grand diplomat. The man had panache and the camp had not broken him yet — at least not on the surface.

In many ways Esa Khan was a traditional Afghan; in his style of dressing, his beard and his old fashioned courtesy. When we first met I was on his ground, and he therefore showed me the hospitality I would have received as my due if we'd met in Afghanistan. He had made up his mind that, in spite of being herded in and out of locked gates, and having to ask permission for almost everything outside the routine of his daily life, in his imagination we were back in Afghanistan and he was the host and I was his guest — his dignity was unassailable. He smiled and charmed, but underneath it all he was a worried man. There were dark lines under his eyes and he squeezed his hands restlessly, there was a quick energy about him but clearly he had much on his mind. I sensed that Esa Khan was a self-made man and wondered if some of the 'young Turks on the block' were challenging his authority, some of the younger, better-educated Iraqis for instance, but I was wrong, something else was troubling him.

The time had come for him to make the decision of whether to return to Afghanistan voluntarily and accept the government's repatriation package of two thousand dollars — families were to receive ten thousand dollars — and a free airfare.

By now he understood that his case was a run-of-the-mill affair to Australian authorities — a man fleeing conscription to the Taliban army — and challenging the decision of the Review Tribunal was unlikely to bring him much joy. He had spent more than three and a half years in detention at Port Hedland; ACM managers came, and went, but Esa Khan remained.

Everybody knew Esa Khan by name, even the guards, and they called him 'the Warlord', but behind the smiles was a grudging admiration, the closest thing to respect that I ever saw the guards show to anyone. You had to admire a man who, when his idea for an activities' room with computer and sewing machine was turned down yet again, told the ACM second-in-command, 'Look, I've been here three years, six months and twelve days. I've been here longer than you; we had such a room when we had six hundred detainees, now we're down to a hundred and fifty, it would be easy. I think I know more about running this centre than you.'

Katie liked Esa Khan too and understood that he worked hard on behalf of the Afghans in the camp and was representing them as best he could; on seemingly small matters perhaps, but these are essential when lives are filled with unrelieved boredom. Such things as permission to celebrate an Afghan festival, which was always difficult to achieve, were the small gifts he negotiated on behalf of his fellow Afghans. But the other nationalities didn't understand his games and it was said that he wasn't always as vocal as the Iranians and Iraqis on the committee when it came to confrontations. Generally at Hedland the guards liked the Afghans more because, as a group, they are seen to be more cooperative, while the Iraqis appear more volatile and shout when they get angry or excited. Sri Lankan Tamils are also well regarded although, at times, in camps like Villawood, in New South Wales, they need protection from Muslims ready to have a go at the 'cow worshippers' as they are called behind their backs and sometimes even to their faces.

Lawyer Marg le Sueur had first introduced me to Esa Khan by giving me his name and number so that we could communicate. I caught my plane, registered at the backpackers' quarters of the nearby caravan park at

Cooke's Point and, hauling a suitcase of clothes and other items as gifts, made my way to the detention centre to meet this remarkable survivor. It was the suitcase of clothes which brought me undone, but which broke the ice in the end. By error I'd packed two pairs of green-coloured tights, meant for an Iranian woman friend, in the wrong case and they'd gone to Esa Khan and his younger compatriot, Afzal — who'd never seen women's tights before in his young sheltered life. The two men were completely befuddled, rather shocked and not a little embarrassed to find these strange garments packed in with their coats, shirts and trousers, although we laughed about it later. Now I'm glad I made that mistake — their laughter was genuine; it became an ongoing joke between us and there really isn't much to laugh at in detention centres in Australia.

The two men were great friends and Afzal submitted to the older man's bouts of benevolent tyranny like a younger brother should. Occasionally, Esa Khan chided Afzal for becoming too western with his ponytail, baseball cap worn backwards and his penchant for pop music. But they were family to each other. Twenty-three year old Afzal worried about his mother and younger brother who had fled Kandahar: he'd had no word for three and a half years and the efforts of the International Red Cross to find his widowed mother had come to nought.

He had the dreamy eyes of a poet and, in the down-to-earth words of Sister Mary, Afzal was ready to 'fall in love with a brick wall'; he had so much love to give. He tried hard to keep himself busy. Esa Khan worried about what would happen to his friend if he left — we were all worried.

Katie becomes very upset when she remembers this young man, who has served nearly three and a half years for the 'crime' of running away from a pro-Taliban warlord who'd killed his father and was now after Afzal's head. She knew he was desperately lonely, but too shy to talk to the young female university students when they visited periodically, unlike the more urbane Iraqis who thought all their Christmases had come at once when the news leaked out that young women had come to visit. 'Girls!' they cried. Young men like Afzal miss their mothers tremendously for they come from a culture where a mother's love for her sons is the strongest of all emotional ties and is duly reciprocated. Female teachers and volunteers often find young men breaking down in their company and crying that they haven't seen their mothers for so many years and how much they miss them and love them.

Not long after I returned to Perth, Esa Khan telephoned me with the news that he'd made up his mind to accept the government's offer of the $2,000 repatriation and a free ride home. He sounded in good spirits — it was now time for me to keep my promise.

TO WHOM IT MAY CONCERN

Esa Khan Andar is returning voluntarily to Afghanistan from Australia. I offer the following comments by way of assisting him to find employment on his return home.

...

In my travels to India, Pakistan and Bangladesh I regularly liaise with local NGOs and international development agencies ... in my opinion Mr Esa Khan would be ideally suited to work with Foreign Aid Agencies or local NGOs in Afghanistan. He is fluent in at least four languages, including Pashto, Dari and English, and while in Australia obtained official accreditation as a level 1 translator.

Added to this he has all the attributes of a skilled negotiator which he has honed in his years in Australia where, because of our current refugee policy, (which does no credit to Australia), he found himself in detention.

Through talking to the detention centre management and the volunteers who visited, including Catholic nuns and church ministers, I know he was regarded as the leader of the Afghans at the centre and was seen to carry out this role with good will and intelligence. For many years he was the detainees representative on the Residents' Committee and was able to negotiate his way through a veritable 'minefield' caused by cultural misunderstandings and the overall despairing environment of a camp population of sometimes 600 people.

I would say he specialised in problem solving and managed to ease tensions between the Management and its diverse, vulnerable population. He carried this out with dignity and had the reputation of being cooperative without being sycophantic.

On meeting him for the first time I was impressed by his energy and focus which stood out in an environment where many people become angry or depressed. He rose above circumstances which would have toppled other men and enjoys my respect. He also enjoys a joke, and is used to the idiosyncratic ways of foreigners. His personal style has been to meet adversity with patience and determination.

In summary, Esa Khan is a survivor and knows how to 'manage' people. Men like Esa Khan are sorely needed to help rebuild Afghanistan. He has an impressive array of skills which I hope will be put to good use. I have no hesitation in recommending him to work in difficult environments which demand intercultural sensitivity, intelligence, and a sense of responsibility and leadership.

The last time we met was at the Perth Detention Centre the day before he was due to leave. Katie and I were there to farewell him but once again Esa Khan turned us into guests while he played host. He carried out this difficult feat in the tiny cramped visitors' room at Perth Airport where mainly students and tourists who've overstayed their welcome remain for twenty-four hours before being deported. In one corner sat a young African and his girlfriend silently holding hands, another Afghan detainee and his two visitors were crammed next to us and two young Turkish men, who'd overstayed their tourist visas, sat with the loves of their lives from whom they would soon be separated; they talked, hugged and cried — there was absolutely no privacy whatsoever.

Somewhere inside this small centre is a man called Stephen Khan, a Kashmiri nationalist who has been kept in detention for four years now: one year in Port Hedland and three in the small centre at the Perth Airport where men sleep ten to a room. He refuses to sign the papers allowing the government to send him back to India where he fears, with good cause, he would be arrested, gaoled and probably tortured by Indian Security Forces as a known militant — to his own people he is a freedom fighter. Esa Khan had caught up with Stephen Khan inside and reported that he seemed as resolute as ever, but was suffering from severe depression.

I said goodbye to Esa Khan that night; three months later word reached us that he was in Kabul, working for an Afghan development NGO.

Katie will soon be returning to Ireland for good and I don't blame her for giving up on us. She carries with her traces of her own personal trauma. 'To be honest,' she said, 'these days I almost detach myself from my words because it is easier for me, or else I go downhill.'

We tell each other how amazing it is that people can

come out of the detention experience and not hate us. Later, however, I remember the words of psychiatrist Louise Newman, which make me stop and think. 'Children are banding together like feral children,' she said, 'like children in orphanages, protecting each other because their parents can't any more — and we are allowing this to happen in Australia.'

There are hundreds of stories waiting to be told from behind the wires and one day they will be revealed when people are no longer afraid to speak out. These are stories happening on our own doorstep, not far away in some repressive regime with a poor record on human rights. People imprisoned in our remote camps have no voice and their slim chances of receiving Australia's magic pieces of paper for temporary stay will disappear if they are critical or seen to be 'ungrateful': their chances will be diminished and all their suffering in vain. Those standing outside the wire with their temporary visas gag themselves in a state of complete uncertainty, living half lives as they wait for their status to be determined once and for all: the first batch of TPVs is due to expire in mid 2003.

The student activists who raise money to drive their protest buses, visiting the remote centres, talk amongst themselves and their campus circles but avoid the spotlight of the media worry that they'll be punished by not being allowed to visit the detainees who've become their friends, and they could not bear that. Sara, the student, tells me, 'I know our visits are looked forward to up north, every time we protest it counters the letters they read in the papers — the "We don't want you go home" letters. We wave our banners and yell "Azadi", which means freedom in Pashto, and they have hope.'

Psychiatrists and other professionals who walked away from detention camps while they could still bear to live with themselves, break the silence by giving evidence to the National Inquiry into Children Under Detention, and writing articles. Other organisations, including many ethnic associations, are afraid to speak out for fear their government funding will be cut.

Many activists believe that sometime in the future there will be a Royal Commission; those responsible will then be judged as having ignored our obligation to the United Nations Convention protecting the Rights of Children we signed in 1990. The findings of the National Inquiry into Children in Detention will present its report to Parliament in 2003. It will make compelling reading and as evidence that surely no one can deny and still retain their credibility — although this has not stopped some politicians in the past.

One day I hope that the people who really own these stories will feel that their time has come and they can speak out. I know that many of them are tired of telling their stories over and over again like a broken record and that is why I have only shared the story of one of my friends, a man who chose voluntary repatriation back to Afghanistan — God help him. He gave me permission to tell his story when the long hand of DIMIA could harm him no further. My other friends are still here behind the wires and I do not want them to feel like animals in a zoo.

The heart of the stories I have shared with you is not about our Border Protection Policy or who is a bona fide refugee and who is an 'economic refugee', but what has been happening out of sight in our detention centres: how we treat people who, according to international law, have done nothing illegal by seeking asylum in Australia. This is now part of our history and the pages make shameful reading.

The real heroes are the men, women and children who sold everything and risked all to come to Australia, never realising they would end up behind razor wire in desert camps, their lives on hold.

There are also stories to be told of Australians who did not turn their backs; who mounted resistance against what was unjust and contemptible. This keeps hope alive and it has grown from such small beginnings into a large coalition of organisations and individuals around Australia. I see some similarities with the anti-Vietnam War Movement in the seventies which was union-based, campus-based and drew into its fold the mothers of Australia who hated conscription.

At present this new movement is smaller and broader based and the unions have turned their backs. What it badly needs is mothers around Australia to open their eyes and see that little 'Ahmed' or 'Wahab' or 'Mariam', playing in the dirt and dust of our remote camps and losing the joy of childhood, could easily be called 'John' or 'Alex' or 'Marilyn', and might easily be their own.

I like to think that these are the Australians the asylum seekers will remember in the future wherever they may be. What memories of Australia will my friend Esa Khan hold as he tries to rebuild his twice-shattered life in Afghanistan? What memories will they all hold of the land of the 'fair go'? How will we live with ourselves? Does it really matter? I think it does.

Epilogue

When the first edition of *Caravanserai* was finished in 1994 I knew that I was writing a story without an ending, that a neatly rounded conclusion was not possible. Only time and future generations of Australian Muslims could answer many of the questions raised, was my thinking as I put my human documentary to bed. I believed we were entering a phase where Muslims would continue to establish their presence without making waves as they had done for all of their settlement history; the few anti-Muslim incidents around the time of the Gulf War were a minor aberration in community relations which we could all learn from. Ten years later I realise I was mistaken. Muslims did not learn from that earlier Middle East crisis; neither did mainstream Australians and sections of the media.

But that was hidden from me at the time. Summing up my impressions of that earlier journey among Muslims in 1994, I wrote that some of the images I'd encountered were endearing while others were irritating; some were admirable, others less worthy; many were contradictory; but all of them were very human and in stark contrast to the alien, threatening figures embedded in stereotypes. The Muslim and Arab stereotype, I argued, was not only a simplification but also a distortion. The words I wrote then still ring true and there is an even more urgent need that they be understood.

What is constantly ignored by 'Muslim watchers' in Australia is the enormous diversity among Australian

Muslims, for everyone is not cut from the one cloth: differences in education, socioeconomic background, ethnicity, customs and religious outlook play their part, moving in and out of people's lives in ways they are not even aware of. And of course that is what makes Muslims so Australian: they are part of the diversity which characterises modern Australia. Muslims like Rokaya the poet from Jordan, Dede from Indonesia, Sameena from India and all the others contribute to that diversity which enriches us all; even those who move back in alarm have been touched by it.

What is stubbornly underplayed by almost everyone, including media and Muslims alike, is the existence of differing degrees of religious attachment. 'Not everyone is as religious as everyone else,' a woman from South Africa said to me early on in my travels. But this is a 'secret' most orthodox Muslims want hidden. Just as the media thinks of Islam as a monolith, that is what the devout want to present: a sanitised perfect Muslim community, praying shoulder to shoulder — but that doesn't exist in Australia or anywhere else for that matter. Muslims need to understand that people with ordinary human weaknesses are more appealing to most people than those who claim moral perfection.

The majority of Muslims make accommodations in adapting their religious lives to Australian society, and throw their energies into negotiating a way to remain Muslim in a secular, non-Muslim society. They are motivated by a desire to enhance their families' life chances. Coming to Australia means living in a democratic, secular society offering freedom of religion — the price they pay is minority status. Others, however, deny the changes they sense taking place and try to return to the past, where the lure of a golden age calls in a comfortable and familiar voice.

History tells us the Irish were not always beloved or welcomed into the Anglican and Presbyterian establishments in nineteenth-century Australia, but that has changed. I often glimpse interesting parallels between the two immigrant communities: the Irish and Muslim diaspora. Among the Irish there were hard-core Church Catholics, Irish nationalists with little religion, labourers and lawyers with varying degrees of religion — especially in the Australian Labor Party — and the cultural Irish in pubs and clubs and the wider community. To outsiders, all Irish were the same, and while certain insiders sometimes wished all Irish were one obedient flock, reality was more diverse. I sometimes say to friends in jest, 'If you can love "a Mick", you can love a Muslim!'

Ten years ago Muslims across Australia were more or less a contented lot; they had freedom of religion, could build their mosques and schools with less trouble from local councils; the law was even-handed; racism and religious vilification were officially decried; women were not scared of being recognised as Muslim; the Gulf War was over and the isolated incidents where buses were stoned and some Muslims called traitor and abused were quickly dealt with by our political leaders.

Looking back now, I recall a remarkable time of institutions around Australia speaking out in defence of Australian Muslims and Arabs. Clear, unequivocal statements were made. The prime minister, state parliaments, churches, unions and human rights groups around Australia stood up and effectively said to the bigots and the tabloid media, 'Leave our Muslims alone, they are Australians.' But September 11 changed all that. So far I have not witnessed the same level of political reassurance and support this time around except perhaps from Australian church leaders and educational institutions. Where once it was only the social misfits who showed their racism, now the voices of prejudice are drawn from a wider spectrum.

After September 11, almost overnight, relations between Australia's Muslim and non-Muslim populations changed. The average Australian was frightened and repulsed by Muslims. In turn, many Muslims began to feel that Australia was no longer a safe place for them. There was tension where there had been none before.

Events which happened in 2001 have damaged the dignity, self-esteem and morale of Australian Muslims. But I believe recovery is possible — if we recognise that we've reached a watershed in community relations — and this is something which Muslims have to open their eyes to as well; they must heed the lessons they ignored ten years ago. Non-Muslims on the other hand must understand that Australian Muslims should not be held to ransom for events that happen overseas.

At present we are witnessing a public reaction against Australian Indonesians in the wake of the tragic Bali blasts of 12 October 2002 similar to the reaction towards Muslims 'of Middle Eastern appearance' after September 11. People, it seems, need to put a face to their fear.

Australians are still in mourning, but this is no justification for turning against Indonesian Muslims, long accepted as gentle immigrants representing a more syncretic, moderate version of Islam. A small minority of extremists in Indonesia does not change this. Nor does it excuse the middle-aged couple who stalked teachers and primary school pupils from a local Islamic school on an excursion to the Perth Zoo, muttering obscenities and general abuse at the bewildered children.Their act of intolerance was contemptible — but what horrified me more was that not a single bystander intervened; they all turned away.

As I revisited old friends and familiar places I found Muslim activists everywhere acknowledging 2001 as a defining moment in their existence as a religious community. In the past there had been much talk about entering into dialogue with the wider community, but it never moved much beyond interfaith meetings and was more rhetorical than real. Now the leadership of Mosque communities was seen to be dropping its fortress mentality. Almost overnight Muslims had become the most unpopular group in Australian society and they were coming to an understanding that they needed to emphasise to fellow citizens a sense of shared values. They needed deeper and more regular dialogue instead of the occasional fending off of criticism.

New alliances must be built. Muslims can benefit from dialogue with religious people who realise that Christianity, Judaism and Islam have much in common due to their shared origins in the Middle East. Muslims should also realise that secular liberals and democrats are also their allies because they value tolerance and freedom of expression. It would be unfortunate if the climate is set by Christian fundamentalists attacking Muslims as terrible non-believers, and Muslims in reply, calling everyone else *kafirs*. Mutual antipathy can only lead to further breakdown and tabloid headlines. Now that religion is a surrogate for race Muslims leaders should move closer to their natural allies, the anti-racist human rights groups in Australia which means they should consider remaining silent on some issues such as homosexuality. This is not a matter of infringing freedom of speech on one hand, nor denying a person's right to decide their own sexual preference on the other, but a strategic sense is needed here. They are fooling themselves by throwing in their lot with anti-gay groups.

It is also time for 'the invisible Muslims' to speak out. Most Australian Muslims do not live in mosque communities nor are they easily identifiable by their dress

— it is the 'visible Muslims' living in, or near mosque communities who bear the brunt of overt prejudice in society and the 'invisible Muslims' who usually keep their heads down. Their lack of participation allows the media to think they have captured Muslim opinion in Australia by sending a reporter and a cameraman to the nearest mosque on Friday.

Perhaps a more open mindset will come from the younger generation of Australian-born leaders — I sense that this is not far away. This new generation may provide new local leaders who understand Australian society, speak English fluently and are more egalitarian and representative. The day may come when we no longer have to import imams and shaykhs from Egypt, Lebanon, Malaysia, Indonesia and Turkey but rely on our own 'locally grown' variety.

The efforts of young Muslims to learn more about their religion attracts scant media attention and yet it is a more accurate indicator of change than kerbside media interviews with sullen and often angry young people. The younger generation's desire to learn more about their religion parallels the Muslim women's movement a decade ago which came out of a reaction to the Gulf War. International events and a feeling of challenge have helped create this socio-religious and political wave of interest among young people — it is happening at different levels among the educated and the less educated, and reflects their diversity of opinion and religious attachment. Feeling marginalised politicises people, and there is great sympathy for the Palestinian cause and a feeling of deep resentment that the world seems so indifferent to the plight of the Palestinian people.

Australia is at last developing an Australian Muslim intelligentsia, children of refugees and a second generation, many of whose parents worked in unskilled and semiskilled occupations in factories and small shops and made the sacrifices all immigrant parents make. Young Muslims in the twenty-first century will be better equipped in terms of confidence and skills to reduce the social distance which exists between them and non-Muslims.

But at a personal level, young Muslims still have the same problems that I had growing up in Australia all those years ago. They still hear the same fears about Australian popular culture expressed by their elders. But wiser heads among parents know that, 'Muslim kids need to understand their own way of life and *choose* to follow — choice and not coercion is the way!'

'Their own way of life.' What exactly does this mean? Children do not share parental nightmares. Most will at some time or other in their lives either experience some aspect of life in the fast lane, like the charming, confident Soban, or toy with the idea of 'crossing over', 'taking on a double life' like beautiful confused Zahra whom I recently tracked down only to discover that she had remarried, was happily wearing *hijab* and had become a practising Muslim. Readers may also be interested to learn that I could find no trace of Denise; she had long disappeared with Snooky, her dog, and a quantity of her wedding jewellery, never to be heard of again by her husband, who at least had his permanent residency papers to console him.

Others, like Wafia's three beautiful daughters, believe they can remain Muslims — not necessarily in exactly the same mould as their parents, but Australian Muslims. 'Many parents get hung up on ritual as a way of coping with their minority status and the open ways of Australia,' said one young man about his parents.

Some young people may take the more painful route, turn their backs and walk away, perhaps returning years later when, in the words of Musa, wise beyond his years, having tried to change their identity and call themselves Tom, they wake up one morning crying and not knowing why. As he said, 'You can try to please your parents, but you yourself remain very unhappy. Or you can try to work out a new position.'

In the wake of everything that has happened over recent years that is what many Australian Muslims, young and old, are trying to do: to work out a new position. To do this they need reassurance that they are not the enemy, that they are recognised as Australians. Perhaps it is also time for mainstream Australians to work out a new position as well, one that recognises Islamophobia as a poison that diminishes us all.

Terrible events took place in 2001 and 2002 and I think they may have changed us forever. They were of different magnitude but all of them impacted on the lives of Australians everywhere, including Australian Muslims and the asylum seekers locked out of sight in our desert gulags. This scandal will haunt us in the years to come, going down in our history books as one of our darkest pages yet recorded: the demonisation of damaged people for political gain. Australia's political leadership has focused on emotion, not facts, by coupling border protection with terrorism and refugee issues. As a country which preaches human rights to other nations in the region we need to take a long hard look at ourselves: we may not like what we see, but we can change it, if we have the will and the compassion to act.

I like to believe that the Australia of my romanticised caravanserai of the twentieth century has not disappeared for good. 'A sanctuary of more permanent abode' is how I whimsically phrased it at the time. I think it is still there waiting to emerge again, although the innocence and peace of mind we as Australians have taken for granted all these years has suffered. Fear and hate makes monsters of us all and it happens almost overnight, eating away at neighbourly exchanges, at our sense of decency and in our denial of what is wrong. But we can put away these things, for as one of my Muslim friends reminded me not so long ago, 'I believe in the intrinsic fairness of Australians; they are incredible people, truly original, and underneath it all they are fair.'

And maybe we are after all.

Photograph: Wendy D'Souza

Hanifa Deen is a Western Australian writer of Pakistani ancestry. She is a great believer in women reinventing themselves and her career has spanned teaching, research, the public service, the media and now — in what she calls the final leg of her journey — writing. *Caravanserai* won the NSW Premier's Literary Award in 1996 and was shortlisted for the Nita B Kibble Award. Hanifa's second book *Broken Bangles* was shortlisted for the 1998 Western Australian Premier's Book Award.

Glossary

Al'ham dulillah	praise be to Allah.
Allahu Akbar	God is Most Great.
azan	call to prayer.
Bismillah	in the name of Allah.
Eid ul-Fitr	festival at the end of Ramadan.
Eid ul-Adha	festival of sacrifice.
fajr	dawn prayer — first of the five daily prayers.
futoor	breaking fast at sunset.
Hadith	a collection of teachings of the Prophet Muhammad and stories about his life; one of these teachings.
haj	pilgrimage to Mecca; one of the Five Pillars of Islam.
haji	title conferred on a man who has completed the haj.
hajiah	title conferred on a woman who has completed the haj.
halal	religiously permitted, e.g. halal meat has been slaughtered according to Islamic ritual requirements.
haram	religiously prohibited or forbidden.
hijab	head covering or women's clothing that follows Islamic principles.
imam	leader of prayers; official attached to mosque.
iman	faith.
Insha'Allah	God willing.
isha	evening prayer — last of the five daily prayers.
jihad	a struggle or fight to bring about an Islamic order — can mean either an internal struggle with the self or an external one with an enemy.

jumma — group or assembly; Friday communal prayer.
kafir — unbeliever.
Kalima — the Word.
Maghreb — after-sunset prayer — the fourth of the five daily prayers.
mehr — dowry paid by groom to his bride before wedding ceremony.
Masha'Allah — as may please Allah, expression used when excited, surprised or wishing to express admiration.
masjid — usually a small mosque.
muezzin — the man who calls people to prayers.
nafs — internal human desires e.g. greed, pride.
najis — impure or unclean.
nargeelah — water pipe used for smoking tobacco.
nikab — full covering and veil.
nikah — wedding ceremony.
niyyat — intentions.
qtbar — sermon.
qurbani — annual donation of a sheep or money to buy an animal for the poor to sacrifice during Eid ul-Adha.
Ramadan (Ramazan) — one of the Five Pillars of Islam; the month of fasting; Ramadam is Arabic, Ramazan is Urdu.
Sahaba — the Companions of the Prophet.
salaam alaikum — peace be with you — Islamic greeting.
salat — prayer; one of the Five Pillars.
sawm — fasting.
Shahadah — obligatory declaration of faith: 'There is no god but God and Muhammad is His Prophet.' One of the Five Pillars.
shaitan — Satan, the devil.
Shari'ah — the law or entire corpus of rules guiding Muslim life; derived from diverse sources including the Qur'an and Hadith.
shaykh — religiously trained scholar; also sheikh.

Shi'a	stream of Islam whose adherents believe that the legitimate succession of the caliphs derives from Ali, the fourth caliph, who was the Prophet's cousin and son-in-law (husband of the Prophet's daughter Fatima).
shirik or shirk	idolatry; worship of false gods.
shura	literally 'consultation', deriving from the commendation to Muslims to consult together and reach consensus.
sobh	morning prayer — second of the five daily prayers.
Sufi	one who practises the mystical tradition of Islam.
suhoor	early morning meal before sunrise during Ramadan.
Sunna	practice; a collection of the sayings, actions and traditions of the Prophet recorded from oral histories after his death.
Sunni	majority stream of Islam whose adherents accept the entire first generation of Muslim leaders as legitimate, in contrast with the Shi'a, who accept only Caliph Ali and his descendants.
sura	a chapter in the Qur'an.
tafsir	scholarly written commentary on the Qur'an.
talaq	pronouncement of repudiation used in divorce.
ulemma	scholars, religious teachers.
ummah	the community of Islam.
zakat	almsgiving; one of the Five Pillars.
zohr	noon prayer — third of the five daily prayers

Index